942.1 P
Porter, Stephen.
  The tower of London
30049002989870

OCT   2014

D1271669

Piqua Public Library
116 West High Street
Piqua, Ohio 45356

Discarded

The Tower of
LONDON

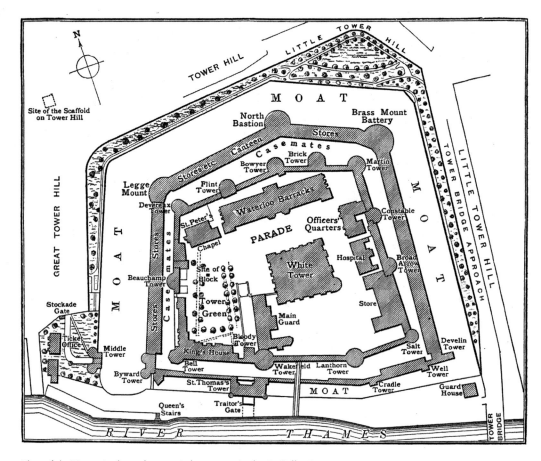

Plan of the Tower in the early twentieth century. Author's Collection.

The Tower of
LONDON
THE BIOGRAPHY

Piqua Public Library
116 West High Street
Piqua. Ohio 45356

STEPHEN PORTER

AMBERLEY

942.1 P
Porter, Stephen.
The tower of London
3004002989870

Cover illustrations:
Front and front flap detail: The White Tower. This copy of a late fifteenth-century manuscript illumination shows the Tower of London much as it was in mid-fifteenth-century. Courtesy of Jonathan Reeve JR992b4p640 14501550. *Back cover*: The south-east corner of the White Tower. Courtesy of Stephen Porter. Back flap: The elephant given to Henry III drawn by Matthew Paris and kept in the Tower of London. Courtesy of Jonathan Reeve JR2225b99plateXVI 12001300.

First published 2012
Amberley Publishing
The Hill, Stroud
Gloucestershire, GL5 4EP

www.amberleybooks.com

Copyright © Stephen Porter, 2012

The right of Stephen Porter to be identified as the Author
of this work has been asserted in accordance with the
Copyrights, Designs and Patents Act 1988.

All rights reserved. No part of this book may be reprinted
or reproduced or utilised in any form or by any electronic,
mechanical or other means, now known or hereafter invented,
including photocopying and recording, or in any information
storage or retrieval system, without the permission in writing
from the Publishers.

British Library Cataloguing in Publication Data.
A catalogue record for this book is available from the British Library.

ISBN 978 1 4456 0381 0

Typesetting and Origination by Amberley Publishing.
Printed in the UK.

CONTENTS

OCT   2014

ACKNOWLEDGEMENTS

In writing the history of such a complex group of buildings over a period of more than 900 years, I have been fortunate to be able to draw on the work of those writers who have preceded me. In particular, I am grateful to Geoffrey Parnell and the late R. Allen Brown for their work on the fabric; to Anna Keay for her edition of the 1597 survey; to the late Howard Blackmore for his inventory of the Armouries' collection of ordnance; to Peter Hammond for his assessment of the nineteenth century; and to the contributors, too numerous to mention individually, to the *Oxford Dictionary of National Biography*. Dr Michael Turner of English Heritage alerted me to material that I was unaware of. Jonathan Reeve at Amberley Publishing has provided cheerful encouragement, and Peter Day and Gillian Tindall were good enough to read the manuscript and suggest improvements, for which I am most grateful. My wife Carolyn has, as ever, been a fount of support and assistance, and made prudent observations as we went around the site through rain and shine.

I

THE TOWER THROUGH TIME

'The history of the Tower of London is a distillation of the history of England', wrote the Japanese author Natsume Soseki, after his visit in 1900. A professor of English, he was asked by his government to undertake a period of study in England. Just two days after arriving in London, he went to the Tower; its reputation had spread far beyond the British Isles, as it became indisputably the most famous castle in the world. The Tower's attraction lay not only in the buildings, and their distinctive profile on the north bank of the Thames, but also in its associations and the centuries of life within its walls. Like many other visitors, what Soseki found so fascinating was the sense of place and the presence of the past in the present; the appeal of those who had been within its walls, as well as the history of the fabric itself.

Soseki's visit came during a period when the association of notable people with places and buildings was being investigated and recorded. Birthplaces and the houses where the famous had lived were being traced and increasingly the connection was marked with a plaque. That was also the case at the Tower, and as historians researched and understood its history, including the building chronology, so they gave attention to those who had lived and, more especially, been imprisoned there. Some of the prisoners had become associated with a part of the buildings, where they were believed to have been incarcerated, and those traditions took such firm root that correcting the associations proved to be difficult, when they were found to be inaccurate.

At various times the Tower served as a fortress and a royal palace. It contained the royal wardrobe and regalia, was a focus of ceremonies, functioned as the state prison, housed a garrison and a military arsenal and was a stronghold for the deposit of bullion. The Royal Mint was there, as was the royal collection of exotic animals; the records of government and the courts were stored in it, its buildings housed an observatory for a short time and the Ordnance Survey's office for fifty years. It provided the backdrop for executions on Tower Hill, the arrival of distinguished persons at Tower Wharf and, for a much shorter period, a beach alongside the Thames. The cannon on its walls were fired in anger and in celebration.

Most of the Tower's roles were established during the Middle Ages and were lost thereafter: the palace and the wardrobe during the seventeenth century, the artillery arsenal by the early eighteenth, the menagerie, record office and Ordnance Survey in the mid-nineteenth, and the military depot towards the end of the twentieth century. Buildings were destroyed, by fire and demolition, especially during the nineteenth century, when parts of the structure were pulled down to remove what were regarded as inauthentic accretions, and so recapture the appearance of the medieval Tower. In the twentieth century that process was deplored, together with what became considered as the previous over-emphasis on imprisonment and torture, to the neglect of other aspects of the Tower's history.

By the twenty-first century the wheel had turned again, with reconstructions of medieval interiors installed in surviving parts of the royal palace, containing furniture and hangings based on medieval designs and staffed by period interpreters in costume. Exhibitions devoted to 'Prisoners of the Tower' and 'Torture at the Tower' were opened, and a seasonal encampment with reproduction medieval artillery was set up outside the walls. The displays of armour and weapons, and the regalia, were periodically redesigned and rearranged, while the number of visitors increased and kept on increasing. Each generation finds a way of interpreting and presenting the many facets of the Tower's past.

To Soseki the Tower represented the 'all-burying current of time flowing backwards and fragments of ancient times floating up into the present age'. He looked for and imagined associations with the famous names from English history, which gave the place a special aura: Richard II, Henry VI, the Princes in the Tower, Archbishop Cranmer, Sir Thomas Wyatt, Lady Jane Grey, Sir Walter Raleigh, Guy Fawkes and those prisoners who carved epigraphs on the walls of the Beauchamp and Salt towers.

As royal rivalries and political purges were played out over the centuries, those consigned to the Tower included kings and queens, princes and princesses, politicians and prelates, conspirators and coiners, poets and playwrights. Some prisoners escaped and attracted a certain celebrity for their exploits. Others used their period of enforced restraint to focus their thoughts and ideals, encapsulating these in their writings: not the least of the Tower's important associations is with the significant books which were written there. And from the early nineteenth century the Tower featured in historical novels, then an expanding genre. A few prisoners died within the walls, more were executed on Tower Hill, many attracted attention in their imprisonment, from supporters and opponents, as well as from the wider public who were fascinated to see the rich and powerful brought so low. That fascination partly explains the size of the crowds that turned out on those occasions when someone of prominence was executed.

The Tower was a symbol of royal authority and state power. Its history was intertwined with events, often of national importance, which affected those who worked there and the prisoners who were detained within it. Also significant were the relations between the men in charge of the fortress and the growing metropolis beyond its gates, and with the authorities governing the City of London from the Guildhall. All of this long and complex history stemmed from a decision made by the first of the Norman rulers to build a stronghold adjoining the Thames, beside the capital of his newly acquired kingdom.

2

FOUNDATION & EARLY HISTORY

The first fortifications in the south-east corner of London were built by William the Conqueror, soon after he had captured the city in 1066. The White Tower was begun a dozen years later and the other defences were developed and enlarged during the twelfth and thirteenth centuries, so that at the end of Edward I's reign, in 1307, the Tower had become a large and imposing castle.

William came to the English throne as the result of the uncertainty over the succession, the unresolved problem of Edward the Confessor's reign of almost twenty-three years, from 1043 until his death in early January 1066. He died childless and the two claimants were William, who may have been promised the crown by Edward as early as 1051, and Harold, Earl of Wessex, the son and heir of Earl Godwine, Edward's father-in-law. Godwine had been a dominant character at court during the second part of Edward's reign, when the earlier Norman influence had been reduced. But Harold was in Normandy in 1064 or 1065 and took part with William in a campaign against the Count of Brittany. He may have been there to confirm Edward's earlier offer of the crown to William, although that is by no means certain, and his visit could have been the accidental outcome of his ship being blown badly off course during a storm.

Norman writers and the depictions of the Bayeaux Tapestry later claimed that while in Normandy Harold took an oath on sacred relics swearing his allegiance to William and that by taking the throne he broke that oath, thereby committing both perjury and blasphemy. Harold's offence was justification enough for William to mount an invasion. His expedition was helped by another incursion in early September, when an army under King Harald Hardrada of Norway and Harold's disaffected brother Tostig landed in northern England. Their army was defeated by Harold at the battle of Stamford Bridge, near York, on 25 September, where both were killed. Harold then marched his forces to Sussex to confront the Norman army, which had been given time to establish itself. In the battle of Hastings on 14 October William's forces were victorious and Harold was killed.

After their victory the Normans advanced to Dover and then Canterbury. Meanwhile, opposition to the invaders had become focused on London, where it was orchestrated by Asgar the Staller, an exceptionally wealthy nobleman with estates in nine counties, who had been wounded at Hastings. According to the contemporary 'Song of the Battle of Hastings', Asgar 'commanded all the chief men of the city and the affairs of the community'. The Witan, the council called by the Anglo-Saxon kings, Ealdred, Archbishop of York, Edwin, Earl of Mercia, and Mokere, Earl of Northumberland, together with the citizens of London, chose Edgar the Aetheling as king, 'just as was his natural right'. He was the grandson of Edmund Ironside, king in 1016, and great-nephew of Edward the Confessor. The Londoners could provide 'a numerous and formidable force' and they were joined by so many others willing to fight that 'they could hardly be housed even in this large town'. Guy, Bishop of Amiens, stressed the city's military strength: 'Protected on the left side by walls, on the right side by the river, it neither fears enemies nor dreads being taken by storm.'

The walls were those erected by the Romans around AD 200, over two miles long, that enclosed Londinium, with a length of wall that ran alongside the Thames, to provide protection against raiders. That section, in the south-east corner, was remodelled in the late third century with the addition of a new wall. The walls still provided effective defences, as Aethelred and King Oláf of Norway discovered in 1009, when they attacked London to eject the Danes, who held what a chronicler described as 'the fortified town', to distinguish it from Southwark, which was 'a large market town'.

The Normans crossed Kent and Surrey, while a detachment of 500 knights approached Southwark and were attacked by Edgar's men, who were defeated. Nevertheless, the Normans could not hope to force the crossing at London Bridge against determined opposition and, after setting Southwark on fire, they rejoined the main army on its march westwards, before turning north to cross the Thames at Wallingford. The army then marched through Buckinghamshire into Bedfordshire and Hertfordshire, devastating the countryside and pillaging the inhabitants as it went, aiming to cut London off from its supplies. Eventually many of the English submitted to William at Berkhamsted. One of the Anglo-Saxon chroniclers reported that those who did so included 'all the best men from London' and commented that the submission came, 'from necessity when the most harm was done – and it was great folly that it was not done thus earlier'. But London had not been pacified and, as autumn turned into winter, the Normans then marched to Westminster, where, according to one account, the soldiers built siege engines and prepared to attack the city.

In the event, those weapons were not needed, for when Asgar attempted to negotiate with William he was politically outmanoeuvred, and the gate at Ludgate was opened to the duke's troops. But within the city the advance guard met resistance and was attacked by Edgar's supporters '*in platea urbis*' – an open space or perhaps wide street, possibly Cheapside. The chronicler who reported the skirmish, William of Jumièges, described how the Normans 'at once engaged them in battle, causing no little mourning to the City because of the very many deaths of her own sons and citizens'. In 1988 eleven bodies were uncovered outside Ludgate, on the banks of the River Fleet. They were covered with stones and may have been dismembered, and could have been casualties in the battle for London late in 1066. That battle was not prolonged, and those members of the Witan and the prominent Londoners who had not already submitted to William now went to Westminster to do so, taking 'all the hostages he named and required', although they acted, according to Bishop Guy, 'with downcast bearing'.

That marked the end of resistance and William was crowned in Westminster Abbey on Christmas Day. But the nervous apprehension of his soldiers, following the hostility that they had encountered, may explain their reaction to the great shout within the abbey when he was acclaimed, which they feared was the beginning of a riot, or even a rebellion. They responded by firing nearby houses: 'without reason they started to set fire to the city'. In the confusion and panic that ensued, most of the congregation fled, leaving only the senior clergy and some monks in the sanctuary to complete the coronation ceremony.

The Normans were not accustomed to dealing with such a large city, with a population of approximately 15,000, and William of Poitiers referred to 'the inconstancy of the numerous and hostile inhabitants'. And so William withdrew to Barking until fortifications had been built, 'against the fickleness of the vast and fierce populace'. These were Baynard's Castle and Montfitchet's Tower, close together west of Ludgate, and another at the south-east corner of the city, just within the city walls. They provided accommodation for a garrison and points from which the citizens could be overawed.

The fortification in the south-east corner initially consisted of an irregularly shaped enclosure. It was bounded by the existing city wall on its east and south sides, and by a ditch and bank, presumably topped with palisades, which ran south-westwards from the east wall and then turned south to join the south wall close to the site of the future Bloody Tower. The area enclosed covered roughly one and a quarter acres, contrived within the defensive walls first erected approximately 850 years earlier.

It is not known whether it contained a motte (an earthen mound) or keep. A motte could be thrown up quickly; the Bayeux Tapestry shows the Normans creating one at Hastings in the period of just over two weeks between their landing and the battle. At least eighty-four castles, and probably far more, were built by them in England before the end of the century, most of them consisting of a motte and bailey. If the enclosure in the south-east corner of London did contain a motte, it is likely that all traces of it were destroyed by the great stone keep that the Normans later erected there.

That keep was begun by William the Conqueror and completed during the reign of his son, William II (William Rufus, 1087–1100). Its erection was overseen by Gundulf, a protégé of Lanfranc, appointed Archbishop of Canterbury in 1070. Gundulf had been a monk at Bec and later at Caen, where he and Lanfranc had built William the Conqueror's abbey of St Etienne. An able administrator,

Gundulf served Lanfranc at Canterbury as head of his household, before being consecrated Bishop of Rochester in March 1077. The register of the cathedral there has a reference to the donation of some property by Edmer Aenhande, a wealthy London citizen, which states that the bishop was lodging with Aenhande, 'while the same Gundulf, by command of King William the Great, was supervising the work of the great tower of London'. The start of the building work is traditionally attributed to 1078, when Gundulf was in his mid-fifties. He was also responsible for building Rochester Cathedral and the outer walls of the castle there, which cost him £60, and a submission to William II described him as 'very competent and skilful at building in stone'.

The keep at London probably was completed within twenty years. It is of Caen stone, 118 feet from east to west and 107 feet from north to south, and 90 feet high to the battlements. The walls are twelve to fifteen feet thick at the base and eleven feet thick in the upper storey. There are turrets at each corner; that in the north-east is cylindrical and projects beyond the lines of the walls, and carries a stairway connecting all of the stages. The other turrets are rectangular; the stairways in those at the south-west and north-west corners gave access to the battlements from the upper floor, not from the entrance floor. The turret in the south-east corner stands above the chapel of St John, the apse of which projects beyond the line of the east wall, above a crypt and sub-crypt. The evidence of the foundations shows that the projection was a change to the original intention, which was to create a rectangular corner.

Access to the tower was at first-floor level at the west end of the south front. The outer door was reached by a timber stairway, but that was later replaced by a rectangular fore-building, to provide extra defence. The addition may have been made during the twelfth century, perhaps during the reign of Henry II (1154–89). In 1172–3 the comparatively large sum of £60 was expended on the Tower and other payments were made later in the decade, although there is nothing in the accounts to indicate that the work paid for included the fore-building.

Within the Tower were two storeys above a basement; the top storey was the royal floor and had a gallery around it, the storey below it was also residential, and the building probably contained an armoury. A cross wall running north to south divided the interior and the eastern side was further divided by an east-to-west wall, so that the royal floor consisted of a hall, chamber and chapel. When a floor was inserted to create an extra storey above the royal floor, possibly in the early seventeenth century, the chapel of St John was left open to its original height. The chapel is fifty-five and a half feet long, thirty-one feet broad and thirty-two feet high, with a gallery running all around it, supported on massive pillars that form aisles and an ambulatory. In 1177–8 lead was bought to cover 'the chapel in the Tower', and in 1240 work ordered during the reign of Henry III (1216–72) included

the whole Chapel of St. John Evangelist in the said Tower to be Whited. And ... three Glass Windows in the same Chapel to be made; to wit, one on the North side, with a certain little Mary holding her Child; the other on the South Part with the Image of the Trinity; and the Third, of St. John the Apostle and Evangelist on the same South Part.

The rood was to be 'Painted well and with good Colours', and images were to be made 'of St. Edward holding a Ring, and giving and reaching it out to St. John Evangelist'.

It seems likely that a curtain wall was erected after the Tower was completed. Presumably it ran along the north and west sections of the fortification created in 1066. That work was being carried out in 1097, according to an entry in the *Anglo-Saxon Chronicle*, which states that 'many shires, whose work pertained to London, were badly afflicted through the wall which they constructed around the Tower, and through the bridge which was well-nigh washed away, and through work on the king's hall which was constructed at Westminster'. Those who were compelled to work on those projects would mostly have been peasants, who had to neglect work on their own holdings, 'and many a man was afflicted with that'. The other major building project under way in London during William Rufus's reign was the rebuilding of St Paul's Cathedral, destroyed by fire in 1087, 'with many other churches and the largest and noblest part of all the city'.

Westminster Hall was built by Rufus, adjoining the eleventh-century royal residence probably erected by Edward the Confessor. The Tower provided another royal palace, described by William Fitz Stephen in the 1170s as '*ars palatina*', which was 'a fortress of great size and strength, the court and walls of which are erected upon a very deep foundation, the mortar used in the building being tempered with the blood of beasts'. As a fortress, it would have impressed and intimidated Londoners and visitors by its sheer bulk, and its novelty, as a stone castle. Indeed, its only rival in terms of structure and size in late eleventh-century England was the great keep which the Normans built at Colchester. That was slightly larger and was similar in many respects: the apse of its chapel also projects beyond the line of the wall. Both may have been modelled on the great tower of the Norman fortress at Rouen, destroyed in 1204.

The great keep at London gave its name to the castle which was developed from those Norman beginnings. The fortress did not become known as the Castle of London, or London Castle, but the whole complex was designated the Tower of London. The eleventh-century keep itself took the name the White Tower, but this was not adopted until after the building was whitewashed. According to orders issued in 1240, the leaden rainwater pipes 'of the Great Tower, from the Top of the said Tower; through which the Rain Water must fall down' were to be lengthened, 'to make them come down even to the Ground. So that the Wall of the said Tower, lately whitened anew, may by no means decay, nor easily break out, by reason of the Rain Water dropping down.' The order went on to instruct those in charge of the building, 'to whiten the whole old Wall about the often mentioned Tower'. After that general whitewashing, the Norman keep came to be described as the White Tower.

William II was killed while hunting in the New Forest, on 2 August 1100. His younger brother Henry immediately claimed the throne and made his claim stick, despite the rights of his older brother Robert. William had been unpopular, especially with some sections of the church, partly because of the heavy taxation which he had levied, much of which was to fund his military campaigns. His most effective and enterprising financial administrator had been Ranulf Flambard, who by 1088 was the custodian of vacant church lands, which were a profitable source of revenue. By the late 1090s Flambard was acting as one of the regents in the king's absence and was created Bishop of Durham in May 1099. Perhaps to gain popularity and support for his seizure of the throne, Henry had him arrested, within sixteen days of claiming the crown, and imprisoned in the Tower. After six months of imprisonment there, he contrived his escape in February 1101. A rope was smuggled in to him in a pitcher of wine. He treated his guards to a banquet and they became so intoxicated by the wine that he could carry out his planned escape. 'When they were completely drunk and snoring soundly, the bishop produced the rope and tied it to the column which stood in the middle of a window of the tower: holding his pastoral staff with him, he climbed down the rope.' All did not go as well as planned; he scuffed his bare hands on the rope and when he reached the bottom found that it was not long enough, so he had to drop to the ground. But friends were waiting for him with horses, as arranged, and he was able to make good his escape and take a boat to Normandy. His mother came with him. Apparently she had to endure the sailors' insulting comments that she was a one-eyed witch.

Flambard was probably both the first state prisoner confined in the Tower and the first prisoner to escape from it. And he made further trouble for the king. According to the *Anglo-Saxon Chronicle*, 'it was mostly his doing and instigation that this year [1101] the earl Robert sought out this land with hostility', in an attempt to seize the throne from Henry. Yet Flambard maintained contact with the king and in 1106 was able to return to England and take possession of the see of Durham.

The Constable of the Tower, William de Mandeville, was punished for his negligence in allowing Flambard to escape, with the very heavy fine of more than £2,200 and the confiscation of three valuable manors in Essex and Hertfordshire until the fine was paid. William's father, Geoffrey de Mandeville, was the first Constable, appointed by William the Conqueror, and served as sheriff of Essex, Hertfordshire, London and Middlesex. Despite the damage done to the family's wealth by the fine, William's son, also Geoffrey, restored its position and gained influence by expanding his own power and playing off the two sides in the civil war between Stephen and Matilda. He was created Earl of Essex in 1141, in which year a charter granted him hereditary custody of the Tower. Geoffrey died three years later after being wounded attacking a royal castle. He was succeeded by his eldest son, another Geoffrey, who, in turn, was succeeded in 1166 by his younger brother, William, the third earl. But the de Mandeville's custodianship of the Tower was withheld from this William. The family had held it for over eighty years, but not unchallenged. The Treaty of Westminster in 1153 between the warring sides in the civil war named Richard de Lucy, who had remained steadfastly loyal to Stephen throughout, as guardian of the Tower and of Windsor Castle.

As well as the responsibility and potential power which the post of Constable conferred, it provided an income through emoluments and perquisites. Tolls had to be paid by some ships, such as two flagons of wine from a wine ship, a bundle of rushes from a vessel carrying that cargo, and mussels, oysters and cockles from others. Cattle that fell into the river from London Bridge were the Constable's, as were all swans on the river below the bridge, and any flotsam and jetsam. As the number of state prisoners consigned to the Tower increased, it became customary for the Constable and his deputy to claim fees from them and their retinues. The first recorded appointment of a deputy, designated Lieutenant of the Tower, was made in 1189.

Essex remained loyal to the king during the troubled later years of his reign and carried the crown at the coronation of

Richard I, who succeeded to the throne on his father's death in July 1189. Richard was eager to be off on a crusade, with Philip of France, and as part of the arrangements he made for the government of England in his absence he created Essex as joint justiciar, with the Bishop of Durham, Hugh de Puiset, granted authority north of the Humber. But Essex died in November, within two months of his appointment, and the office was then granted to William Longchamp, who had been appointed Chancellor as part of Richard's arrangements for his absence. Richard left England on 11 December 1189 and under Longchamp's direction work soon began on the enlargement of the Tower. Over the following eleven months the substantial sum of £2,881 1s 10d was spent by the Constable on work at the Tower. This was roughly twice Henry II's outlay on building a new castle at Orford, Suffolk, between 1165 and 1173.

The work undertaken by Longchamp involved almost doubling the area of the Tower, by enlarging the outer bailey westwards towards the city. A curtain wall was built running south of west to the point where the Beauchamp Tower was later built. A gatehouse was constructed there; the continuation of Tower Street on its present alignment would reach the line of Longchamp's new wall at that point. The wall was then continued southwards to the river, where the Bell Tower was erected, and eastwards from that tower to join the existing defences. It may be that the Wardrobe Tower was built during this phase, east of the White Tower on the line of the existing curtain wall. Longchamp's workmen also dug a ditch, no less than nineteen feet deep, outside the new wall, apparently 'hoping that the water from the Thames would flow through it'. That did not occur, perhaps because, if the river water did fill the ditch at high tide, the sluices required to retain it in the ditch as the tide receded were faulty. Nevertheless, by the end of 1190 the Tower was a much larger and more strongly defended castle than it had been at Richard's accession. The political situation in his absence was such that, according to Richard of Devizes, across England 'castles were strengthened, towns fortified, ditches dug'.

While Richard was away at the crusade a power struggle developed between his brother John and Longchamp. John had been granted considerable authority by Richard and he and his armed retinue progressed around the country. But Longchamp had the greater power, as co-justiciar, Chancellor, papal legate and Keeper of the King's Seal. Yet because of his personality, background and administrative actions he grew increasingly unpopular, resented by both the barons and the clergy. The chronicler William of Newburgh wrote that he was generally seen as 'an intolerable tyrant'.

To strengthen his position, Longchamp attempted to gain control over castles within the counties assigned to John and in 1191 began to bring in mercenaries from abroad. A formal agreement between the two sides was reached in July, but the dispute flared up again when Longchamp's men seized John's half-brother Geoffrey Plantagenet, Archbishop of York, after he had landed at Dover. John reacted by marching on Longchamp at Windsor. Longchamp moved to the Tower, but was followed to London by John, who was welcomed by the citizens with a torchlight procession. John called a meeting in St Paul's on 8 October, attended by nobles, bishops and citizens, which recognised him as Richard's heir. Longchamp did not resist and the Tower was surrendered after three days, without a siege; Longchamp, stripped of his offices by the great council, left England. His commanders probably recognised that to attempt to hold the fortress in defiance of the hostile citizenry would have been difficult and ultimately futile.

In return for its support, John granted London commune status. A commune was an association of citizens who swore to uphold or extend their rights, which were taken to include choice of a civic leader, known as a mayor. It briefly had such a status in 1141, but no mayor was recorded to have been chosen at that time. The first *de facto* mayor was Henry Fitz Ailwin, an alderman since 1168, who was described as mayor in 1194 and held the post until his death in 1212. He faced a serious challenge, however, in 1196, which arose because of the increased taxation required to raise the ransom of 150,000 marks paid to free Richard I from captivity by the emperor Henry VI. The citizens believed that the civic leaders, including the mayor and members of the commune, taxed themselves lightly and so placed a disproportionate burden on the ordinary citizens.

They found a leader in William Fitz Osbert, whose supporters were prepared to break into the richer citizens' houses to seize the 'tax money'. The discontent became such a threat that Fitz Osbert's supporters were attacked by royal soldiers. During the ensuing clash Fitz Osbert himself killed one of the king's men. He sought sanctuary in St Mary le Bow church, but the right of sanctuary was not respected, the building was set on fire to smoke him out and he was wounded when he emerged. Fitz Osbert was taken to the Tower, before being tried and executed at Tyburn. Essentially, the episode had been a civic dispute into which the government had been drawn.

Such opposition to royal authority did not endear the Londoners to Richard or to John, who succeeded to the throne in 1199, but John eventually conceded the principle of an elected mayor in a charter granted in 1215. He did so in an attempt to retain London's loyalty as his relations with the barons deteriorated. That did gain him some support, but a faction of the citizens backed the rebellious barons, and on Sunday 17 May they allowed their forces into the city, while most citizens were at mass. The mayor was replaced by one of the baronial committee which negotiated with the king. Meanwhile, the Tower remained in the possession of the king's garrison, and the barons' forces were reported to be preparing siege weapons, in an attempt to force its surrender. Emboldened by their control of London and subsequent defections to their cause, the barons pressed their demands and at Runnymede in mid-June the king accepted the terms of Magna Carta.

An agreement probably drawn up at the same time provided for the Archbishop of Canterbury, Stephen Langton, to take possession of the Tower until 15 August, while the barons retained control of the city, and beyond that if the terms of the charter had not been met. The barons would be unlikely to relinquish London, at any time, and indeed relations between the king and his barons worsened again, with the king recruiting mercenaries on the Continent. Civil war began during the autumn of 1215 and in December a force of French troops reached London, after Prince Louis, the son of Philip II, had accepted the barons' offer of the throne. More soldiers arrived in January and February, as allies of the rebels, and a larger force reached the city with Louis on 21 May. Langton, meanwhile, had set off for Rome. The war dragged on without John being able to pose a threat to London, and he died on 18 October 1216. He was succeeded by his son, as Henry III. A victory over the rebels near Lincoln in May 1217 and a naval encounter near Sandwich three months later, in which Louis's supply fleet was defeated, paved the way for a settlement. Peace was concluded by the Treaty of

Lambeth in September 1217, by which Louis and the French forces withdrew.

The Tower's defences had not been put to the test, and in truth they were becoming increasingly out-of-date, as military technology developed. The whole of the castle was to be much improved and enlarged during Henry's reign (1216–72) and that of his son Edward I (1272–1307). Henry was nine years old when he came to the throne, and much of his kingdom was under French occupation. Once the French had been defeated and peace established, his advisers turned their attention to improving the Tower. From 1220 until the end of the reign, almost £10,000 was spent on it.

A great hall already existed on the south side of the inmost ward, against or close to the curtain wall. In 1220 work began on two new towers, one was a 'new tower next to the king's hall towards the Thames', later known as the Wakefield Tower, and 'the small tower' probably was the Lanthorn Tower, to the east. A stretch of curtain wall ran north from the Wakefield Tower to the Coldharbour Gate, adjoining the west side of the White Tower. This was built during the same phase of work, with projecting circular towers, and was entered from the north side. Within this more strongly defended area the buildings of the royal palace were extended and improved. On its south side, the great hall was rebuilt by 1234, served by a new kitchen and, between them, a 'large and fair' saucery. Two suites of rooms were created, on either side of the great hall, one for the king and the other for the queen, Eleanor of Provence, who he married in 1236. The king's chamber was within the Wakefield Tower and the queen's in the Lanthorn Tower, which was taller than the Wakefield Tower and contained three floors, perhaps even four. In 1246–7 new privy chambers for the king and queen were erected. The buildings were decorated with coloured glass and statues, vines grew within the king's garden, and willow and cherry trees were planted. Despite the great improvements to the royal quarters within the Tower, Henry probably stayed there on only eleven occasions in his long reign of fifty-six years.

The enlargement of the palace buildings was followed, from around 1238, by a programme of work during which the outer defences were considerably extended. A new wall punctuated with towers was built on the east and north sides of the complex, well away from the White Tower and beyond the line of the Roman wall. The Salt Tower, in the south-east corner of the new enclosure, was 140 feet from the Lanthorn Tower, to which it was connected by a stretch of curtain wall. The wall on the east side ran to the Martin Tower at the north-east corner, turning to run on an alignment slightly north of west to the Bowyer Tower, from where it followed a course south of west to the Devereux Tower in the north-west corner.

On the east side this involved taking a considerable piece of land from St Katherine's Hospital, which had suffered some loss when Longchamp's great ditch had been dug, including the destruction of the watermill adjoining the Tower's outer wall. In 1239 compensation of £166 was paid to the prior of Holy Trinity, Aldgate, the Master of St Katherine's, 'for the damage they sustained by the wall and ditch of the Tower of London'. Given the failure of Longchamp's engineers to flood the ditches, to supervise the hydraulic arrangements a Flemish engineer was brought in, John le Fossur (whose name literally means a 'ditch digger'), who succeeded in creating a wet moat around the walls.

A catastrophe occurred in April 1240, according to the chronicler Matthew Paris, when 'a noble gateway which the king had built at great expense' collapsed. A year later a section of the new curtain wall also fell down. Henry III's relations with the Londoners were uneasy and they resented the extension of the castle, which they saw as a threat, carried out 'to their detriment'. And so 'the citizens of London were nothing sorry' when the masonry collapsed and they attributed it to the intervention of their guardian saint, Thomas à Becket.

Writing in the sixteenth century, and using Paris as his source, the historian John Stow placed the location of the two disasters to the west of the White Tower, and so the gateway, erected by Longchamp, would have been the principal entrance from the city. The king ordered that the gateway and wall should be rebuilt, and in September 1241 a writ was issued which ordered that timber and lead should be recovered from 'the tower recently fallen'. The location mentioned by Stow is corroborated by the massive foundations of the Beauchamp Tower and adjoining curtain wall, erected later, evidently to guard against a repeat of the two collapses, which probably were the result of building over the infill of Longchamp's ditch.

One reason for the Londoners' resentment of the enlargement of the castle was that on its west side it encroached on the city and houses were demolished. It is improbable that the area taken in was not built upon, even if the royal officials had managed to maintain some clear space between the defences and the houses. And it is likely that the chapel of St Peter ad Vincula ('St Peter in chains'), which was now within the defences, had been a church serving that neighbourhood. Fitz Stephen mentioned that there were 136 parish churches in London in the 1170s, and St Peter's was probably one of them. The building was refurbished by Henry III in 1240, when it was given a new roof, large glazed windows, and in the nave two 'large and handsome stalls' for the king and queen. A 'great painted beam' across the chapel was to carry a crucifix with Mary and John, and 'on either side of the great cross' were to be placed 'two fair cherubim standing, with cheerful and joyful countenances'. Despite those improvements and embellishments, St Peter ad Vincula was rebuilt by Edward I in 1286–7 as 'a great new chapel', at a cost of £317 8s 3d.

An extensive programme of work was undertaken during the early years of Edward I's reign, beginning in 1275. It continued for ten years and cost £21,000. The western curtain wall, from the Devereux Tower to the Bell Tower, was completed, with the Beauchamp Tower built roughly midway along it in 1281, on the site of the former gateway. A new entrance was created beyond the Bell Tower at the south-west corner, through a barbican, later the Lion Tower, the Middle Tower, which was surrounded by the moat, and the Byward Tower. A visitor who had crossed the drawbridge and causeway and passed through those gates would then have been in an outer ward on land reclaimed from the Thames foreshore. A new curtain wall protected that outer ward on the river side as far as the new St Thomas's Tower, a large water-gate that stood in front of the Wakefield Tower and the adjoining Bloody Tower, its predecessor as the water-gate for the palace.

Around the perimeter of Henry's outer walls, his moat was filled in and a new curtain wall was built, without towers, to enclose them. That wall was lower than Henry's walls, which probably were raised as part of the work. A narrow outer ward was created between the two walls, on the site of Henry's moat. Encircling the new outer wall, a new moat was dug, at considerable expense. The wages bill alone was £2,484 between May 1275 and December

1276, and that sum had risen to £4,150 by the time that the work was completed, in 1281 or soon after. In addition, timber would have been required for piling and shoring, and other costs included the construction of water-mills at both the east and west outfalls of the moat into the Thames, and the wages of Walter of Flanders, who supervised the work. Some of the outlay was recovered by selling the clay extracted to the city's tile-makers. With Edward's extension of the defences, the Tower now occupied roughly eighteen acres.

Henry III had been crowned in a rather hurriedly arranged ceremony at Gloucester soon after his succession. A second, much grander, coronation was celebrated in Westminster Abbey in May 1220. To avoid possible disturbances, the Jewish community in London was moved temporarily into the Tower. The same precaution was taken during the celebrations for Henry's marriage to Eleanor. But during the struggle with the rebellious barons in 1264, not all of the Jews were able to take refuge and some were massacred. The Tower was again a safe haven when Henry III died in 1272 and was succeeded by his son Edward. Henry died on 16 November and nine days later Ben' fil Cok', a London Jew, was described as being 'in hiding in the tower of London because of the king's death'.

Edward's reign brought a change of policy and in 1275 the Statute of the Jewry prohibited them from taking interest and granting mortgages, which effectively ended their involvement in the land market. Many members of the community were imprisoned in the Tower between 1275 and the summer of 1277, in various buildings, including stables. A further bout of persecution in 1279–80 was centred on accusations of coin clipping, part of

Edward I's attempt to revise the coinage. As many as 600 Jews were imprisoned in the Tower, and the figure perhaps represented the head of every Jewish household in England. A contemporary chronicler recorded that more than 280 were hanged. For every Christian executed for coinage offences, more than ten Jews were also executed. Despite that ruthless attack on the community and the continued high levels of taxation to which its members were subjected, they adapted to other types of business still open to them, trading as merchants and probably operating as pawn-brokers.

The 1280s was generally a prosperous decade, and the Jewish community benefited from that. But it continued to attract the king's hostility, which partly reflected suspicion of its members' business probity and partly their refusal to convert to Christianity. Edward's antipathy also owed something to the anti-Jewish policies of other rulers in western Europe. It culminated in 1290 in the expulsion of the remaining 2,000 or so Jews, who were ordered 'to voyde the reaume of Engelond be Alhawen tyme [1 November], upon peyne of lesynge of there heedes'. The Constable of the Tower was partly responsible for supervising the process and took a toll from the 1,461 Jews who embarked within his jurisdiction. Of these, 1,335 paid 4d each and 126 who were poor paid a half of that, so that the constable took 'receipt of 23 pounds and 6 shillings by the said custom at the time of the crossing of the Jews'.

Londoners and the crown had experienced troubled relations, with the king intermittently taking the government of the city into his own hands, returning it on payment of a fine. The tensions existed at lower levels also. Even a seemingly well-intentioned and harmless contest at the quintain in 1253 between young knights and others from the royal household and a group of Londoners degenerated into a brawl and exchange of insults after the

Londoners won the contest. When the king's dispute with the rebel barons under the leadership of Simon de Montfort, Earl of Leicester, deteriorated into civil war, in 1263, a faction among London's ruling elite, led by the mayor, threw in their lot with de Montfort.

The king and queen, their households and council took refuge in the Tower and when the queen attempted to leave to go to Windsor, on 13 July, she was insulted and pelted by the Londoners as her barge approached London Bridge, and had to turn back. The rebels entered the city shortly afterwards, trapping the king in the Tower. Perhaps its defenders could have withstood an attack or even a siege, but the king's political position was so uncomfortable that he chose to come to terms with the rebels and agree to their demands. As in 1191, the military power of the Tower had been balanced by the hostility of the citizens beyond its gates, and the king chose not to put its strength to the test. One of de Montfort's supporters, Hugh le De Spencer, was given command of the Tower, which then remained in the barons' control until de Montfort's death at the Battle of Evesham in 1265 and the subsequent revival of the royal cause.

Another crisis erupted when Sir John Deyville and the Earl of Gloucester, erstwhile rebels who were dissatisfied with the post-war settlement, occupied London for two months in the spring of 1267. The Tower was defended by the garrison under the keen eye of Ottobuono de' Fieschi, Pope Clement IV's legate. Henry eventually relieved the Tower, subdued the city and re-imposed his authority, fining London £13,333 for its disloyalty, and withdrawing its liberties for two years. De' Fieschi returned to Rome and in 1276 became Pope, as Adrian V, although he was pontiff for just thirty-eight days before his sudden death. But London's uneasy relations with the crown continued, so much so that in 1285 Edward withdrew the city's government and did not return it to the mayor and officers for thirteen years.

The digging of the new moat, the building of the outer curtain wall and the completion of the inner curtain provided the concentric lines of defence of a modern castle. Edward's achievement at the Tower can be seen in the context of his great programme of castle-building in Wales. For the castles built in the principality after his first campaign there he drew expertise from Savoy, perhaps because he gave precedence to the work at the Tower, which he did not wish to disrupt by taking his masons away from it. His son Edward II (1307–27) rebuilt the south curtain wall east of St Thomas's Tower and erected a tower between the Watergate and the Wakefield tower, described as the 'tower with the king's wardrobe'. During the long reign of Edward III (1327–77) the Cradle Tower was built on that stretch of wall, in 1348–55, for the king's own use, to give direct access from the river front to the palace buildings. The wharf along the Thames was gradually extended during the fourteenth century, until by around 1400 there was a stone wharf along the whole of the Tower's frontage. That reduced the value of the entrance through the Cradle Tower, which now opened onto the moat.

Other work during the later Middle Ages made changes and embellishments within the complex, but did not extend it. Through its enlargement by Henry III and Edward I, by 1300 the castle had reached its maximum extent and had taken the form which is familiar today.

3

THE TOWER IN THE LATE MIDDLE AGES

Much of the space within the area formed by the double line of enclosing walls was taken up by buildings used by a variety of offices of the crown. They were augmented from time to time, as the need arose. But the medieval Tower never lost its prime functions of fortress, palace and prison, and the pressure on space must at times have been considerable. This was in some ways an uncomfortable neighbour for the city, which itself was expanding. Yet it was also a profitable one. The Tower was an important market for London's merchants and artisans, who provided and made items for the wardrobe, and for the suppliers of food and drink.

By the thirteenth century, government was carried on by the state departments and those of the king's household, the chamber and the wardrobe, with the wardrobe gradually superseding the chamber during the early part of the century. The wardrobe was responsible for acquiring and maintaining the king's possessions, including beds and bedding, garments, hangings, armour and weapons. It obtained fabrics and furs and oversaw the making of clothes from them, as well as being responsible for storing and distributing both the raw materials and finished items, with the many other articles which the household required. The wardrobe also bought food, spices, wine, wax, horses, jewels, gold and silver plate, and its clerks were responsible for the routine expenses incurred by the household, for victualling and maintaining armies and garrisons. Its officers had to account with the exchequer, which they drew on for funds.

During the early years of Henry III's reign the wardrobe was divided between the great wardrobe, which had custody of the household's larger items, and the privy wardrobe, which dealt with routine matters and the king's personal property, including arms and armour. The wardrobe also had the keeping of the small, or privy, seal, distinct from the great seal, which was in the care of the Chancellor. But in 1311 care of the privy seal was separated from the duties of the controller of the wardrobe and the Privy Seal Office subsequently developed as a separate department.

The king was peripatetic for much of the time, travelling around his kingdom and possessions in France, or was with his army on campaign. Some of his household items went with him, but much of the remainder was stored in the Tower, including his personal treasure and regalia. While Edward I was on campaign in Scotland in 1303, valuable items from his treasure stored at St Peter's abbey, Westminster, began to appear in London, presumably stolen. And so the treasure was moved to the Tower for safer keeping and an urgent investigation was begun, with Sir Ralph Sandwich, Constable of the Tower since 1285, as one of the four men appointed to carry it out. The loss was valued at £100,000, in a year when the expenditure of the great wardrobe was almost £140,000. Much was recovered, from London goldsmiths and others, and suspicion of the theft fell on the monks for having, at the very least, colluded with the thieves. The sacristan was a suspect, as he had responsibility for the keeping of the abbey's own treasure, and so, too, was the cellarer. During the summer ten monks were imprisoned in the Tower and two more joined them shortly afterwards.

The king was not satisfied with the first enquiry and ordered another, under Sandwich, and by early October forty-eight monks and thirty-two lay members of the community were incarcerated in the Tower. Examinations of the suspects were held there in January and most of the monks and their servants were released, but ten monks, six of the sacristan's servants and some of the abbey's officials were indicted. The monks successfully claimed immunity from prosecution by pleading benefit of clergy, but were not released until early April 1304. Richard Puddlicot, a former merchant, who was on close terms with the abbey's senior figures, had been the leading miscreant in organising and carrying out the robbery, and he was tried and hanged. The theft was all the more serious because of the crown's desperate shortage of funds, caused by the costs of Edward's wars.

The annual fee of £100 due to Sandwich as Constable had never been paid and after the king's death he pleaded for payment of that and various expenses, including the reconstruction of St Peter ad Vincula in 1285–7. He eventually received £1,750 from Edward II, 'in consideration of his free and praiseworthy service to him and his father'. That could not be said of his successor, John Cromwell, who was alleged to have neglected the palace building to such an extent that rainwater came through the roof of the royal bed-chamber. He was dismissed.

In 1338 John de Flete was appointed 'Keeper of the King's Jewels, Armour and other things in the Tower of London'; he was the first recorded holder of the post. By the early fifteenth century the position had become 'Keeper of the King's Jewels and Treasurer of the Chamber', to which Richard Courtenay was appointed by 1413. The king's possessions were stored in the White Tower and buildings around the inner ward, including, presumably, the Wardrobe Tower, although the name is not recorded until the late sixteenth century. The names of many of the towers were changed through time and became fixed only during the Tudor period. By the reign of Edward II (1307–27) the wardrobe also occupied the Wakefield Tower, which had contained the king's apartments. Edward III (1327–77) used the Lanthorn Tower for his chambers, and St Thomas's Tower was taken over by the wardrobe for storage.

The growing number of items that had to be kept included diplomatic documents and those generated by the household, and so the Tower became a major repository for the crown's archives. It had been used for that purpose since at least 1205–6, when it was recorded that 'the plees of the coroune were pleted in the tour of London'. A century later there were so many documents, and their storage was so badly arranged, that sometimes they could not be found when needed. Some attempt was made to deal with the growing problem. In 1312 the treasurer provided more racks for the storage of documents and in 1320 St John's chapel in the White Tower was fitted with additional racks. In that year Walter Stapledon, Bishop of Exeter, was created Lord High Treasurer and, as part of his administrative reforms, he instituted a sorting of the documents, not only those in the Tower, but also those of the exchequer and treasury kept at Westminster. They were loaded on to barges and taken along the Thames to the Tower.

The actual sorting was done in St John's chapel by the two chamberlains and up to a dozen clerks, and took eighteen months. They rearranged the items and produced two calendars of Anglo-Gascon diplomatic records. That 'great array' was completed in

1322 and another, briefer, sorting was carried out three years later. The exchequer records were returned to Westminster after being sorted, but many of the treasury records remained in the Tower, with those of chancery.

In 1361 the wardrobe acquired from Sir John Beauchamp's executors the house which he had built opposite to the Blackfriars monastery on St Andrew's Hill, south of St Paul's. The wardrobe's bulky goods were moved there from the Wakefield Tower, which was then used for storing the chancery records that had been in the White Tower. The early-fourteenth-century overhaul of the documents had greatly improved record keeping and had continued the Tower's role as a repository of the crown's records. Nevertheless, pressure on storage space continued to grow and in 1377 the site of the Converts House in Chancery Lane was assigned by Edward III to the Keeper of the Rolls of Chancery. Henry III had established the house around 1231 for Jews who had converted to Christianity; after 1290 the house was no longer needed for that purpose. The Chancery clerks were based there and the chapel of the converts provided a new repository.

The Tower had also become the principal storehouse for that section of the privy wardrobe which had custody of military equipment. It included coats of chain mail, shields, suits of armour, helmets and gauntlets, together with swords, lances, spears, axes, bills and daggers, bows and arrows, crossbows and bolts. In the fourteenth century sets of plate armour superseded mail for the knightly class, and shields became redundant. The finest suits of plate armour were imported from Milanese makers, although their skills were gradually acquired by London armourers. In 1380 one Richard Davy was noted to have 'lived in Lombardy and there learnt the mistery of making breastplates', and he was ordered to 'stay in the Tower of London for the purpose of making them for the king's use and instructing others therein'.

As well as being a place of storage and of receipt for confiscated and captured weapons, the Tower increasingly became a centre of arms production, with workshops for carpenters and furnaces for smiths. By the beginning of the fourteenth century those who were being paid included the king's smith, the king's armourer and the maker of the king's crossbows and crossbow bolts. The Keeper of the Artillery in the Tower of London was responsible for all projectile weapons, including siege engines for flinging big stones, arrows and crossbows, and the early holders of the post were crossbow makers.

Cannon came into use during the middle of the century; three were deployed by Edward III at the Battle of Crécy during his campaign in France in 1346, which culminated in the capture of Calais. By that date gunpowder was being manufactured in the Tower, but the cannon were made by founders outside the royal establishment. These early guns were mostly of copper; in 1353 William of Aldgate supplied four 'gunnos de cupro [copper]' and in 1365 nine 'gunnes de cupro' were listed at the Tower. A similar list compiled in 1399 included forty-three cannon 'de cupro et ferro [iron]'. The founders who made the guns generally were bell founders and William Wodeward, who supplied cannon to the king, also held the specialist position of Keeper of the King's Great Clock at Westminster. He cast seventy-three of the eighty-seven new guns bought by the Keeper of the Privy Wardrobe between 1382 and 1388. Most of them weighed between 318 pounds and 380 pounds, although the largest was twice that weight, and were bought at the rate of roughly 4d per pound. Many of the pieces bought by the privy wardrobe were deployed at other castles or were with the armies on campaign. In the 1380s only eleven were retained at the Tower for its defence; nevertheless the storage and maintenance of cannon, associated equipment and gunpowder were to take an increasingly large area within the walls. Even the buildings which formed the royal palace were encroached upon, with stone cannon balls being made in the great hall and chests of armour stored in the queen's chamber.

The armour and personal weapons maintained by the wardrobe were issued for use in tournaments and jousts. The mid-fourteenth century saw the development of suits of armour designed especially for those mock combats. Such pieces were first listed in an inventory drawn up between 1337 and 1341. The large-scale tournaments that involved hundreds, even thousands, of knights required extensive sites and so were held some distance from London. But jousts, which were combats between individuals, could take place in much more restricted areas, with Smithfield, Cheapside, and even London Bridge, commonly used. Those participating in them often processed from the Tower to the site of the joust.

As tournaments declined, jousts became increasingly common during the second half of the thirteenth and the fourteenth centuries. They were held over several days, as long as fifteen days for one staged in London by Edward III in 1342. Such events were major spectacles, providing opportunities for the king to parade distinguished prisoners in procession through London's streets after a successful campaign, and the wardrobe had to provide suitably lavish costumes for the participants and the courtiers who were spectators. Philippa of Hainault, Edward III's queen, was a prominent sponsor of jousts and, towards the end of his reign, so was Alice Perrers, his mistress, who in 1375 rode 'as lady of the sune, fro the tour of London through Chepe; and alwey a lady ledynge a lordys brydell'. Jousts continued to be encouraged by Richard II, who succeeded to the throne as a ten-year-old in 1377. In 1385, 'was a great rydynge fro the tour of London to Westm'; and evere a lord ledde a ladyes bridell', reversing the procedure of ten years earlier. At a joust in October 1390, twenty knights paraded from the Tower to Smithfield, where the combat was to be held.

The Tower was also the starting point of a king's procession through London to Westminster for his coronation. The practice was begun by Edward I in October 1274, although he was an infrequent resident of the Tower during the remainder of his reign. Edward II followed the same procedure for his coronation in February 1308, and the custom of processing through the city from the Tower was continued by every monarch until James II, who declined to observe the tradition in 1685. It also became the practice for the king to create Knights of the Bath on the eve of the coronation. Candidates underwent a purification ritual on the previous day and then kept an overnight vigil in St John's chapel, praying and watching over their arms, before being dubbed by the king.

As well as clothing, treasure and weaponry, the wardrobe was responsible for looking after those exotic animals given to or acquired by the monarch. In 1204 wild beasts for King John were transported to England from Normandy in three ships and they probably included the lions recorded at the Tower in 1210–2. Henry III's coat of arms depicted three leopards and so, in 1235, the Emperor, Frederick II, sent him an appropriate gift of three leopards. Five years later a lion was recorded at the Tower. An equally exotic animal was the polar bear which was given to

Henry in 1251. A muzzle and chain were acquired, and a strong tether to hold the bear when he was swimming in the Thames. The daily allowance for the bear's food was 1s 2d, which compares with the 2d per day for the lion, and 1½d for the lion's keeper. Those allowances and the keepers' wages were paid by the sheriffs of London, who also had to provide a house forty feet by twenty feet for the elephant which Louis IX of France gave to Henry in 1255. Matthew Paris enthusiastically described it as 'the only elephant ever seen in England ... the people flocked together to see the novel sight'. He was among them and not only described the elephant, as about ten years old and ten feet high, but made a coloured drawing of it, showing one of its forelegs tethered to a stake, being tended by its keeper. The elephant died two years after its arrival, and its carcass was buried within the Tower.

By the 1330s the menagerie of lions, leopards and bears may have been in the barbican at the western entrance to the complex, where the Lion Tower housed the king's beasts in the sixteenth century. The office of 'Keeper of the Lions, Lionesses and Leopards in the Tower' was created in the fifteenth century. This was a supervisory or honorary position and its holders were not involved with the daily care of the animals. That continued to be carried out by the keepers, some of whom incurred considerable debts because of the tardy payment of their allowances. And their efforts were not always successful, for in 1436 there 'deyde all the lyons that were in the Tour of London'.

The Mint was a later arrival at the Tower than the menagerie. The number of cities and towns where coins were minted fell steadily from the late eleventh century, until by the mid-thirteenth century their production was concentrated in London and Canterbury. But security seems to have been a low priority and coins were made in workshops in the streets, away from the king's palaces or castles. According to John Stow, 'the Place of Coining, was the Old Exchange', near Sermon Lane, south of St Paul's, which he discovered had been called Sheremoniers Lane in the late thirteenth century. Stow also found evidence that the street had contained 'a Place to be called the Black Loft, of melting Silver; with four Shops adjoining. It may therefore be well supposed, that Lane to take Name of Sheremoniers; such as cut and rounded the Plates, to be coined or stamped into Estarling Pence.'

During the early years of Edward I's reign the operation was centralised and moved into the Tower. It is likely that the move was part of the great recoinage which the king initiated in 1279, for by around 1280 the master worker of the Mint was liable for fees payable to the parson and sexton of St Peter ad Vincula. The practice of clipping silver from the edges of coins had become so common that their value had been reduced. Those coins were to be surrendered and exchanged for new ones, and new denominations were issued. According to the *Great Chronicle of London*: 'the kyng made newe money of silver called half penys and farthynges, alle rounde, of whiche were none sen before'. The third new coin was the groat, which was worth 4*d*. The recoinage began in April 1279 and by the time that it was completed, at the end of 1281, the London mints had struck £357,780. The operation had been overseen by a team of mint-masters from the Continent that included William de Turnemire from Marseilles, who was appointed Master of the Mint.

A further recoinage was begun in 1299 and completed in the following year. That was aimed at replacing similar coins, but of less weight, struck abroad and brought into England, while the more valuable English coins were exported. Perhaps it was to oversee the process that John Sandale was appointed warden of the Mint. He had begun his career as a royal administrator in the wardrobe and had also worked at the exchequer before being appointed Keeper of the Royal Mints in 1298. He went on to be Chancellor of the Exchequer, Treasurer, Dean of St Paul's and, in 1316, Bishop of Winchester. Sandale ordered the erection of a building 400 feet long in the Tower to house the furnaces, which were to be increased in number to thirty. The number of workmen in the Mint was also inadequate for the surge in production, and so 263 experienced coin-makers were brought to London from Paris, Brussels, Bruges, Namur and Brabant.

The location of the Mint's operations may have been, from the first, where it certainly was by the sixteenth century, in the outer ward on the west side, which became known as Mint Street. The curtain walls on both sides would have reduced the obvious risk of a fire that broke out among the furnaces spreading to other buildings. That site would have been just large enough to accommodate the long building that Sandale erected, and it fitted the common description of the Mint as 'the mint below the Tower'.

As the detention of the monks of Westminster demonstrated, the Tower served as the state prison, not only for individuals who had erred politically or administratively, but also for groups of people who had fallen foul of the monarch. The towers that punctuated the new curtain walls of the thirteenth century had considerably increased the accommodation that could be used for such prisoners. Londoners were wary of this, being concerned that citizens could be imprisoned for trying to extend the city's liberties, and so they complained to the king, 'fearing lest that were done to their detriment', which he denied.

A tower would be allocated for the exclusive use of a distinguished prisoner and his retinue, although if the number of attendants was too high, some of them would be housed in the city. The numbers of such prisoners held at the Tower increased during Edward I's wars against the Scots and Welsh, and the campaigns of Edward III in France that continued after his reign and became known as the Hundred Years' War. But monarchs and members of the nobility were not confined to the Tower during the whole of their imprisonment. Although they were commonly housed there at the start of their captivity, so that they could be paraded through London as trophies that were evidence of the king's victories, they were then accommodated elsewhere. Such prisoners were, in any case, allowed to go out riding and hunting, and could be attended by their own servants and bring in their choice of furnishings and possessions.

David II, King of Scotland, was captured at the Battle of Neville's Cross in 1346 and was held in captivity for eleven years, much of that time in the Tower. But he was allowed to go to the north to take part in the negotiations with the Scots in 1351–2, and perhaps again in 1353, and to spend some time in Scotland in 1352. John II of France was taken at the Battle of Poitiers in 1356, with his son Philippe, and after being held in various palaces while his ransom was being discussed, he and Philippe were taken to the Tower in April 1360 from Somerton Castle in Lincolnshire. They arrived with five cartloads of goods, and another came later bringing the instruments of 'John the organist'. Because space in the White Tower was required for the king, his son and their entourage, the chancery records were moved to the Wakefield Tower. When his ransom of half a million pounds had been negotiated and the terms of the Treaty of Bretigny agreed, the French king entertained Edward and Queen Philippa, at a great banquet in the Tower. Later that year, with the first instalment of his ransom paid, he was returned to French soil by Edward the Black Prince, who had captured him. He left three of his sons as a pledge for payment of the remainder of the sum, but one of them, Louis, Duke of Anjou, escaped and did not return. On hearing of this, in 1363 John voluntarily returned to London, where he died at the Savoy, in April 1364.

Ransom played an important role in medieval warfare, as a means for an individual knight to acquire wealth, and for the crown to offset the costs of its campaigns. And so those prisoners who would command a high ransom were detained until the agreed sum was paid, regardless of the diplomatic situation. Charles, Duke of Orléans, was captured by Henry V's army at Agincourt in 1415. As the nephew of the French king, Charles VI, he was a considerable asset, and was held in England, although only initially in the Tower. As the English forces ravaged his estates in the Loire valley, the money for his release could not be raised, and only in the changed military and diplomatic circumstances of the late 1430s could a realistic sum be agreed. It was obtained by a levy taken throughout France and he was released in 1440. His brother Jean, Count of Angoulême, had been sent to England as a hostage and he was freed in 1445, after an imprisonment of thirty years.

Despite the comfortable arrangements for many prisoners, some did attempt to escape. Gruffudd ap Llywelyn was handed over to Henry III in 1341 by his half-brother Dafydd, with the warning that were he to be allowed to go free, there could be further conflict in Wales. He was imprisoned in the Tower, with other

Welsh detainees, and the king gave him a daily allowance and permitted his wife to visit him. But on the night of 1 March 1244 he attempted to escape, making a rope of his bed linen. He fell and his neck was broken.

The conditions in which Roger, Lord Mortimer, and his nephew, also Roger, Earl of March, were imprisoned in 1322 were not so comfortable. They had engaged in an alliance with Thomas, Earl of Lancaster, in an attempt to lessen the De Spencer family's influence over Edward II. After Lancaster was defeated at Boroughbridge, the Mortimers were tried and condemned to death, but their sentence was commuted to imprisonment and they were held in the Tower. The young Mortimer cleverly escaped, 'by giving to his keepers a sleepy drink' at a banquet where the Constable and his officers were 'made intoxicated'. But his uncle remained in confinement until his death in the Tower in August 1326.

In the following month Mortimer, who had taken refuge in France, and Queen Isabella landed with an army at Orwell. Londoners were opposed to the king and after he had left the Tower nominally in the charge of his nine-year-old second son John, Earl of Cornwall, the citizens broke in, 'wrested the keys out of the hands of the constable and delivered all the prisoners'. John was made Keeper of the Tower and the city. During this tumult Walter Stapledon was caught by the citizens before reaching sanctuary in St Paul's and he and at least three others were beheaded in Cheapside, where their bodies were displayed. In the aftermath of this eruption Edward II was captured and, in the following January, was deposed.

Early that summer Sir Hugh de Spencer had taken steps to strengthen the Tower's defences with 'barriers and wooden towers' on all the 'turrets and embrasures' and at all the gates, and had ordered the provision of 'engines and siege machines and other kinds of apparatus of great cost'. His efforts were all to no avail, for the garrison had failed in its loyalty to the king, so that the powerful stronghold had been captured by a crowd of citizens. The episode demonstrated the obvious fact that a fortress is only as strong as the trustworthiness and determination of its defenders. The young Edward III came to the throne and in 1330 toppled Mortimer from his authority and sent him to the Tower. He was executed not within the Tower or on Tower Hill, but at Tyburn, the place of execution for common criminals.

The Tower again succumbed to an attack in 1381, during the Peasants' Revolt. That uprising was partly provoked by the poll tax, a new levy of 1s payable by everyone aged between sixteen and sixty. The rebels from Kent assembled on Blackheath on 12 June and then entered London and those from Essex arrived at the city two days later. Richard II was at the Tower with his mother, Joan of Kent, his uncle, the Earl of Buckingham, Simon Sudbury, Archbishop of Canterbury and Chancellor, Sir Robert Hales, the Treasurer, and a number of earls and other members of the nobility. The Kentish rebels, led by Wat Tyler, ran amok in the city. They looted the shops, set fire to John of Gaunt's palace of the Savoy and 'destroyed several fine houses', attacked the archbishop's palace at Lambeth, captured the Fleet and Marshalsea prisons, burned the lawyers' books at the Temple, and threatened to 'burn and destroy everything'.

On the 14th the king, who was fourteen years old, appeared at one of the towers on the outer walls of the Tower and called to the rebels, with a promise to pardon them if they would disperse. They ignored his offer and so he courageously rode from the

Tower with his entourage for a meeting with the rebels at Mile End. But while they were away from the fortress the rebels from Kent broke in. For some reason, the guards offered no resistance, and the crown's stronghold was overrun by the insurgents, who swarmed around the buildings and released the prisoners. They discovered Sudbury and Hales in St John's chapel, preparing for the worst, and dragged them to Tower Hill, where they were beheaded, together with John Legge, serjeant at law, who was held responsible for the poll tax, and William Appleton, John of Gaunt's physician. The rebels also ransacked the kitchens and bedchambers, forced their way into Joan of Kent's apartments, smashed the furniture, pulled down the wall hangings and cut up the bedding. Although she was insulted and some of the intruders 'invited the king's mother to kiss them', she was able to escape by river to Baynard's Castle. The Tower was not entirely the secure fortress that its builders had envisaged.

When the king returned to London he went to the great wardrobe, not the Tower, and on the following day again met the rebels, in Smithfield. Tyler's behaviour there infuriated members of the royal entourage. One of them insulted Tyler, perhaps to provoke him, and when Tyler tried to attack the courtier Sir William Walworth, the Lord Mayor, intervened. Tyler struck at him with his dagger, but as Walworth was wearing armour he was unhurt and stabbed Tyler in the neck. The wounded Tyler took refuge in St Bartholomew's priory, but was dragged out and executed. The king defused a potentially serious situation by riding ahead of the rebels, telling them to follow him to Clerkenwell, which they did. By 15 June the king was again in control of London and the Tower, and the revolt then petered out.

The causes of those shocking events were analysed by John Wycliffe, who was critical of the policies of the lay and ecclesiastical establishments and sympathetic to the problems faced by the poor. Those who followed his reforming ideas and developed them, the Lollards, were never in a position to influence policy, despite attracting support among a group of courtiers. Richard II's fall came not from popular dissent, but opposition among the nobility. Five leading nobles, who became known as the Lords Appellant, defeated the king's army in 1387 and marched on London, where they confronted Richard in the Tower. He survived the crisis and wrested power back from them in 1389. His mistrust of them lingered and three of them were dealt with in 1397 on charges of treason. When Henry Bolingbroke, Earl of Derby, and Thomas Mowbray, formerly Earl of Nottingham and now Duke of Norfolk, quarrelled in 1398, Richard was given an opportunity to neutralise them, too. The council decided that their differences would be settled by combat, but the king dramatically intervened and banished them both, Mowbray for life and Bolingbroke for ten years. After Bolingbroke's father, John of Gaunt, Duke of Lancaster, died in 1399, the king extended his punishment to a lifetime in exile.

Richard then mounted an expedition to Ireland, with most of his loyal supporters. In his absence Bolingbroke returned to claim his inheritance as Duke of Lancaster and perhaps to challenge the king. On his return from Ireland, Richard found his support to be so meagre that he submitted to Bolingbroke at Flint and, early in September, 'kyng Richard was put into the tour of London tyl tyme that the parlement, whiche began at Westm' on seynt Jeromys day the laste of Septembre; whiche day, in the tour of London, kyng Richard resigned his dignyte'. Bolingbroke took the throne as Henry IV.

The Lollards were prosecuted and punished as heretics, whatever their social background. They formed a category of prisoners that was to become prominent in the sixteenth and early seventeenth centuries; those who would not conform to the church's teachings and theology. Many of those convicted at the heresy trials of Henry IV's reign (1399–1413) were in the Tower for a short time, as they were commonly executed soon after conviction. Sir John Oldcastle, a successful military commander, MP and friend of the king, was less harshly treated in 1413, after an outburst against papal authority at a hearing by the archbishop. He was sent to the Tower for forty days. His friends in London helped him to escape and in 1414 he attempted to raise a Lollard rebellion, which was easily overcome at St Giles-in-the-Fields. He was burnt at Smithfield three years later.

Its political credibility destroyed, Lollardy nevertheless survived throughout the fifteenth century and contributed prisoners to the Tower. They included Richard Hunden, a wool packer, who ate flesh on Fridays, and was 'dampned as a fals heretyk and a lollard, and brent at the Tour hill'. Richard Wyche, a priest who was 'of many lewde folks accepted for an holy man', was also burned there, in 1440, for saying 'that the posterne of the tower shulde synke, as after it dyd, and other fantastical dedys or wordes'.

Similar events to those of the Peasants' Revolt occurred during Jack Cade's rebellion in 1450. The rebels, from Kent, occupied London. James Fiennes, Lord Saye and Sele, the immensely unpopular Lord Treasurer, was first arrested and imprisoned in the Tower and when the rebels occupied the city he was taken out, tried at Guildhall and executed in Cheapside. That evening 'London did arise and came out upon them at ten on the bell ... And from that time until the morrow eight of the bell they were ever fighting upon London Bridge.' The rebellion was quashed, not by the military garrison of the Tower but through the citizens' reaction to the occupation of their city and the rebels' behaviour.

Cade's rebellion came at a time when the English were being driven out of Normandy and were losing the wars in France. Henry V was named heir to the French throne in 1420, but died in 1422, when his heir, Henry VI, was not quite nine months old. A few weeks later the French king, Charles VI, also died and by the Treaty of Troyes of 1420, Henry was King of England and France. He was crowned King of England in Westminster Abbey in 1429 and in December 1431 his coronation as Henry II of France was celebrated in Notre Dame Cathedral in Paris, but not in Reims Cathedral, where by tradition French kings were crowned. Reims was then occupied by the French and their military revival from the early 1430s saw the loss of almost all English possessions in France. The Duke of Somerset was blamed for the defeat at Formigny in April 1450 and his surrender of Caen a few months later, which precipitated the loss of Normandy. He was imprisoned in the Tower later that year until the king intervened and ordered his release. The last battle of the Hundred Years' War was the English defeat at Castillon in Gascony in 1453, which was followed three months later by the surrender of Bordeaux.

Henry VI was an ineffectual monarch and was declared insane in 1453. The Duke of York, acting as regent, consigned Somerset to another spell of imprisonment in the Tower. Two years later Somerset was killed at the Battle of St Albans, the first encounter of a period of intermittent warfare between factions of the aristocracy that was to continue for thirty years. The name 'The Wars of the Roses' was first used by Sir Walter Scott in 1829, in his novel *Anne of Geierstein*.

London attempted to remain aloof from the wars, but by the end of the 1450s probably was more sympathetic to the Yorkists than to the Lancastrians. The citizens experienced fighting at first hand in 1460, during a period of rapid reversal of fortunes: a Yorkist victory at Blore Heath in Staffordshire was followed by the disintegration of their army after a confrontation at Ludford in Shropshire. The Yorkist leaders fled to Calais, but returned and occupied London before setting off to confront the king's army, which was concentrated at Northampton. His supporters left in London were Lord Scales and Lord Hungerford. They had withdrawn to the Tower, which they then endeavoured to hold, but, as a chronicler recorded:

> the Tower was besieged by land and water that no victual might come to them that were within ... they that were within the Tower cast wild fire into the city and shot in small guns, and brend and hurt men and women and children in the streets. And they of London cast great bombards on the further side of the Thames against the Tower and crazed the walls thereof in divers places.

The defenders hoped for relief, but they surrendered after news reached them of the king's defeat at the Battle of Northampton on 10 July. Hungerford and Scales were to be pardoned and allowed to leave, and Hungerford did get away, but Scales was killed by boatmen as he attempted to go to Westminster by boat.

The damage in the city caused by the defenders may partly explain Scales's violent death, and the citizens' opposition to the Lancastrians after their victory at St Albans in February 1461. Fearful that the Lancastrian army would sack their city, the citizens closed Cripplegate against a delegation of Lancastrian knights that arrived to demand its surrender. They also prevented a convoy of supplies for the Lancastrian army from leaving: 'when they with the victuals came to Cripplegate, the commons arose and stopped the carts, and would suffer none to depart out of the City'. Meanwhile, Edward, Earl of March, heir of the Duke of York, who had been killed at the Battle of Wakefield on 30 December 1460, had won a significant victory at Mortimer's Cross and then marched towards London, so the Lancastrians retreated. He entered the city, took control of the Tower, and on 4 March was proclaimed King Edward IV.

Henry VI then went to Scotland, but that was not a safe haven after an Anglo-Scottish truce was agreed in December 1463. Following the Lancastrian defeats at Hedgeley Moor and Hexham in 1464 he was a fugitive, until he was captured in Ribblesdale in July 1465. He spent the next five years in captivity at the Tower. When Edward IV was outmanoeuvred and fled abroad in October 1470, Henry was restored to the throne, but Edward returned and won a decisive victory at Tewkesbury the following spring. Henry was then returned to the Tower; Edward came back to London on 21 May and within a few hours 'King Herry, being inward in prison in the Tower of London, was put to death, the 21st day of May, on a Tuesday night, between eleven and twelve of the clock'. His death must have been sanctioned by Edward, and he, his brother Richard, Duke of Gloucester, 'and many other' were in the fortress at the time. To Philippe de Commynes, in France, it seemed as though it was in the Tower that Henry 'spent the greater part of his life and was finally killed'. Edward, Prince of Wales, was killed at Tewkesbury, and the queen, Margaret of Anjou, a leading figure in the Lancastrian cause, was taken after the battle and brought to the Tower on the day that her husband died. Her political influence was now extinguished. Within a few months she was allowed to leave the Tower, first for Windsor and later for Wallingford Castle, where she lived under the supervision of Alice de la Pole, Dowager Duchess of Suffolk. She returned to France in 1476, on payment of a ransom of 50,000 crowns.

The clear victory of Edward and the Yorkists did not end intrigue and rivalries among the families close to the throne. These were notably between the Woodvilles, the queen's family, the Greys and the Stanleys, and between the king's brothers, George, Duke of Clarence, and Richard, Duke of Gloucester. Clarence married the Earl of Warwick's daughter Isabel, although the king had forbidden the marriage, and the dispute over the Warwick inheritance was one of the causes of the rift between him and Richard. In January and February 1478 a sitting of parliament considered charges against Clarence and he was put on trial. The prosecution was promoted by the king, who had been increasingly exasperated by Clarence's high-handed actions and abuse of power; on his arrest he denounced him as being 'in contempt of the law of the land and a great threat to judges and jurors of the kingdom'. But the king may have been encouraged by the Woodvilles, for the queen perhaps regarded Clarence as a potential threat to the succession of their son Edward, born in 1470. Convicted of treason, Clarence was executed in the Tower on 18 February.

What made Clarence's case unusual in an age marked by the violent deaths of members of the royal family and the nobility, was the report that he was killed not by any conventional means, but was drowned in a butt of malmsey, a strong, sweet wine. That was not repeated by all contemporary chroniclers, although the story was current within five years of his death, and perhaps earlier. According to the Latin scholar Dominic Mancini, who visited England in 1483 on behalf of the Archbishop of Vienne, 'the mode of execution preferred in this case was, that he should die by being plunged in a jar of sweet wine'. Commynes wrote that he was 'put to death in a pipe [cask] of malmsey'. Sir Thomas More later wrote that 'attainted was hee by parliament, and iudged to the death, and therupon hastely drouned in a Butte of Malmesey'. Shakespeare elaborated, giving one of Clarence's murderers the words, 'Take him over the costard with the hilts of thy sword, and then we will chop him in the malmsey-butt in the next room.' To which his fellow murderer replies, 'O excellent devise! make a sop of him.'

During Edward's reign, in 1480, 'This yere were the diches about the Tour newe cast, and the Tour newe repeired.' When he died, unexpectedly, on 9 April 1483, Edward, Prince of Wales was at Ludlow with his half-brother Sir Richard Grey and his uncle, Anthony Woodville, Earl Rivers, while his brother Richard, Duke of York was in London with their mother. The royal entourage eventually set off for the capital and were met at Stony Stratford on 30 April by Richard, Duke of Gloucester, the new king's uncle, and his ally the Duke of Buckingham. After spending a hospitable evening together, on the following day Gloucester took charge of the boy king, Edward, dismissed his household and arrested Grey and Rivers. The royal party then continued to London and by 8 May Richard had been recognised as Protector. On 8 June at a council meeting in the Tower he acted against Lord Hastings, who was arrested and summarily executed. Hastings had been a close advisor of Edward IV and hitherto Richard's ally against the Woodvilles, but perhaps had come to suspect Richard's ambitions. These became clear through a campaign on his behalf that questioned the legitimacy of his nephews, on the grounds that Edward IV had made a previous marriage contract with one Lady Eleanor Butler before he married Elizabeth Woodville, and such an agreement was binding. This laid the groundwork for having the boys declared illegitimate, so that Richard could claim the crown, and his case was justified in sermons, speeches and a manifesto known as *Titulus Regius*.

When news of the coup at Stony Stratford reached London the queen took the young Duke of York with her to sanctuary in Westminster Abbey. On his arrival in the capital, Edward V was treated respectfully and initially taken to the Bishop of London's palace. Only later, by 19 May, was he taken to the Tower, to prepare for his coronation. Cardinal Thomas Bourchier, Archbishop of Canterbury, persuaded the queen to let the Duke of York join his brother there, which he did on 16 June. With both princes in his power, Richard moved to secure the throne for himself; he was elected king by an assembly of notables on 25 June, took the throne as Richard III on the following day and was crowned on 6 July.

Grey and Rivers were executed at Pontefract on 25 June, but what had happened to the princes was not clear and the absence of firm and reliable testimony allowed ample scope for speculation and partisan allegations. Richard did not counter suspicions that the princes were dead by producing them, which would on the one hand have ended the rumours, but, on the other, confirmed to those unhappy with his taking the throne that Edward should remain a focus for their efforts. In July there was a conspiracy uncovered to rescue the boys and restore Edward to the throne. But by September there was a growing presumption that they had been killed, perhaps by Richard, but with the possibility that Buckingham had connived at their deaths, or was responsible for them. (He had a claim to the throne as a descendant of Edward III's son Thomas of Woodstock.) An account which may be contemporary noted that the boys had been 'put to deyth in the Towur of London be the vise of the duke of Buckingham'.

Rumours in some European courts also attributed the princes' deaths to Buckingham. At the French court, Commynes wrote that Buckingham 'had put the two children to death', although elsewhere in his memoirs he noted that Richard 'had his two nephews murdered and made himself king'. Dominic Mancini was in England at the time and wrote that

> all the attendants who had waited upon the king were debarred access to him. He and his brother were withdrawn into the inner apartments of the Tower proper, and day by day began to be seen more rarely behind the bars and windows, till at length they ceased to appear altogether.

He went on to comment that he did not know whether Edward had 'been done away with, and by what manner of death'; his information was incomplete and he depended in some measure on news and gossip provided by others, many of whom would have expressed their own partisan bias. He admitted, though, that he was unable to obtain 'the names of those to be described, the intervals of time, and the secret designs of men in this whole affair'.

Mancini was not alone in fearing for the princes and, as the presumption of Edward V's death spread, those unhappy with Richard's usurpation now began to look to other candidates as king. But a rebellion by Buckingham, Richard's erstwhile ally, in October 1483 was easily defeated and he was executed. Even disaffected Yorkists then turned to the Lancastrian candidate, Henry Tudor, in Brittany; they would hardly have done so if there had been hope that Edward was alive. After a period of growing uncertainty, Tudor invaded and on 22 August 1485 Richard's army was defeated at Bosworth in Leicestershire and he was killed during the battle. Tudor took the throne as Henry VII.

Richard's character was thoroughly blackened by writers under the Tudor dynasty, culminating in the personification of evil depicted by Shakespeare. In truth, that process had already begun during his reign, when his own effective style of propaganda had been turned against him. Only later were alternative interpretations provided, by Sir George Buck, diplomat and Master of the Revels, in the early seventeenth century, and by Horace Walpole in 1768. But not until the mid-twentieth century was the basic view of an evil usurper who was responsible for the murder of his two nephews seriously revised. Much of Richard's reputation derived from the deaths of the boys, the Princes in the Tower, whose fate had become inextricably associated with the fortress where they were assumed to have been murdered. Both Richard II and Henry VI had been killed after they had been deposed, but Edward V and his brother were children, were in Richard's care and he owed them his loyalty, and so his was regarded as a most heinous crime, rather than a move in the political game to secure his own position as king.

The case against Richard was supported by the testimony of Sir James Tyrell, who admitted to his role in the killing of the princes. He had been a long-standing servant of Richard and his close association with him gave his confession plausibility. Tyrell successfully transferred his loyalty to Henry, but in 1502 was convicted of treason and executed. He confessed to his part in the princes' deaths during the four days between his conviction and execution. The confession does not survive, but was reported by later writers, including Sir Thomas More, probably writing eleven years after Tyrell's death, and Polydore Vergil, both of whom were hostile to Richard. According to their accounts, Richard ordered the Constable of the Tower, Sir Robert Brackenbury, to have the boys killed and when he demurred Tyrell was assigned the task. More admitted that he had heard differing accounts of the princes' deaths, preferring 'that way that I have so heard by such men and such means as me thinketh it were hard but it should be true'. In his account, the boys were 'both shut up' and all but one of their servants withdrawn. Tyrell chose Miles Forest, one of their four gaolers, and John Dighton to do the deed, and one night the two men smothered the boys in their beds. On Tyrell's orders they then buried the bodies 'at the stair foot, meetly deep in the ground, under a great heap of stones'. Despite that description of the place, no bodies were produced by Henry VII, to deter potential pretenders from claiming their identity. Even so, Tyrell's explanation was a convenient one for Henry by removing suspicion that the boys may have survived Richard's reign and had been put to death on his instructions. It could not be verified by Brackenbury, who had died at Bosworth, but Dighton was released after Tyrell's execution and later was said to have been 'the principal means of divulging this tradition'.

In July 1674 workmen rebuilding the stone stairs to the chapel in the White Tower uncovered a chest buried below those stairs. According to Christopher Wren, it lay 'about ten feet deep in the ground'. The chest contained bones, which the workmen threw out with other debris, but they had to recover them when their possible significance as the remains of the princes was realised. They were found to be 'bones of two striplings', which were 'proportionable to the ages of those two Brothers viz. about thirteen and eleven years', and so were assumed to be theirs. In the following February Wren was instructed to design 'a white Marble Coffin for the supposed bodyes of ye two Princes lately found in ye Tower of London', which was buried in Henry VII's chapel in Westminster Abbey.

In 1933 the coffin was opened and the bones were examined by Professor Wright, Dean of the London Hospital Medical College and President of the Anatomical Society of Great Britain and Ireland. He concluded that they did indeed belong to two children roughly of the age of the princes in 1483. Later reconsiderations, based on photographs taken in 1933, questioned his findings, pointing out that there could be no such certainty either of the precise year of death, which Professor Wright put at 1483, not 1485, or of the ages at death. It has also been wondered how the chest could be buried in such a position surreptitiously without building work that would attract attention.

Francis Bacon's account, written in the early seventeenth century, agreed with More's in stating that initially the princes were 'buried under the stairs, and some stones cast upon them', but added that, as the king thought that place 'too base for them that were king's children', on another night they were 'removed by the priest of the Tower and buried by him in some place which, by means of the priest's death soon after, could not be known'. Where the 'other place' was could not be established, nor was there an explanation why the bodies of two children other than the princes should have been deposited in a chest within the White Tower and not buried conventionally in consecrated ground.

Richard III's death ended the long period of Plantagenet rule, during which the Tower had acquired a range of functions, developing as a centre of royal administration, as well as a fortress and palace. It endured a siege, yet its garrison failed to defend it on other occasions, when the crown's rebellious subjects overran it. The Tower was also the state prison and a place of execution, where the unexplained deaths of members of the royal family occurred, but on the other hand was a source of pageantry that gave the crown a lively presence on the fringe of the City.

4

UNDER THE EARLY TUDORS

The victory at Bosworth put Henry VII on the throne and marked a change of dynasty, but that did not affect the Tower. It continued to have a distinct identity among the crown's buildings, and a role in domestic matters and military affairs. The new king did have a significant input to the Tower's history early in his reign, when he appointed a small force of about 200 men, to be a bodyguard. It was a part of his household, 'so that they should never leave his side'. According to Polydore Vergil 'he was the first of all the Kings of England to have a bodyguard, a feature he is said to have acquired from the sovereigns of France'. From it developed the Yeomen Warders, who were responsible for guarding the Tower.

Henry's accession did not end the political strife that had erupted into sporadic warfare for over thirty-five years. He needed to raise armies from time to time, to put down rebellions and to support his foreign policy. These included the force which defeated the Yorkist army that invaded from Ireland in 1487, promoting Lambert Simnel as a claimant to the throne: he was supposedly Edward, Earl of Warwick, the Duke of Clarence's son. Less threatening uprisings occurred in Yorkshire, Warwickshire and Worcestershire, but in 1497 a serious rebellion which originated in Cornwall saw a considerable body of rebels march across southern England and occupy Blackheath, where they were utterly defeated by a large royal army. The rebellion had been provoked largely by the taxation levied to defend northern England from a Scottish invasion in support of Perkin Warbeck, another pretender to the throne who posed an intermittent threat for much of the 1490s. He gained support in Ireland as well as Scotland, and in the aftermath of the Cornish rising he raised a rebellion in the South West. The force which he gathered was large enough to besiege Exeter, before it melted away and he surrendered and was imprisoned in the Tower. Henry's armies were retained for only a short time, although the military stores in the Tower were maintained in peace and war.

With the development of siege artillery, the Tower became increasingly obsolete as a fortress, but it continued to serve as a military base, arms depot, storehouse and workshop. It was the focus for military operations, such as the invasion of France in 1492, when, according to Bacon, there 'was drawn together a great and puissant army into the city of London ... rising in the whole to the number of five and twenty thousand foot, and sixteen hundred horse'. In 1496–7, the Venetian ambassador's secretary commented that

the diligent watch that is now kept over the Tower of London, was never so before the reign of Henry the Seventh, who keeps there a great store of heavy artillery, and hand-guns, bombards, arquebuses, and battle-axes; but not in that quantity that I should have supposed; it must be owned, however, that the ammunition of bows, arrows, and cross-bows in the said Tower, is very large and fine.

His observation is supported by an inventory of 1496, which shows that the Ordnance Office had custody of sixty-three guns, but 9,253 bows and 27,804 arrows. The artillery deployed in the campaign against Scotland in the following year consisted of eighteen cannon, six 'serpentines', and thirty-two lighter pieces known as falcons. The larger cannon taken from the Tower for that operation included a 'Curtowe of brasse named the toure', presumably because it had been made at the foundry within the fortress.

The ordnance workshops, the furnaces in the Mint and the military storehouses were perhaps unsavoury neighbours for a palace, yet Henry VII continued to use the Tower as a royal residence, as had his predecessors. He also staged entertainments there, such as a tournament held within the walls in 1501. The royal accommodation was improved, with the erection of a new tower in 1501 and a long gallery five years later. The tower was on the south side of the Lanthorn Tower. It had two floors above the ground level; the upper one contained a library. As this was at the heart of the king's apartments within the royal lodgings, it is clear that its purpose was to serve as the king's library. The long gallery connected the Salt Tower with the Lanthorn Tower and overlooked gardens on both sides. It provided a suitable room for taking exercise when the weather was inclement. On its north side a room was built as a new council chamber, where the Privy Council held its meetings when it assembled in the Tower. It had previously used a chamber in the Lanthorn Tower.

The advantage of the Tower being both the state prison and a royal palace was illustrated in Sir Francis Bacon's description of the fall of Sir William Stanley, Lord Chamberlain and hitherto one of Henry's supporters. The king was aware that Sir Robert

Clifford was in England and might have important intelligence, so, after Christmas and Epiphany had been celebrated at Westminster, early in January 1495 he moved the court to the Tower. There, Clifford could be questioned without attracting attention by having him taken from the court, 'the court and prison being within the cincture [circumference] of one wall'. Clifford's evidence that Stanley acknowledged Perkin Warbeck's claim was enough to have Stanley condemned. He was arrested, imprisoned in the Tower and beheaded on Tower Hill.

Some prisoners were held at the Tower indefinitely, because they were so closely related to the king as to be potential claimants. The Earl of Warwick had attended Richard III's coronation in 1483, but he had subsequently been kept a prisoner at Sheriff Hutton in Yorkshire. He had a stronger claim to the throne than did Richard, or Henry, who had him removed to the Tower in 1485. There he remained, although he was paraded through London to St Paul's in 1487 to show that he was alive and that Simnel, who purported to be Warwick, was an impersonator. After Warbeck's surrender he joined Warwick in the Tower, and, after insinuating himself with the servants, plotted an escape, including Warwick in the process. Four servants of the Lieutenant, Sir John Digby, were suborned and instructed to get the keys from Digby one night so that they could release Warbeck and Warwick. Polydore Vergil explained to his readers that Warwick was weary of his long imprisonment and that he 'had been imprisoned since childhood, so far removed from the sight of man and beast that he could not easily tell a chicken from a goose'. The plot was betrayed and Warbeck and Warwick were executed in 1499, Warbeck at Tyburn and Warwick, the last of the Plantagenet male line, on Tower Hill.

Another potential claimant to the throne imprisoned in the Tower was Edmund de la Pole, Earl of Suffolk. After his involvement in a murder in the parish of All Hallows by the Tower in 1498 he fled abroad, but surrendered to the king's authority at Calais in 1506. He spent the remainder of his life in captivity, and was executed in 1513. Implicated with Suffolk was another Yorkist lord, William Courtenay, Earl of Devon, who was arrested in 1502 and remained a prisoner in the Tower until he was moved to Calais in 1507.

The later years of Henry VII's reign were marked by his increasing accumulation of treasure, much of it extracted from the taxpayer by Sir Richard Empson and Edmund Dudley. Their ruthless methods made them immensely unpopular; they imprisoned those who prevaricated, when faced by their demands, until a fine was paid. Among the prominent men who fell foul of their methods was Sir William Capell, a draper, who had served as lord mayor in 1503–4. His chief claim to fame at that stage, according to John Stow's later account, was that he had 'caused a cage in every ward to be set for punishing of vagabonds', and he had been knighted by Henry VII. The king was anxious to improve the standard of the coinage by reducing the inflow of foreign coins and the practice of clipping. Sir William was accused of having 'knowledge of false monies' and not being assiduous in pursuing the offenders. He was subjected to a heavy fine by Empson and Dudley, who followed that up with an even larger one, which Sir William refused to pay. He was then imprisoned in the Tower, during the king's life. Henry died on 21 April 1509, Empson and Dudley were arrested three days later and imprisoned in the Tower, while Sir William was released and served the balance of the mayoral year 1509–10, after the death of Thomas Bradbury. Also harassed by Empson and Dudley were the former lord mayors Sir Lawrence Aylmer and Thomas Kneysworth, and two former sheriffs, all of whom were imprisoned 'under some pretext or other of exceeding their commission in the execution of their offices'.

Both Empson and Dudley were convicted of treason, but were not executed until 17 August the following year. Dudley was held in the Tower and made an unsuccessful attempt to escape, before settling down to writing. He composed a petition to the new king, Henry VIII, and also a longer work, which is headed, 'This book named the Tree of Common Wealth, was by Edmund Dudley, esquire, late counsellor of King Henry VIIth, the same Edmund at the compiling hereof being prisoner in the Tower.' In the text Dudley developed his concept of the state as a commonwealth which resembled a mighty tree 'growing in a faire feilde or pasture, under the shadowe or Coverte whereof all the beasts, both the fatte and the leane, are protected and comforted from heate and colde as the tyme requireth'. Its five roots are the love of God, justice, truth or fidelity, concord or unity, and peace, and it produces five fruits, which have to be pursued by each part of society, carefully peeled and their cores removed, and consumed with the 'payned sauce' of the Dread of God. Dudley made observations on various aspects of the state of the nation and the behaviour, failings and misconduct among some sections of society, including the clergy. In places comments were directed at the king, presumably in the hope that Henry would read the book, be impressed and pardon him. But that did not happen. Dudley's ideas on the commonwealth of England were fairly conventional for the time, but his book was a considerable achievement for someone imprisoned under sentence of death, uncertain when the axe would fall.

The living apartments in the royal palace of Westminster were destroyed by fire in 1512, but Henry VIII did not use the Tower as a palace. His court was peripatetic for much of the time, moving from one royal residence to another and staying with members of the nobility and senior clergy. In London the king used the accommodation in Baynard's Castle, near Blackfriars, which had been improved by his father, and between 1515 and 1523 he erected Bridewell Palace nearby, which was built around two courtyards, with a large gatehouse fronting the river. In the longer term York Place became available to him. That was the London palace of the Archbishops of York; the current incumbent was Thomas Wolsey, cardinal and Henry's chief minister until his fall from power in 1529, when the place was appropriated by the king. Renamed Whitehall Palace, it became the principal royal palace in the capital, covering more than twenty-three acres, an even larger area than the Tower. Around London the king could stay at Windsor Castle, Eltham Palace, the palaces erected by his father at Richmond and Greenwich, and another of Wolsey's great houses, the one at Hampton Court, which became a favourite of Henry's. As a hunting lodge he erected Nonsuch Palace, near Esher and a convenient distance from Hampton Court. Even with the improvements carried out at the Tower by his father, the royal apartments in the fortress could not rival the new renaissance palaces and their sophisticated settings.

The Tower underwent some changes in the early part of Henry's reign, despite his preference for his other residences. The new library in the king's apartments was dismantled and it was made a room for private devotion, with an altar and prayer desk. A new jewel house was built in 1508, against the south side of the White Tower. This became used for storing 'the kyngs plate', those items that were taken out for use in other royal buildings, while the older jewel house was used for the permanent collection of valuables. In 1514 new 'storehouses and coining houses in the Tower' were erected for the mint, and during that decade the Brick Tower was remodelled, as a residence for the Master of the Ordnance. The security of the complex remained important. Ordinances issued by Henry three months after he came to the throne 'for the yeomen of the Guard and other soldiers in the Tower of London', ordered that they were not to be absent without leave and that no more than one-third of them should be away at any time.

The largest military operation which Henry undertook early in his reign was an expedition to the Low Countries in 1513, with an army of 25,000 men. During the ensuing campaign the English and their Imperial allies won a victory over the French at the Battle of the Spurs, and captured Tournai and Thérouanne. The campaign continued into 1514. In the absence of the English army and its commanders, the Scots mounted an invasion, led by James IV. They were defeated at Flodden in Northumberland, in September 1513, by an army commanded by the Earl of Surrey, and James was killed. Surrey's army had been hastily assembled, but probably was of roughly the same strength as that under Henry's command in the Low Countries.

The military establishment in the Tower was especially busy during these wars, and when the Venetian envoy Pietro Pasqualigo visited in 1515 he noted tersely that 'besides the lions and leopards, [we] were shown the King's bronze artillery, mounted on 400 carriages, very fine; also bows, arrows and pikes for 40,000 infantry'.

A fire in 1512 gutted the chapel of St Peter ad Vincula, but it was not rebuilt until after the war, in 1519–20. The building has a simple plan, with two aisles of equal width, the north one slightly shorter than the principal one, with a small bell-tower at the north-west corner. The chapel was erected while Sir Richard Cholmondeley was Lieutenant, and in 1522 he had a fine tomb built for himself and his wife, which has their recumbent effigies on an alabaster chest. It was not uncommon for a tomb to be both commissioned and built under the direction of the person commemorated, but Cholmondeley was more than a little premature, for he did not die until 1544.

Cholmondeley attracted criticism for his actions during the Evil May Day riot of 1517, when some London apprentices and young men went on the rampage, attacking foreigners and their premises. Sebastian Giustinian explained to the Signory of Venice that the apprentices and others 'rose up and went to divers parts of the city inhabited by French and Flemish artificers and mechanics, sacked their houses and wounded many of them, though it was not understood that any were killed'. The disorders did not threaten the security of the Tower and the riot was directed against immigrant workers, not the government. Nevertheless, as Edward Hall related, 'while this ruffling continued, Syr Richard Cholmeley knight, Lieutenant of the Towre, no great frende to the citie, in a frantyke fury losed certain peces of ordinaunce, & shot into the citie, whiche did little harme, howbeit his good wyl apered'. That account is supported in a letter despatched to Mantua a few days after the riot had been subdued, which mentioned that 'Cannon were fired to intimidate the town'. Such action was unlikely to make for cordial relations between the City and the authorities in the Tower.

No further rioting broke out in London during the remainder of Henry's reign, but the potential threat of a restive city evidently remained in the government's consciousness, for in 1534 the Holy Roman Emperor's ambassador, Eustace Chapuys, reported that 'guns have been placed on the top of the Tower commanding the city. This has made many persons muse.' In the following year the roof of the White Tower was reinforced, to support the artillery pieces. New cupolas, topped with weathervanes, were added to the four turrets on the White Tower at about the same time, replacing the earlier conical-shaped features.

The work at the White Tower was part of a much wider restoration, set on foot by Thomas Cromwell. A survey probably made in 1532 had revealed how dilapidated parts of the buildings had become, including the woodwork of floors, staircases and roofs in several of the buildings. Not all of the work recommended was carried out. For example, the verdict on the state of Coldharbour Tower was that 'the moste pte of it to be taken downe', but no extensive repairs were recorded, let alone the rebuilding suggested by the survey.

Cromwell's overhaul of the buildings was undertaken in time for the coronation of Anne Boleyn on 1 June 1533. The king had married her the previous January, having at long last achieved his objective of annulling his marriage to Katherine of Aragon. Their only child to survive infancy was a girl, Mary, and the failure to produce a male heir had caused the king growing anxiety. He had become convinced that this marriage was unlawful, because Katherine had previously been married to his elder brother, Arthur, who had died in 1502. She would not consent to an annulment, nor would the Pope, who was in the power of her nephew, the Holy Roman Emperor Charles V: his troops had sacked Rome in

1527. It had been Wolsey's failure to secure an annulment which had caused his fall from power.

To prepare the Tower for the coronation of the new queen, the approach to the entrance from Tower Hill was improved and embellished, with new paving laid between the gate and the Lion Tower and 'crestes and coynes' added to the bridge leading to the gate. The upper storey of St Thomas's Tower was rebuilt and two chambers created for two officers with major roles in the ceremony. They were the Earl of Oxford, the Lord Great Chamberlain, who was responsible for arranging the coronation, and Lord Sandys, who, as the Lord Chamberlain of the Household, oversaw all ceremonies within the royal palaces. The buildings within the inner ward were renovated and decorated, with the great hall repaired, but not 'taken downe and newe made', as recommended in the survey. However, some work was more extensive than the survey advised. It identified the roofs and floors of the privy chamber and dining chamber as requiring repair, but in fact they were replaced. And an apartment was created for the queen at the west end of the great hall and reached from it by 'dyverse steppis of free stone'. The new room that was to be the queen's great chamber was a timber-framed structure on a brick plinth, fifty-nine feet by twenty-six feet, with 'a great carrall window'. New windows built elsewhere included a set of three in 'the King's dining chamber' that consisted of a broad one seven feet wide flanked by two narrower ones.

Within the king's apartments, repairs were carried out to two of the principal public rooms, the watching chamber and the presence chamber. Timber frames were also made for two chambers 'next the King's closet', one of them fifty-two feet long and the other 'within the same' twenty-three feet long. Within his closet was installed 'an altar wrought round about the edges with antique, and a coffer with tills thereto for the priest to say mass on'. In addition, a completely new building was erected during this phase of work, connecting the Wardrobe Tower, adjoining the White Tower, with the Broad Arrow Tower on the inner curtain wall. For this a 'new frame' of timber was constructed, 101 feet by 24 feet. The building was described as 'a warderobe for the kyng'. The king's wardrobe was now split into two sections, the 'robes' and the 'beds', but it is likely that both of them used the buildings in the Tower as a repository.

During this extensive programme of repair and renovation, it was found necessary to install 'a bell in the White Tower to call workmen to and from work'. They included carpenters, joiners, sawyers, bricklayers, masons, tilers, plasterers, painters and the plumbers, whose work included renewing the lead roofs of several buildings and towers. The estimated cost for the whole of the work was £3,593 4s 1d, although what was implemented was by no means what was originally recommended. The claim in a list of Cromwell's services to the crown, while he was the king's chief minister, that he had 'repaired the tower of London' was fully justified.

On 29 May 1533 the lord mayor, aldermen and representatives of the livery companies in the City went to Greenwich in a flotilla of forty-eight barges, richly decorated with 'the banars and penanntes of armis of their craftes, the which were beaten of fyne gould'. They returned with the new queen in her barge, painted with her colours, and carrying 'many banners', accompanied by as many as 100 or 120 other barges, serenaded by 'many drums, trumpets, flutes, and hautbois'. More than 200 other boats followed the queen's flotilla. When her barge drew level with

Wapping mills, cannon at the Tower fired a salute, four at a time. At Tower Wharf she was received by the Lieutenant, the heralds and officers of the household, then by Lord Sandys, the Earl of Oxford, the Earl of Essex, Lord William Howard, deputising for his brother the Duke of Norfolk, the Earl Marshal, other lords, and the Bishops of Winchester and London. The king greeted her within the Tower.

On the following day eighteen Knights of the Bath were created in a 'long chamber' within the Tower, in the presence of many of the nobility. Eighteen baths had been prepared for them, with rails from which hangings were draped. Another sixty-three men were knighted 'with the sword'. On the Saturday the queen went in a long procession to Westminster, and on the Sunday she was crowned in the abbey.

Henry VIII did not stay in the Tower again, but Anne returned three years later, as a prisoner. She gave birth to a daughter, Elizabeth, just over three months after her coronation, on 7 September. In the following summer a second baby was stillborn, and in January 1536 a pregnancy ended in the miscarriage of a boy. Not only had she failed to produce the male heir that the king was so desperate for, but he had begun to tire of her, and she had many enemies at court. These had not included Cromwell, but in 1536 he turned against her, regarding her influence as obstructing the change in foreign policy that most of the government supported. He questioned Mark Smeaton, a young musician and a member of Anne's circle, and with the information which he obtained approached the king, who was attending the May Day joust at Greenwich, and sowed the seeds of suspicion in his mind. Henry abruptly left Greenwich and rode back to London with only a handful of attendants. During the journey the king pressed one of them, Henry Norris, about his relationship with the queen, but he 'wold confess no thinge to the Kynge, where upon he was committed to the towre in the mornynge'. On the following day the queen was arrested at Greenwich and taken to the Tower. When she disembarked at Tower Wharf, to be admitted as a prisoner, cannon at the Tower were fired. Alexander Aless, a Scotsman in London at the time, heard the firing and explained in a letter that 'such is the custom when any of the nobility of the realm are conveyed to that fortress, there to be imprisoned'. Smeaton and Anne's brother George, Viscount Rochford, were also incarcerated in the Tower, and later that week they were joined by four other courtiers.

Anne was lodged in the queen's apartments that she had occupied three years before. The great hall was prepared for the trials of Anne and Rochford, with a 'great scaffold' erected in the centre and 'benches and seates for the lords'. On the dais at one end was a throne under a canopy, for the Duke of Norfolk, representing the king. The trials were held on 15 May, with a jury consisting of almost thirty peers. The verdicts were not in doubt and Anne was condemned to 'be burnt here within the Tower of London on the Green, else to have thy head smitten off, as the King's pleasure shall be further known of the same'.

At an earlier trial the courtiers who had been imprisoned had been found guilty of high treason; they and Rochford were executed on Tower Hill on 17 May. Among them was Sir Francis Weston, one of those created a Knight of the Bath before Anne's coronation. Her execution was delayed until the 20th so that Cromwell's order that foreign dignitaries should not be present could be enforced. She was beheaded on a scaffold erected on Tower Green, probably on the north side of the White Tower, in front of a crowd said to have numbered 'a thousand people'. As a special consideration, granted by the king, the execution was carried out with a sword in the 'French fashion', not an axe, by an executioner brought over from Calais for the purpose, who was 'dressed like the rest, and not as an executioner'. Anne and her brother were buried in St Peter ad Vincula.

Anne's circle included a number of people who were committed Protestants and under Henry VIII proceedings were taken against heretics and traditionalists, especially after the break with Rome and the creation of a national church. Those who opposed the king's will in such matters did so at their peril, but many continued to favour the old faith, including some factions at court. The king's failure to secure the dynasty through the birth of a son imperilled those with a claim to the throne. When Lord Thomas Howard met and fell in love with the king's niece Lady Margaret Douglas, and agreed to marry, he put himself at risk. Sure enough, when their agreement to marry became known both were arrested and consigned to the Tower, in July 1536, 'for making a privie contract of matrimonie'. He was condemned to death for treason by an Act of Attainder and, although that was not carried out, he remained in the Tower, where he died on 31 October 1537. After his death, Margaret 'that had lyen in prison in the Tower of London for love betwene him and her' was pardoned and released, 'howbeit, she tooke his death very heavilie'.

Sir Thomas More was the most senior political figure to lose his life in the reign. As a young man he considered entering the priesthood, but chose instead to follow in his father's footsteps and train for the law, at Lincoln's Inn. During that time he took part in the spiritual exercises of the Carthusian monks at the

Charterhouse in Smithfield. William Roper, his son-in-law and biographer, wrote that More was 'religiously lyvinge' in the Charterhouse, implying that he lodged within the precincts, but according to the humanist scholar Erasmus, who he first met in 1499, he lived 'near the Charterhouse'. More's friendship with Erasmus grew and he became one of the circle of European humanist scholars. His abilities as a lawyer also attracted attention and Wolsey employed him in diplomatic negotiations. Somewhat reluctantly, More was drawn into the king's service. While he was on a diplomatic mission to the Low Countries in 1515 he began to write *Utopia*, published in the following year, in which he depicted an imaginary well-governed commonwealth, using the setting to explore the social problems of contemporary England. At the same time he was writing his *History of Richard III*, and other works followed.

More's career in the king's service developed. He was appointed to the Privy Council in 1517, was made Under-Treasurer and was knighted in 1521, and was Speaker of the House of Commons in the parliament of 1523. The king appointed him Chancellor on Wolsey's fall in 1529. But More was opposed to the annulment of Henry's marriage with Katherine. As the controversy grew his position became so uncomfortable that he resigned, in May 1532. The king's exasperation with More's 'obstinacy' increased, and so did his hostility towards him. According to Roper, when the king realised that he could not persuade More, 'then lo went he about by terror and threats to drive him thereunto'. But to no avail, and after More refused to swear to the Act of Succession which rejected papal authority, he was imprisoned in the Tower in April 1534. So was John Fisher, Bishop of Rochester, whose scruples caused him to follow a similar path to More and to refuse to swear.

Sir Edmund Walsingham met More when he arrived at the Tower. Walsingham had been appointed Lieutenant in 1521, a position which gave him responsibility for the prisoners, whose fees supplemented his annual salary of £100. Other members of the Tower staff were entitled to perquisites, such as the porter, who could take a new prisoner's 'upper garment'. When he asked More for his, he wittily offered him his cap, not his cloak: 'No sir, quoth the porter, I must have your gown.' More was housed in a chamber which was roughly eighteen feet by twenty feet, in one of the towers, perhaps the Beauchamp Tower or the Bell Tower. He was permitted a servant during his imprisonment, John Wood, whose weekly allowance was a half of that of his master. The wearisome months of imprisonment were put to good use. Like Dudley, More took the opportunity to write, completing a series of tracts on the Eucharist and writing two more substantial works, *The Sadness of Christ* and the *Dialogue of Comfort*. Both deal with the subject of Christ's passion, as encouragement during times of persecution and as a preparation for martyrdom.

In November 1534 a new Act of Succession was passed, remedying the defects of the first, and so, too, was the Act of Supremacy, which stated that the king 'shall be taken, accepted and reputed the only supreme head of the Church of England'. The Treason Act, passed in the same parliamentary session, declared that treason could be committed by words, as well as by actions. And so denying the king's headship of the English church became a treasonable offence, as was calling the king or queen a heretic or schismatic, and treason was punishable by death. Parliament also passed two Acts of Attainder, one of them directed against More, for 'intending to sow sedition' by refusing to take the oaths. The object of the other Act of Attainder was Fisher, who was held in the Tower for fourteen months until, convicted of treason, he was beheaded on Tower Hill in June 1535. That was the course which the government would take with More.

During More's imprisonment, senior figures, including Cromwell, tried to persuade, or browbeat, him to modify his views, at least to be flexible enough to take the required oaths, but he would not. On 1 July 1535 he was tried on an indictment which alleged that he had 'falsely, traitorously and maliciously' denied the king his right to be head of the church, by not taking the oaths required by the Acts of Succession and Supremacy. He was found guilty and five days later was taken out of the fortress to the scaffold on Tower Hill, a rickety structure which was 'so weak that it was ready to fall'. More said to Walsingham, 'I pray you, Master Lieutenant, see me safe up, and for my coming down let me shift for myself.' Like Fisher, he was beheaded, and not subjected to the ghastly penalty commonly inflicted on those executed for treason, that of being hanged, disembowelled, beheaded and quartered.

Members of the Carthusian order were also intractable opponents of the changes to the English church. John Houghton became prior of the London Charterhouse in 1531, and he and his monks, a half of whom were under thirty-five years old when he became prior, faced the same dilemma as More and Fisher. In 1534 they subscribed to the first Act of Succession. Nevertheless, their misgivings were such that Houghton and the procurator, Hugh Middlemore, were briefly incarcerated in the Tower before they were persuaded to swear, and it required three visits to the Charterhouse by the king's commissioners to obtain the oath from all of the monks. But many members of the community who had taken that step felt unable to acknowledge the king as head of the English church, expressed in the Act of Supremacy. Houghton was the first to be imprisoned; he and the priors of the Carthusian houses of Axholme and Beauvale were held in the Tower for five weeks, tried under the Treason Act, and executed at Tyburn in May 1535. Sir Thomas More watched as they were taken out of the Tower to their execution, commenting to his daughter that they were 'as cheerfully going to their deaths as bridegrooms to their marriage'. During that summer three other senior members of the London Charterhouse were imprisoned there, for four weeks, before their execution. In all ten monks and six lay brothers of the priory lost their lives for opposing the king's policy and the house was dissolved.

The dissolution of the religious houses provoked such opposition that 'divers abbottes and monkes were putt in the Tower for treason'. Walsingham's prisoners included Lawrence Cooke, Prior of Doncaster, the vicar of Louth, who was one of a dozen men convicted and executed in London after an uprising in Lincolnshire, and Robert Salisbury, the Abbot of Vale Crucis. Thomas Abell was first imprisoned in 1532, for a publication opposing the king's right to annul his marriage, and then again in 1533, and was then kept in the Tower until his execution in 1540. On the day that Abell was executed, so were Richard Featherstone, former chaplain of Katherine of Aragon and tutor to Mary, and Edward Powell, for denying the royal supremacy; also Robert Barnes, Thomas Gerard and William Jerome, 'which three parsons were of the newe sect', for heresy. Not all prisoners maintained their beliefs during their imprisonment. The courtier Sir Nicholas Carew converted from Catholicism to evangelical Protestantism before he was beheaded in March 1539, and was thankful for his incarceration, according to the chronicler Edward

Hall, 'giving God most hearty thanks that ever he came in the prison of the Tower, where he first savoured the life and sweetness of God's most holy word, meaning the Bible in English, which there he read by means of one Thomas Phelips then Keeper'.

The English Catholics who had fled abroad included Reginald Pole, later cardinal. His brother Henry Pole, Lord Montague, grandson of George, Duke of Clarence, together with the Marquess of Exeter, grandson of Edward IV, were arrested in 1538 and charged with plotting treason. The government feared that Emperor Charles V and King François I of France were considering a joint invasion of England; it was against that background that both Montague and Exeter were imprisoned in the Tower and then executed. Margaret Pole, Countess of Salisbury and mother of Reginald and Henry, was also questioned, on suspicion of engaging in a treasonable correspondence with Reginald. She was being held in the Tower by November 1539, where a waiting woman was allowed to attend her. In March and April 1541 bills for clothes and other items for the countess, totalling £15 2s, were paid by the government, so it may have come as a surprise when shortly afterwards, on 27 May, she was taken to the block, where she suffered a particularly badly botched beheading. The execution took place 'in a corner of the Tower, in presence of so few people that until evening the truth was still doubted', according to the French envoy Charles de Marillac. He added that her fate 'was the more difficult to believe as she had been long prisoner, was of noble lineage, above 80 years old, and had been punished by the loss of one son and banishment of the other, and the total ruin of her house'.

It may be that her execution was prompted by a policy, which Marillac claimed he had on good authority, that 'before St. John's tide [24 June], they reckon to empty the Tower of the prisoners now there for treason'. If so, execution was a drastic solution to the growing problem of overcrowding at the Tower. It had become so great by December that year that, when the Council considered detaining half a dozen people, Walsingham responded

> there are not rooms to lodge them all severally in the Tower, unless the King's and Queen's lodgings be taken. Beg that the King will send hither his double key or permit them to alter the locks, or else signify whether the great personages may be committed to the Tower and the rest to other custodies until rooms may be prepared for them.

Space had to be found for one of 'the great personages' in 1542, when another queen was brought to the Tower and executed. Henry's third wife, after Anne Boleyn, had been Jane Seymour, who gave birth to the longed-for male heir, Edward, in October 1537. But the queen died twelve days after the birth. Henry next married Anne of Cleves, but found her singularly unattractive and the marriage was dissolved after seven months. The Howard family then saw an opportunity to further their interests by drawing the king's attention to Katherine, grand-daughter of Thomas Howard, second Duke of Norfolk. Henry and Katherine were married in July 1540. But her behaviour drew suspicion of adultery and when the king was informed, on 6 November 1541, he abandoned her. The charges against her were confirmed and on 22 November she was deprived of her status as queen and detained at Syon. Katherine was taken to the Tower by barge on 10 February 1542, for execution, having been condemned not by a trial but by an Act of Attainder for high treason, for her adultery. Also condemned was one of her ladies, Jane Boleyn, Viscountess Rochford, widow of Anne's brother George Boleyn. They were beheaded on a scaffold on Tower Green on 13 February and buried in St Peter ad Vincula. Francis Dereham and Thomas Culpeper, who were implicated in her behaviour, were executed after a brief imprisonment in the Tower.

The king's chief minister, Thomas Cromwell, also spent a short time at the Tower, following his sudden fall from power in 1540. Arrested at a council meeting on 10 June, he was taken directly there by barge. Although the king had not appointed him Chancellor, he had been the key figure in dealing with the break with Rome and its legislative consequences, and with the Dissolution of the Monasteries. Among the various factors that contributed to his fall was the king's disastrous marriage to Anne of Cleves, which, for diplomatic reasons, he had arranged. He was condemned by an Act of Attainder for a range of offences that included treason, heresy and corruption, and he was executed seven weeks after his arrest. On the same day Lord Hungerford was executed, for treason. It may be that his fate was linked in some way with that of Cromwell, although Maraillac wrote that he was 'attainted of sodomy, of having forced his own daughter, and having practised magic and invocation of devils'.

After Cromwell's fall, Henry's foreign policy turned bellicose, with campaigns against Scotland and a war with France, from 1542. As Stephen Gardiner, Bishop of Winchester, wrote, 'We are at war with France and Scotland, we have enmity with the Bishop of Rome; we have no assured friendship with the Emperor.' The war with Scotland began with an English victory at the Battle of Solway Moss in November 1542. Among the prisoners were twenty-three 'principal lords and gentlemen', who were conveyed to the Tower. The king evidently had agreed that the royal apartments could be used for prisoners, for various rooms in them were prepared for the influx, including the king's great chamber, dining chamber, bed-chamber, closet and gallery, where windows were repaired 'Agenyst the comying in of the prisoners of skottland'. Small wonder that Charles Wriothesley, Windsor Herald and a member of the king's household, wrote that when they arrived at the Tower 'that night they had great chere and riche lodginge prepared for them'.

An invasion of France in 1544 produced the capture of Boulogne, but French plans for an invasion of England posed a serious threat. In the following year they landed a force of 5,000 men on the Isle of Wight, although it was withdrawn after a naval encounter in the Solent, in which the *Mary Rose*, the pride of the English fleet, sank in a squall. The wars were ruinously expensive for the crown, damaging to the trade of 'all our merchants that traffic through the narrow seas', and a strain on the military resources from the Tower. These consisted of an ever-increasing number of both cannon and smaller guns, and more traditional weapons and equipment. An inventory compiled in 1547 listed the cannon with their projectiles, many suits of armour, thousands of bows, bowstrings and sheaves of arrows, and edged weapons.

The ordnance storehouse had been reported to be in such a bad condition in 1533 that it was 'lykly to falle downe' and the repairs carried out did not solve the problem. Despite the crown's parlous financial state, it was replaced in 1545–7 with a new storehouse on the existing site, described as 'Above the grene upon the hyll'. The description of the new building as 'one house' does not convey its scale, for it was the place 'Wherin all the kinges maiesties Store and provicon of Artillerie Ordinnce and other Municons maye be kepte and garded and bestowed'. It consisted of twenty-one bays and occupied much of the ground adjoining the inner curtain wall north of the White Tower.

The Tower's guns had a ceremonial, as well as martial, function, when a flotilla passed on special occasions and as part of national celebrations. In June 1536, when Jane Seymour was proclaimed queen at Greenwich, she and the king then travelled by barge to Westminster, escorted by many other vessels. As they drew level with the Tower, 'their was shott above fower hundred peeces of ordinance, and all the Tower walls towardes the water side were sett with great streamers and banners'. The celebrations that greeted the birth of Prince Edward included 'a great peale of gonnes' at the Tower, and that night 'there was shott at the Tower above tow thousand gonns'. Four years after Queen Jane had travelled along the Thames in procession, Anne of Cleves was welcomed to London in the same way, and on that occasion the salute from the Tower was said to have consisted of 'above a thousand chambers of ordinance, which made a noyse like thunder'. Katherine Howard's flotilla was also greeted with a salute by the Tower's gunners. Henry's sixth marriage, to Katherine Parr in July 1543, was not celebrated in the same way; the wedding was a modest ceremony at Hampton Court, attended by just eighteen people.

As Henry VIII became increasingly aged and decrepit, he began to negotiate to end the war with France. The French ambassador Claude D'Annebault came to England in August 1546 to conclude a treaty between the two nations. He was given a typically well-organised and impressive welcome, travelling by barge from Greenwich to Tower Wharf. When he arrived there, according to

Wriothesley, 'the Towre shott such terrible shott as heaven and earth should have gonne togeether', and Hall described it as 'a terrible peale of ordinaunce'. Presumably, the scale of the salute reflected the importance of the occasion and the ambassador's rank, but also was designed to impress him with the power of the English artillery. After his ears had been so seriously assailed, he rode on into the City, to be received by the lord mayor and aldermen.

Peace with France brought stability in foreign affairs, but with Prince Edward still a minor, the religious future of the kingdom remained in doubt. Conservatives and reformers manoeuvred and schemed so as to be in a decisive position to gain control when Henry died. Among those caught in the web of their rivalry was Anne Askew, a convinced reformer from a minor gentry family in Lincolnshire. She was attempting to obtain a divorce from her husband, who had so strongly objected to her religious views that he allegedly 'vyolentlye drove her oute of hyse howse'. In London she attracted hostile attention for expressing her faith, was arrested, questioned and released, but in June 1546 was again detained and appeared before a court at Guildhall, which convicted her of heresy. She was then taken to the Tower and tortured on the rack. Torture was unusual and in this case unlawful, for she was a woman, was of gentle birth, and already had been condemned by the court at Guildhall. Her treatment was known outside government circles, for a London merchant wrote that 'she hath ben rakked sins her condempnacion'. Hopeful that she had contacts at court who would be discredited if she revealed their connections and reformist beliefs, the conservatives were desperate to extract information from her.

According to an account attributed to Anne, even two privy councillors, Sir Richard Rich and Thomas, Lord Wriothesley, the Lord Chancellor, went so far as 'to rack me with their own hands, till I was nigh dead'. They were disappointed, for she did not, perhaps could not, incriminate those whose reputations they were hoping to besmirch. Walsingham had relinquished his post as Lieutenant in 1543 and his successor, Sir Anthony Knyvet, refused Wriothesley's order to continue to rack Anne. She was moved to a house to recover from her ordeal before being taken to Newgate and then, on 16 July, to Smithfield, where she was burned as a heretic. The effects of the torture were obvious, for she 'was so racked that she could not stand'.

Political machinations rather than religious beliefs contributed to the fall of two senior members of the Howard family. The Howards had survived the execution of Queen Katherine and its consequences, and while Thomas, 3rd Duke of Norfolk, was a Catholic, his son Henry, Earl of Surrey, tended towards evangelical Protestantism. Norfolk had married Anne, a daughter of Edward IV, and with his position at court it may be that he hoped, perhaps expected, to become regent on the king's death. Surrey had been commander in France and succeeded in holding Boulogne against a siege. Errors of military judgement prompted his recall, but it was for the heraldic offence of quartering his own arms with those of Edward the Confessor, the ancient arms of England, that he was arrested, on 12 December 1546, and marched through the city to the Tower. His father was detained on the same day and joined him there.

Surrey's potential allies at court had wearied of his arrogance and ambition and other charges were laid against him. Norfolk admitted his fault, that he had 'concealed high treason, in keeping secret the false acts of my son, Henry earl of Surrey, in using the arms of St. Edward the Confessor, which pertain only to kings'. That admission was written on 12 January 1547. On the following day Surrey was tried and found guilty and a week later was executed on Tower Hill. He was a notable poet, described as both the poet earl and the father of the sonnet, and during his imprisonment in the Tower he composed paraphrases of Psalms 55, 73 and 88. His father was condemned by an Act of Attainder on 27 January, but saved by the king's death on the following day.

During the reigns of the first two Tudor monarchs the role of the Tower had begun to change. It remained the state prison, but, despite improvements to the royal apartments, went out of favour as a palace. On the other hand, its functions as military storehouse had grown in scale, and the other departments housed there continued to give it the character of a workaday establishment as well as a fortress.

5

THE LATE TUDOR TOWER

Royal building under the later Tudors was more limited than in the reigns of Henry VII and Henry VIII. Within London, Henry VIII's children relied largely on Whitehall Palace and St James's Palace, and perceptions of the Tower altered as its use as a royal residence virtually ended. According to Holinshed, the Tower had become 'rather an armorie and house of munition, and thereunto a place for the safekeeping of offenders, than a palace roiall for a king or queen to soiurne in'. But its other functions continued, indeed were expanded, and it became notable as the state's prison, especially for those accused of treason. Visitors, the officers of the great fortress and the prisoners themselves recorded their impressions of the conditions of life in the Tower.

The nine-year-old Edward was proclaimed king on 31 January 1547 and later that day went to the Tower to prepare for his coronation. With the Howards' influence in abeyance, Edward Seymour, his maternal uncle and Earl of Hertford, was in the ascendant and he took over the reins of government as Lord Protector. Before the coronation he was created Duke of Somerset. While Edward was at the Tower, the lord mayor, aldermen and others waited upon him so that he could confirm the lord mayor's election. In a rather strange ceremony, the king knelt before the Lord Protector and was knighted by him; the king then took the sword and knighted the lord mayor, Henry Huberthorn, and William Portman, a judge of the King's Bench. The knighting of the sovereign by a subject was said to have been done to fulfil Henry VIII's wish. After a stay of three weeks the king processed through London to Westminster to be crowned.

Somerset's period of power drew to an end in October 1549, after dangerous rebellions in the West Country and East Anglia and a dubious foreign policy that had involved England in wars with France and Scotland. Earlier that year he had seen off a threat from his brother Thomas Seymour, Lord Sudeley, who was arrested in the middle of January and imprisoned in the Tower before being condemned for treason and beheaded on Tower Hill on 20 March. He was buried in the Tower. On his fall from power, Somerset and a number of his close associates were also detained in the Tower, including William Cecil, who, as Lord Burghley, was to be Elizabeth's chief minister. Other senior figures had been arrested unobtrusively, such as Thomas Cromwell, but when Somerset was delivered to the custody of the Constable, Sir John Gage, he was part of a cavalcade consisting of 'diuers Lordes, knightes, and gentlemen' accompanied by no less than 400 horsemen in livery. These processed from Holborn through Newgate, and after they had entered the City they were joined by the lord mayor, both the sheriffs and other senior figures. From Holborn Bridge to Tower Hill there were 'certaine Aldermen or theyr deputies sitting on horseback in euery streat, with a nomber of householders standinge by them with billes in their handes, in euery quarter, as he [Somerset] passed through the streates'.

Somerset was replaced by John Dudley, created Earl of Warwick at the outset of the reign and Duke of Northumberland in 1551. After more than four months in the Tower, Somerset was released and resumed an active role in government, but he was suspected of being dissatisfied with an inferior position. When he was said to have openly spoken of considering a coup that would have involved the execution of Northumberland, the seizure of the Tower and the raising of the Londoners in his support, he was again arrested and returned to the Tower in October 1551. This time there was to be no reprieve and he was executed on Tower Hill three months later, on 22 January.

For some, incarceration did not mean isolation. Although excluded from day-to-day politics and with his direct contacts controlled, a high-ranking prisoner could nevertheless put forward his views and attempt to have an impact on policy. Stephen Gardiner was a conservative theologian who had been an influential figure under Henry VIII, and had been created Bishop of Winchester in 1531. Increasingly uncomfortable with the religious changes in the later years of Henry's reign, he was strongly opposed to those made under Somerset and Northumberland. Freed from a spell of imprisonment in the Fleet, he was later invited to preach a sermon before the king that would demonstrate his support for the regime's Protestant policies. He accepted the invitation and preached the sermon, in June 1548, but what he said was not what was required, for 'the morrow after he was sent to the Towre of London'. There he set about writing tracts justifying his position and responding to those of Protestant writers, so much so that after a hearing in February 1551 the Privy Council ordered that his paper, pens and ink should be taken away, to staunch the flow of his writings, and he was deprived of his bishopric. The council's prohibition evidently was futile, for further treatises from his pen followed. Cuthbert Tunstall also took the opportunity provided by being sequestered in the Tower to write. Deprived of the bishopric of Durham during Northumberland's administration, he completed a treatise on the Eucharist and also found time to edit for publication a tract by his cousin John Redman, formerly chaplain to Henry VIII and later head of King's Hall, Cambridge.

Others suffered more grotesque punishments than imprisonment, for adhering to their faith. In one case recorded by Charles Wriothesley in the month after Gardiner was imprisoned, 'a priest was drawen from the Towre of London into Smythfield and their hanged, headed, and quartred and his membres and bowells brent'. Smithfield, not Tower Hill, was the preferred place of execution throughout the mid-sixteenth century for those put to death for their faith, both Catholics and Protestants. Many of them were not held in the Tower before being condemned, but in other prisons in the capital.

In early 1553 the young king's health began to fail. What seemed to be a heavy cold failed to clear and his condition deteriorated. He and Northumberland planned that his half-sister Mary should not have the crown, and on 21 May Northumberland's son, Lord Guilford Dudley, was married to Lady Jane Grey, Edward's cousin and the preferred Protestant heir. She was the daughter of Henry Grey, Marquess of Dorset and Duke of Suffolk, and Frances, the daughter of Henry VIII's younger sister Mary. Jane was, therefore, a strong claimant to the throne, if Mary and Elizabeth were barred from the succession on the grounds of illegitimacy. This was the course that Edward followed in a document on the succession and his will, in which he excluded his two half-sisters and nominated 'the Lady Jane' as his successor. Following his death, on 6 July, Northumberland began to implement Edward's intentions. On

10 July, Jane and Guilford went by water to the Tower, and later that afternoon she was proclaimed queen.

Northumberland had failed to secure Mary and she prudently withdrew to Norfolk, where she found so much support that she quickly raised an army. This could not be ignored and Northumberland set out from London to confront it, but many of his men deserted when it became apparent that his forces were no match for Mary's, and he had little choice but to surrender to her. She made her entry into London on 3 August and went to the Tower, where she was met by Gage and Sir John Bridges, the Lieutenant. As part of the celebrations, 'there was such a terrible and great shott of guns shot within the Tower and all about the Tower wharfe that the lyke hath not bene heard'.

On Tower Green the Duke of Norfolk, Stephen Gardiner and Edward Courtenay knelt and asked Mary for pardon. Despite his reprieve in 1547, Norfolk had spent the whole of Edward's reign as a prisoner in the Tower, neither being granted a release or imprisonment elsewhere. Loyal to the Catholic religion of her mother, Katherine of Aragon, and sympathetic to conservative figures such as Norfolk and Gardiner, Mary did pardon them and ordered their release. As Earl Marshal, Norfolk bore the crown at her coronation, Gardiner resumed his bishopric of Winchester, and both were again sworn as members of the Privy Council. Courtenay's release ended fifteen years of imprisonment, and yet he was still only twenty-five years old.

Jane's incipient reign was over after just nine days. She had entered the Tower to prepare for her coronation, but it had become her prison, from which she was not to emerge alive. It also served as Northumberland's prison briefly, until his execution on Tower Hill. William Parr, Marquess of Northampton, who had acted with him to thwart Mary's accession, was first imprisoned in the Tower and charged with treason and then, in December, was released. But the religious change that followed Mary's accession saw the imprisonment in the Tower of Thomas Cranmer, Archbishop of Canterbury, Nicholas Ridley, Bishop of London, Hugh Latimer, Bishop of Worcester, and the evangelical preacher John Bradford. Overcrowding was so acute during the following winter that the four men had to share accommodation, which allowed them to co-ordinate their response to the charges which they were inevitably to face. In March the former bishops were taken to Oxford and John Bradford to the King's Bench prison in Southwark. All four men were burned at the stake, Latimer and Ridley in Oxford, Bradford at Smithfield in 1555, and Cranmer in Oxford in the following year.

One of the reasons for the overcrowding in the Tower in 1554 was the rebellion of Sir Thomas Wyatt. This grew out of dissatisfaction with Mary's policies and especially her proposed marriage to Philip of Spain. That prospect raised fears of a Catholic dynasty and England's subservience to Spain, and fear that the power of local magnates and gentry would be eroded. Plots were hatched to raise rebellions in the provinces, but only in Kent did an uprising take place, led by Wyatt. When a force of Londoners sent to suppress the rising defected to him, he was encouraged to think that he might be able to capture London, and the rebels entered Southwark on 3 February. But Mary and her government stood firm, as did the Londoners, who prevented Wyatt's men from crossing London Bridge.

During this confrontation, a boat carrying one of the Tower's Lieutenant's servants was fired on and its waterman was killed.

The Lieutenant retaliated by firing some of the Tower's cannon, described as 'great peces of ordenance', including those on the White Tower. Their shot were directed 'full against the foote of the bridge and agaynst Southwarke, and the ij. Steples of saincte Tooles [Olaf's] and sainct Marie Overies'. The inhabitants then pleaded with Wyatt to withdraw his men, to prevent 'the utter desolation of this boroughe, with the shott of [the Tower] layed and chardged towardes us'. Vulnerable to that artillery fire and, in any case, thwarted by the Londoners' refusal to allow them across the bridge, his men marched away, crossed the Thames at Kingston and entered London from the west, reaching Ludgate before being defeated.

In the aftermath of the rebellion the government arrested those suspected of involvement and eleven men were admitted to the Tower as prisoners in the space of two days. The Marquess of Northampton spent another two months there before being released for lack of evidence, and Edward Courtenay, who had been created Earl of Devon by Mary in September, was returned to the Tower in mid-February, moved to Fotheringay in May and released in 1555 (he died in Italy shortly afterwards). Those taken to the Tower also included the princess Elizabeth, who would have come to the throne had the rebels succeeded in deposing Mary. Even on the scaffold Wyatt denied that he had any support from Elizabeth, but she was imprisoned in the Tower for two months until transferred to Woodstock Palace. Elizabeth survived, despite calls for her execution, from Gardiner among others, but Wyatt's rebellion proved to be fatal for Lady Jane, her husband and her father. Convicted of treason in November but spared, Jane and Guilford were now both executed, on 12 February, she within the Tower, an acknowledgement of her royal status, and

Previous page: 1. Duke William confers arms and armour on Earl Harold.
Above: 2. Duke William of Normandy defeated King Harold's army near Hastings in October 1066 and went on to occupy London.

Left: 3. St John's chapel within the White Tower, painted by John Fulleylove *c.* 1907.
Opposite: 4. The south-east corner of the White Tower, which contains St John's chapel, and the ruins of the Wardrobe Tower.

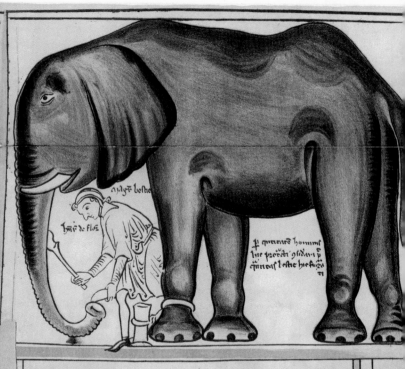

Animal huiuſmo
di teemarič pur
iſſema eximia
figuratur. elephâ
dicitur. et eſt reg
omniū iumentoꝛū
ſicut leo beſtiarū
aqla auiū. balena
ſiue ceto uel cetꝰ pi
est. ⁊ draco ſpentim
iumenta dicuntur
ąiꝟia que ďantur
a co honinū iuuan
men laboꝛ. ut eqꝰ
aſinꝰ. ⁊ ſimilia. er
quo eſt maximū
coꝛ. elephat. Quem
q̇i iuſepturꝰ frequē
ter de ſo fit ſmo ⁊
raro ⁊ꝛili uiďeur
occideriſ ⸱ da ⁊ u
hꝑ pagina figuraď
⁊ figurū pⁱꝰ
deſcriber
ur

ſubnigri. fuliginei ſiue tereſtriſ coloriſ eſt. nilloꝛ piloꝛ. inſtar alioꝛ
animaliū. ornatuſ tegmine ut muniꞇ. Nullus uero uñm allꞃ eleph
uiſuſ eſt ſicut nec cornuſ albuſ ut cignuſ niger. Unde oratꞇ in expl
penultima. Siue elephat albuſ uulgi couiceꞇ oꝛa⸱ Spꝛauet popuſⁱ
ludiſ attenturſ⸱ ⁊ é. Sedm aūt pliniū. yſidoriū ⁊ alioſ naturaleſ filoſo
phoſ⸱ india ⁊ eí parteſ contmine elephanteſ producit⸱ Qui in aqꝯ
ꝗꝓ draconū inſidiaſ igniceꝯ pariūt. Dracones eñí elephantinū ſau
guinē ad cor auide ſiciunt reſtigeriſ⸱ Quando aūt draco ipſū ele
phanꞇ cupit occupare⸱ illaqat ⁊ conectit pedeſ eí cauda ſua. ut ſic
ſpiriſ inceatū pſternat ⁊ infectat morſibꝯ⸱ uenenoſiſ. et ſugat ab
inſecto ſanguinem genitū. Eſt elephat atal pōderoſū. tereſtre ac ro
buſtū. Qui cū neceſſe habeat a dracone ſauciuſ ⁊ moriturꝰ cade⸱ eadė
ultro ſꞇ dracone. ut ſic duⁱſpenſ⸱ forſam montuuſ triumphet de ini
mico. ſicut legitur de ſamſone. Et qꝫ int omia greſſibilia maximū
atal eſt ⁊ deforme⸱ ⸫ lepra morbuſ elephantiꝰ ꝗ ſit inſanitatem
⁊ deformitate. Animal ḡ⸱ ad pugnandū docibile eſt ⁊ obediēſ. Ec ſi
leo ꝓuocetur ad iram ⁊ pugnam ꝓpⁱe caude flagello⸱ ſic elephaꞇ
uiſo ſanguꞇ ꝓprio maximo ut ſucco a morſ ⁊ uulſ expꝛeſſo⸱ ꝗ
ſanguiſ ꝓtendit ſimilitudine ſophiſtice cliꝯꝰ⸱ a cuuurd bel
liū ⁊ ad irā ꝓuocatur⸱ ꝗ hoſteſ acerbiꝰ origuͭ. Pondꝰ iuuane
portat ita ut ꝓpugnaciſaca machinam cū uiginti ⁊ uiꞇatiſ ⁊ coꝛ
bauilet neceſſariꝰ. ⁊ ſeiꝑm loꝛicatū. Magin forteſ ⁊ adulti plg
tiginta prout legit in libro machabeoꝝ pⁱmo capⁱtꝉo nondecmꝫ
de elephante regalⁱ loꝛicato ꝗn eleazar fortiſſⁱmⁱ ⁊ audaciſſⁱmⁱ
peremit ab eodem ꝩempⁱuſ ⁊ oppꝛeſſuſ. In plⁱo uero exiſtit ele

6. A section of the western wall of the inmost ward, perhaps part of Henry III's rebuilding of the 1220s and 1230s.

Right: 7. The staircase in the north-west corner of the White Tower.
Opposite: 5. The elephant given to Henry III by Louis IX of France in 1255 and kept in the Tower of London. Drawn by Matthew Paris, he described it as 'the only elephant ever seen in England'.

8. The Beauchamp Tower was built during Edward I's rebuilding of the western defences. The tower was used to house prisoners. It was refaced in the early 1850s as part of the Victorian restoration of the Tower.

Above left: 9. The Beauchamp Tower was built on the site of the gateway in the outer wall, which was at the end of Great Tower Street, as seen in John Fulleylove's painting of *c.* 1907.
Above right: 10. The Byward Tower is the inner gateway of Edward I's defences fronting the main entrance to the Tower.

11. Richard II's reign came to an ignominious end in 1399, when he was compelled to abdicate, in the Tower.

Above left: 12. The interior of the Bloody Tower, with the mechanism for raising and lowering the portcullis, painted by John Fulleylove *c.* 1907.

Above right: 13. Part of the reconstruction of 1992–3 by Historic Royal Palaces in the upper chamber of the Wakefield Tower of the palace as it may have looked in the thirteenth century.

Left: 14. Charles, Duke of Orléans, nephew of the French king, Charles V, was captured at Agincourt in 1415 and brought to England pending the payment of a ransom. He was not released until 1440, although he did not spend the whole of his captivity in the Tower. This late-fifteenth-century illustration shows him looking out of a window watching for the messenger bringing the arrangements for his release, greeting the messenger, signing the release and then riding away with an escort.

Opposite: 15. Henry VI was deposed and was presumed killed in the Tower in 1471. This portrait of the king is on the screen in St Catherine's church, Ludham, Norfolk.

Above: 16. The room which is presented as the one where, according to tradition, Henry VI was killed. Since 1923 an annual ceremony has been held there on the anniversary of his death.

Left: 17. Edward V succeeded his father Edward IV in 1483 and was deposed in the same year by his uncle, who became Richard III. Edward and his brother Richard are presumed to have been murdered in the Tower.

RICARDVS. III.

18. Richard III carried out the coup which secured the throne in the Tower.

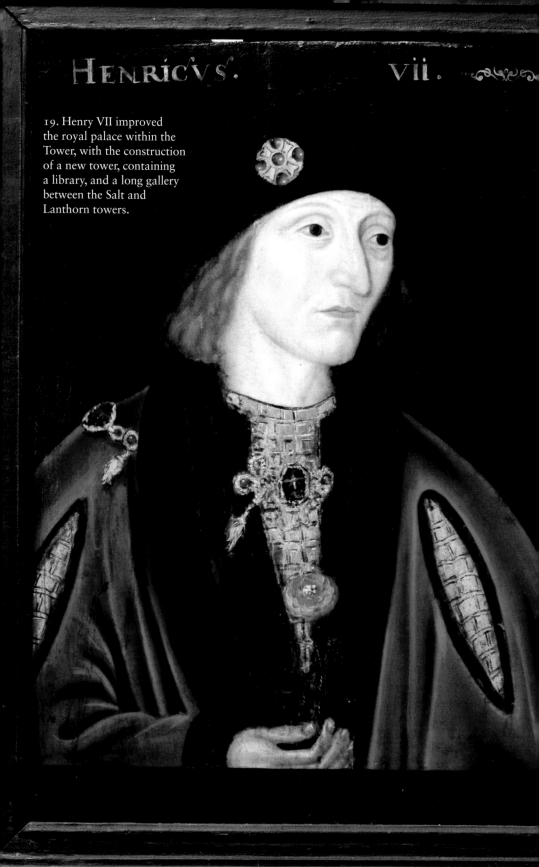

HENRICVS. VII.

19. Henry VII improved
the royal palace within the
Tower, with the construction
of a new tower, containing
a library, and a long gallery
between the Salt and
Lanthorn towers.

20. Sir Thomas More, who had been Chancellor, was imprisoned in the Tower for opposing Henry VIII's break with Rome. He was executed on Tower Hill in July 1535.

21. Anne Boleyn, who was married to Henry VIII in June 1533. She was imprisoned in the Tower three years later and executed on Tower Green in May 1536.

22. Anne Boleyn preparing for her execution. The executioner is shown holding a sword, not an axe, which was an unusual aspect of her beheading.

Above left: 23. Henry VIII, by Hans Holbein.
Above right: 24. Anne Boleyn's falcon badge, carved among the graffiti in the Tower.

26. Traitor's Gate beneath St Thomas's Tower, the Tower's Watergate. The name has been used for the gate since the early seventeenth century; in 1611 it was described as 'the Bridg called Traitores staires'.

Above: 27. The effigies of Henry Howard, Earl of Surrey, and his wife Frances, in St Michael's church, Framlingham. He was imprisoned in the Tower and executed on Tower Hill in January 1547. The monument dates from 1614. *Opposite*: 25. Katherine Howard, beheaded by a single axe blow on Monday 13 February 1542 on Tower Green.

Left: 28. Lady Jane Grey was placed on the throne by her father-in-law, the Duke of Northumberland, before being deposed after a reign of just nine days, and later executed, as was her husband, following Sir Thomas Wyatt's rebellion. She became one of the most lamented of the Tower's famous prisoners.

Above: 29. The Dudley rebus in the Beauchamp Tower, with verses beneath. This contains the symbols of Lady Jane Grey's husband Lord Guilford Dudley, who was executed, and his brothers, who were imprisoned in the Tower. *Left*: 30. Charles II was the last monarch to process from the Tower to Westminster before his coronation. Portrait by the school of Peter Lely.

31. The Cradle Tower on the outer wall, from where John Gerard, a Roman Catholic priest, escaped in 1598 by crossing the moat by rope. The upper part of the Tower was removed in 1777 and rebuilt in 1878–9 as part of the Victorian restoration.

Above: 32. Claes Visscher's view of 1616 shows the Tower closely hemmed in by buildings. The fortress was sometimes compared to a town, because of the many buildings within its walls.

Left: 33. George Villiers, 2nd Duke of Buckingham, who was a leading courtier and erstwhile political ally of Charles II, but was imprisoned in the Tower in 1677, having alienated the king by claiming that Charles had prorogued parliament illegally.

34. The Tower from the north-west of Tower Hill, *c.* 1820.

Above left: 35. Anthony Ashley-Cooper, Earl of Shaftesbury, a leading Whig and prominent opponent of the king during the Exclusion Crisis of the late 1670s and early 1680s, who was imprisoned in the Tower in 1681. This portrait is by a follower of John Greenhill.

Above right: 36. The Duke of Wellington was Constable of the Tower from 1826 until his death in 1852. He was opposed to the fortress becoming an attraction for visitors and wished to maintain it solely as a military base. This portrait is by Henry Perronet Briggs.

37. The Duke of Wellington laid the foundation stone of the Waterloo Barracks of 1845, built to replace the Grand Storehouse destroyed by fire in 1841.

Above left: 38. The subject of the Princes was taken up by Sir John Millais, in 1878. He depicted them as two frightened boys at the foot of a dark staircase.

Above right: 39. The instruments of execution and torture as displayed in the early twentieth century. The iron frame in the foreground is the scavenger's daughter, which kept the prisoner in a crouching position. It was said to have been 'devysed by Mr Skavington, sometyme Lieutenant of the Tower' and according to Miles Coverdale, in 1564, the victim's body 'standeth double, the head being drawen towardes the feete'.

40. The place on Tower Green to the south of St Peter ad Vincula marked in 1866 as the site of the scaffold, on Queen Victoria's instructions. Almost certainly it is in the wrong place.

41. The Middle Tower at the entrance to the fortress, painted by John Fulleylove *c.* 1907.

42. The Tower photographed from the north-west *c.* 1920.

Above left: 43. The Bloody Tower and Wakefield Tower looking east *c.* 1907, painted by John Fulleylove. *Above right*: 44. The gateway to the Bloody Tower and the entrance to the Wakefield Tower, where the royal regalia were displayed, painted by John Fulleylove *c.* 1907.

45. The Tower, with Tower Wharf cleared and set out as a place for recreation, shown in a water-colour by John Fulleylove *c.* 1907.

Above left: 46. The Tower from the Thames, in a colour lithograph from the early twentieth century by Charles Wilkinson. *Above right*: 47. A policeman clearing children off the strip of shingle adjoining Tower Wharf in advance of the rising tide, *c.* 1930. In 1935 an artificial beach was created there which remained in use for thirty years.

Above left: 48. The Byward and Bell towers and a section of the curtain wall, as depicted by John Fulleylove *c.* 1907. *Above right*: 49. The Head Warder in state dress, *c.* 1930. *Left*: 50. The gateway of the Bloody Tower and the Traitor's Gate beyond, painted by E. W. Haslehust *c.* 1924.

51. The Tower as seen from the river, by Mortimer Menpes (1855–1938).

52. The Norman keep became known as the White Tower after it was whitewashed in the thirteenth century. During the long period when coal was London's fuel a dark grime concealed its whiteness.

53. Six ravens are kept at the Tower, their wings clipped to prevent them flying away when they are out of their pen. The tradition that the monarchy will fall if there are no ravens at the Tower dates from the late nineteenth century.

54. Tower Green with two of the resident ravens, painted by John Fulleylove *c.* 1907.

55. The City British Legion band playing in the ditch on the site of the moat in 1933. Relations between the authorities in the Tower and the nearby parishes were not always comfortable, and this was the first time that the band had been allowed to bring the public there during a performance.

56. Cleaning and restoration of the fabric in the late twentieth century gave the Tower a picturesque image, in contrast with its earlier reputation as a grim fortress and prison.

57. A barrage balloon over the Tower in 1939. A number of buildings within the Tower were destroyed by bombing during the Second World War.

58. The chapel of St Peter ad Vincula on the north side of Tower Green, in 2011.

59. Reconstructed medieval siege artillery in the former moat.

60. The wooden stairway to the newly reopened doorway on the south side of the White Tower was erected in 1973, reconstructing the original arrangement of the eleventh century.

he on Tower Hill. Both were buried in St Peter ad Vincula. On the 23rd her father was executed, having failed to raise a rebellion in the Midlands.

Mary married Philip despite the opposition to the match, but they did not have children, and so when she died, on 17 November 1558, Elizabeth succeeded to the throne. She was then at Hatfield House in Hertfordshire and when she travelled to London a few days later she did not go directly to the Tower but first went to Lord North's mansion at the Charterhouse. She stayed there for five days before processing to the Tower, where she remained until 5 December. She returned to the Tower for two days to prepare for her coronation, which took place on 15 January. As part of her policy to settle the church, the Bishops of Winchester and Lincoln were sent to the Tower in April, and some of those senior clergymen who refused to subscribe to the Oath of Supremacy were subsequently imprisoned there, including the Archbishop of York and five other bishops. Elizabeth's church was to be Protestant, and outward conformity, at least, would be required.

While attention naturally focused on those great events and on the senior figures admitted to the Tower, others continued to be imprisoned there charged with less portentous crimes. A Frenchman accused of coining was held in the southern tower of the Byward Tower, where he was killed by rubble when some gunpowder was detonated accidentally. The tower was so damaged that it had to be 'new builded'; the warder responsible for that tower was arrested for keeping prisoners close to a cache of gunpowder. Before Christmas 1553 a counterfeiter named Harvey escaped from the Tower and had reached a ship in the river before being caught. He was returned and a few weeks later taken to Tyburn for execution.

By the time of Elizabeth's accession parts of the Tower palace were becoming dilapidated. A survey taken a few months after her coronation described the great hall as being 'in very greate decaye so as it is lyke to fall if it be not provided for in convenient tyme'. The various departments competed for space, and the Ordnance Office was using rooms within the royal apartments for storage by the 1560s. Although it could not have been foreseen, because of Elizabeth's long reign the apartments did not in fact have to be renovated for another coronation for forty-four years.

One of the major decisions taken early in her reign was to undertake a recoinage, to restore the silver content which had been reduced by successive debasements from the early 1540s. The Mint already was a busy part of the Tower, with twenty-two salaried staff in 1552. During Mary's reign, and as part of her marriage agreement, it had minted coins for the Spanish government. In 1554 experiments were made with a 'great mill', although they seem to have been abortive and five years later all of its ironwork and other 'waste yron' were sold, to pay for a new armoury. Elizabeth's recoinage required additional plant and storage for the coins that were called in. A new refining house was built close to the White Tower and a set of buildings was erected between the inner and outer curtain walls on the east side of the Tower, known as the 'upper mint'. These were completed by the end of 1560, but the recoinage did not get underway for another few months. It was carried out by a German firm of refiners, referred to as 'Straungers Alamayne Fyners'. Its workers suffered from metal poisoning, which killed some of them.

The queen acknowledged the importance of the recoinage by visiting the Tower in July 1561, spending most of the day there, 'and went and saw all her mints. And they gave the Queen certain pieces of gold and ... the Lord of Hunsdon had one and my lord Marquis of Northampton.' By the time that the recoinage was completed in September 1562, new coins valued at £783,248 had been issued. After that surge of activity, work at the Mint returned to its former level, but a new blanching house was built in 1566 and a new office twenty years later. By the 1580s the Mint's buildings ran around the space between the curtain walls, from the 'nether mint' on the west side to the 'upper mint' structures close to the Salt Tower.

Pressure on the accommodation for prisoners varied, according to the number incarcerated at any one time, and their rank. In September 1562, twenty-two people were listed as prisoners in the Tower. Nine of them were the senior clergymen imprisoned early in the reign, and the list was headed by Lady Katherine Grey and the Earl of Hertford. Katherine was a younger sister of Lady Jane Grey, descended from Henry VII and, by Henry VIII's will, the heir to the throne. Her marriage to Henry Howard, son of the Earl of Pembroke, had been annulled soon after Mary's accession. Other matches were then suggested for her, but by an Act of 1536 a member of the royal family required the sovereign's consent to their marriage. Katherine did not obtain Elizabeth's approval when she married Edward Seymour, Earl of Hertford and son of the former Lord Protector, late in 1560. She then conceived and, unable to conceal her pregnancy, had to admit her marriage. The queen was so indignant that she ordered Katherine's imprisonment in the Tower, where a boy, Edward, was born in September 1561. Hertford was recalled from Paris and also sent to the Tower, while an investigation into the circumstances of the marriage, which had been conducted clandestinely, concluded that it had not been valid. Edward was thereby officially illegitimate, although he was allowed to use the courtesy title of Lord Beauchamp.

In the Tower husband and wife were kept apart, but the Lieutenant did not strictly enforce his orders and allowed them to visit each other. Katherine again became pregnant, giving birth to a second son in 1563. Hertford was fined £15,000 by the Star Chamber court for deflowering a royal virgin. He was released from the Tower during the plague epidemic of 1563, but detained in various country houses until 1571. The queen was unforgiving in Katherine's case, and she was imprisoned until her death in 1568. She was also incensed by the marriage of Katherine's sister Mary to Thomas Keys, the queen's Sergeant Porter, in 1565. Both were detained, although not in the Tower.

Elizabeth's attitude to marriages contracted without her knowledge by those in court circles had not softened almost thirty years later. Sir Walter Raleigh married one of her maids-of-honour, Elizabeth Throgmorton, in 1592. The bride was already pregnant; husband and wife were both sent to the Tower and imprisoned there for several months.

One reason for Elizabeth's implacability regarding the Hertford case was her sensitivity over the succession. The alternative heir to Katherine and Mary Grey was Mary, Queen of Scots, who would restore Catholicism. Plots to displace Elizabeth from the throne commonly involved replacing her with Mary. An early scheme of this kind, involving sorcery, was planned by a group of Catholics in Essex. This came to light in 1561 with the arrest and interrogation of a priest, John Coxe. Fortune-tellers were believed to have discovered that 'the Queen would not live till Christmas, and the old laws should up again in spite of all that would say nay'. Among those arrested in the wake of Coxe's revelations was Sir Edward Waldegrave, a religious conservative, who was imprisoned in the Tower, and died there in September 1561.

Other plots followed, of varying degrees of sophistication and threat. The most high-ranking of those incarcerated in the Tower for plotting to displace the queen was Thomas Howard, 4th Duke of Norfolk. He was born in 1538 and succeeded his grandfather as duke and Earl Marshal of England in 1554. Descended from Edward I, he was the only duke and first subject and as such had a prominent position at court, but his political rivals thwarted his ambitions. Norfolk had dealings with the Florentine banker Roberto Ridolfi, who was widely connected with senior figures at Elizabeth's court. Ridolfi, who may have acted as a double-agent, was at the centre of a conspiracy to depose Elizabeth and replace her with Mary, Queen of Scots, who was to marry Norfolk. A rising in England with foreign support would place Mary on the English throne, and she would also regain her throne in Scotland. Roman Catholicism would be restored.

Norfolk's general disaffection and conduct were such that he spent several months in the Tower in 1569 before being released to house arrest at his mansion at the Charterhouse, which he had bought from Lord North's son. The plotters then successfully approached him. John Lesley, Bishop of Ross, visited him at the Charterhouse on a number of occasions and Ridolfi went there at least twice. The plot was unravelled by the government in 1571, when Norfolk's secretary was interrogated in the Tower. An incriminatory letter was found under a mat close to the duke's bedchamber in the Charterhouse, and the key to the cipher in which it was written was later discovered hidden between roof tiles. Norfolk's role as leader of an insurrectionary force that was to co-operate with an invading Spanish army and seize Elizabeth was revealed. He was returned to the Tower and in January 1572 was convicted of high treason and condemned to death. Yet Elizabeth prevaricated for more than four months, reluctant to send her cousin to the block. Eventually she resigned herself to the inevitable: Norfolk was executed on Tower Hill on 2 June, and was buried in St Peter ad Vincula.

On his death the queen waived the crown's right to his estates, which should have been forfeit because of his treason, and they passed to his eldest son, Philip Howard. Philip held the courtesy title of Earl of Surrey (his father's title having been extinguished), until he succeeded his grandfather as Earl of Arundel in 1580. In the early 1580s he followed in his father's footsteps and corresponded with Mary, and in 1584 he was received into the Roman Catholic Church. Not surprisingly, his activities aroused the suspicion of the government. Following an unsuccessful attempt to leave the country without the queen's permission, in April 1585 he was imprisoned in the Tower. He was attainted in 1589 and condemned to death, and, although the sentence was not carried out, he remained a prisoner for the rest of his life. He spent his time in the Tower writing religious treatises and translating other works. After he died there, in October 1595, there was a rumour that he had been poisoned by his cook.

A Latin inscription on a wall inside the Beauchamp Tower translates as, 'The more suffering for Christ in this world the more glory with Christ in the next. Arundell June 22 1587.' The earl was just one of dozens of prisoners who left their mark on the walls of the Tower, especially in the Beauchamp and Salt towers. Most carved their names, perhaps with a verse and in some cases within a decorative panel. One of the most elaborate is a panel commemorating the five sons of the Duke of Northumberland, who were imprisoned in the early years of Mary's reign. Above the name 'John Dvdle', the centre-piece depicts a bear and lion supporting a ragged staff, encircled by a pattern consisting of roses, oak leaves, gillyflowers and honeysuckle, respectively the symbols of Ambrose (later Earl of Warwick), Robert (later Earl of Leicester), Guilford (executed in 1555) and Henry (killed at St Quentin in 1558).

Much more complex was the astronomical clock in the Salt Tower. The clock and calendar are surrounded by numerals, signs of the days and months, and the symbols of the zodiac. It has the inscription, 'Hew Draper of Brystow made thys spheer the 30 daye of Maye anno 1561.' He was a tavern-keeper interested in astronomy who found himself accused of dabbling in sorcery directed against Sir William St Loe and his wife Elizabeth. Sir William was appointed captain of the guard to Elizabeth in 1559, and it may have been the St Loes' position at court that was the reason for Draper being confined to the Tower, and not a prison in Bristol. Elizabeth St Loe's second husband had been Sir William Cavendish, who died in 1557, and, after St Loe's death, in 1565, she married the Earl of Shrewsbury, and became known to posterity as Bess of Hardwick.

Most tablets and inscriptions were plain and crudely executed. Some prisoners who left their memorials in this way carved the letters 'ihs', with a bar on top of the h, the symbol of the Jesuits. After the Papal Bull *Regnans in Excelsis* of 1570, which declared Elizabeth a heretic and deposed from her titles, the laws and penalties directed at Catholics were strengthened, and priests were liable to be arrested on charges of treason. Although the Catholic inscriptions were an act of defiance, declaring the faith of the prisoner, they were subsequently covered over, not defaced or removed. Other prisoners simply recorded their presence. One man evidently found the sheer tedium of confinement taxing and wrote, 'Close prisoner 8 monethes 32 wekes 224 dayes 5376 houres.'

Close prisoners were allowed little freedom, while others were less constrained and could walk about parts of the site adjoining their rooms. Some were allowed visitors and considerable flexibility, and they were described as those having 'liberty of the Tower'. Harsh conditions would have been inappropriate for those held there to signify the queen's displeasure with a servant of the crown who had acted against her wishes, such as Sir William Davison. After service as a diplomat, Davison was appointed one of the secretaries of state in 1586 and among his duties was custody of the warrant for the execution of Mary, Queen of Scots, who was condemned after her trial in October. The warrant was drafted in December and Elizabeth signed it on 1 February. She instructed Davison not to release it until it had been sealed, but it was sent and not recalled. When Elizabeth was told of Mary's execution, she blamed Davison for breaking her trust by releasing it. He was sent to the Tower, where he was held for twenty months, as well as being subject to a large fine. But he retained his post as secretary and continued to draw the salary for the remainder of his life. It seemed that he had been the scapegoat for Elizabeth's authorisation of the death in her custody of a monarch, who was also her cousin. While in the Tower Davison wrote a justification of his actions, and a description of Ireland.

No purpose-built prison block was erected and the accommodation of prisoners in the towers made the application of tight security arrangements difficult. And the degree of supervision varied. When William Creighton, a 'Scottish Jesuit', was imprisoned in the Martin Tower he had a room above that of Nicholas Roscarrock, a Cornishman suspected of 'intelligence with Jesuits and priests'. Roscarrock 'did often times by some device, open two doors which were between their lodgings and so they conferred at pleasure'. Moreover, Creighton handed letters to Roscarrock, whose room was close to the ground, and he passed them out of his window 'to a little maiden', and they were taken out of the Tower. Items could also be brought in. Henry Percy, 8th Earl of Northumberland, was imprisoned in the Tower for the third time in 1584, on suspicion of involvement in Francis Throckmorton's plot against Elizabeth. One morning in June 1585 he was found dead in his bed, from a pistol shot through the heart. His servant had bought the weapon from a London gunsmith and had taken it into the Tower. Although some Catholics claimed that Northumberland had been murdered, an inquest found that he had taken his own life.

Control over those holding positions within the Tower was also less than stringent, so far as their religion was concerned. The Elizabethan settlement was lenient towards some of those nonconformists who did not challenge the established church. Members of the Family of Love, a sect founded by the Dutch mystic Hendrik Niclaes in 1540, were tolerated even in positions close to the crown. They included some of the yeomen warders, officers of the Jewel House, the armouries and the wardrobe; in the early seventeenth century the keeper of the lions was a Familist. Despite the Familists being denounced by orthodox

Anglican clergy, and a burst of persecution between 1578 and 1581, for most of the reigns of Elizabeth and James I those holding posts at the Tower were permitted to retain them.

Such tolerance contrasted with the harshness to which some prisoners were subjected, including torture. Prominent writers such as Sir Thomas Smith, in the sixteenth century, and the great jurist Sir Edward Coke, in the early seventeenth, stated that torture was unknown in the English legal system. Sir William Blackstone, in his *Commentaries on the Laws of England*, published in the 1760s, justified those comments when he made the distinction that the rack, the favoured method of extracting information, had been 'occasionally used as an engine of State, not of Law'. The Privy Council kept close control of the process and a warrant was required authorising the use of torture on a specific prisoner. Just eighty-one such warrants were issued between 1540 and 1640, fifty-three of them during Elizabeth's reign (1558–1603). Of the eighty-one warrants, forty-eight authorised torture in the Tower, in cases ranging from horse theft and robbery to sedition and treason. Only nine were designated as 'religious' cases, although others which did have a religious basis would have been counted as treason.

The rack was used in at least thirty-one of the cases in the Tower. It consisted of a rectangular iron frame within which were three wooden rollers, across which a prisoner was spread-eagled, tied by his limbs. The outer ones were turned gradually and the central one, which had iron teeth, supported the prisoner's torso, so that the rack's operator could leave the room while the officers took down the victim's information. The rack in the Tower was last used in 1640. Manacles were used in six cases where the form of torture was specified, perhaps as a supplement to the rack, but in seventeen of the Tower cases the implement was not described. A prisoner could also be subjected to acute discomfort, rather than actual torture, by being kept, perhaps for a few days, where he could neither stand nor lie down. Known as 'little ease', this space was mentioned in 1534, but by 1604 was reported to be disused. It may have been in the base of the Salt Tower, although that is not certain, and in 1604 the term 'little ease' was also applied to the implement of torture known as Skeffington's daughter: 'An Engyne devysed by Mr Skavington, sometyme Lieutenant of the Tower, called Skavingtons daughters, or Little Ease.'

Manacles were the form of torture used to try to extract information from John Gerard, a Catholic priest. He was born in Derbyshire in 1564 and was educated at Oxford. His father had been imprisoned in the Tower for two years in the early 1570s, for his part in a plot to rescue Mary, Queen of Scots, from captivity at Tutbury Castle. So it may not have been a surprise when, in 1581, John announced his intention of joining the Jesuits. After a spell of imprisonment in London, he travelled to Rome, where he entered the Society of Jesus in 1588. He landed in England later that year and served as a priest to recusant families until he was captured in 1594. In 1597 he was transferred to the Tower. Gerard described his experiences. He was imprisoned in the Salt Tower, 'a large tall tower, three storeys high with lock-ups in each storey'. The first room in which he was held had been occupied by another Jesuit priest, Henry Walpole, three years earlier, for Gerard discovered his name 'cut with a chisel on the wall'. For his first night the warder left 'a little straw' for him to sleep on, 'for beds are not provided in this prison, but the prisoner must find his own bed and any other furniture he wants, on condition that they go to the

Lieutenant of the Tower, even if the prisoner is liberated'. A bed and some clothing were provided by his friends.

After initial questioning Gerard was shown the warrant from the Privy Council directed to the Lieutenant, Sir Richard Berkeley: 'You shall by virtue hereof cause him to be put to the manacles and such other torture as is used in that place.' Gerard was then taken to the torture-room, which was 'underground and dark ... a vast place and every device and instrument of torture was there'. This probably describes the sub-crypt of the chapel in the White Tower. His wrists were put into iron gauntlets and an iron rod was passed between them, the rod was then attached to a large post and the support was removed, so that the prisoner was suspended, with his feet clear of the floor. That happened on two occasions and when he was taken to the torture-room for the third time he was threatened with the rack, but was not put on it. Gerard later wrote of the compassion shown him by his warder and the officers, including Berkeley, and he was not tortured twice a day until he gave the information they wanted, as had been ordered.

The torture left his hands swollen and it was three weeks before he could move his fingers enough to hold a knife, and six months later he still had 'a certain numbness' in them. After the initial spell of torture, he was largely left alone, but was not allowed to have visitors. He paid his warder to carry letters between him and his friends, although he was, of course, breaking the regulations by doing so. The food varied according to the prisoner's social rank, and with no distinction regarding religion. Gerard admitted that the fare 'was plentiful – every day they gave me six small rolls of very good bread', and his friends sent him 'sweetmeats and other delicacies'.

He also made contact with John Arden, a prisoner in the Cradle Tower, the next tower along the wall. Arden had been incarcerated since 1587 for suspected complicity in the Babington Plot to replace Elizabeth with Mary. Gerard's warder was also responsible for Arden and was persuaded to let Gerard visit him. When he did so Gerard saw that 'it might be possible for a man to lower himself with a rope from the roof of the tower on to the wall beyond the moat'. This he and Arden achieved, having made arrangements with their friends in the city. A ball attached to a length of thread was thrown from the roof of the Cradle Tower to their accomplices on the bank, who attached to it a rope fixed to a stake driven into the ground. The rope was then pulled up and tied to a gun on the roof, and the prisoners, with difficulty, worked their way down it to join their friends, who were waiting with a boat. They got clean away. Their warder had been an accomplice, by carrying letters and allowing Gerard to go to the Cradle Tower in the evening. Warned by a fellow warder, he also made his escape.

Gerard's warder had previously declined the offer of a hefty sum of money to co-operate by, in Gerard's words, 'letting me walk out of the prison, as I could easily do in borrowed clothes'. His phrase suggests that his friends thought it would be that easy. Many people were allowed to come and go from the fortress, to work, or to bring supplies to those employed in the various departments, and 'curious people' went in to look at the lions and other animals. Researchers who wished to consult the records were also admitted. In 1601 the corporation of Stratford-upon-Avon paid its solicitor the 13s 4d 'that he layed out for us in searchinge in the Rowles in the tower & othe[r] where'.

The staff did take some basic security measures. For example, when Paul Hentzner, from Brandenburg, and his companions arrived for a visit in 1598, he wrote, 'Upon entering, we were obliged to leave our swords at the gate, and deliver them to the guard.' And an overnight curfew was enforced; a bell rung at five o'clock in the afternoon warned those who were not resident to leave before the gates were locked. But no record was taken of those entering, or the purpose of their visit.

The Tower was on the sight-seeing itinerary of many visitors from abroad. Lupold von Wedel, from Pomerania, was there in 1585, and recorded his impressions of a 'great castle surrounded by a moat and walls and garrisoned by soldiers'. He looked around the arsenal, commenting on the cannon balls stacked in pyramids, and the wardrobe, with its 'gilt bedsteads, curtains, tapestries, tablecovers, cushions … all royally wrought in gold and silver … [and] some chairs which were upholstered with velvet and gold brocade and inlaid with silver and gold'. He noted that in the Mint, 'many persons were sitting and working continuously'. At the treasury he and his companions were allowed to look into, but not enter, the room which was 'full of silver gilt and pure gold plate'. He admired the workmanship of many of the pieces and wondered at the value of those made of 'pure and finest gold'.

The plate and jewels drew admiration, and the menagerie's lions and lionesses, a lynx, a wolf, an eagle and a large porcupine, were a curiosity, but the Tower's value as a fortress was questioned. Baron Waldstein, from Moravia, who was in London in 1600, acknowledged that the Tower was 'defended with several moats, encircled by triple walls', but it had not been adapted, by the addition of arrow-headed bastions to the line of stone walls and towers, to withstand artillery fire. A few years later the Venetian ambassador Nicolo Molin observed that 'it has neither bulwarks nor bastions nor other fortifications'. The walls did not even have a lining of earth and would have been breached by cannon fire. But with the erection of artillery defences downstream and the development of the navy, it was judged that enemy forces were unlikely to penetrate along the Thames as far as London. Enveloped by the growing metropolis, with suburbs along the north bank of the Thames almost to Limehouse, defence of the fortress would have been difficult.

Despite its military weaknesses, the Tower could still have a potential function in intimidating the citizens. Waldstein saw sixteen cannon on the White Tower, 'which are trained upon the City'. It could be a valuable tool in domestic politics and give those controlling it an influence in decision-making. This was shown by an investigation in 1595, which uncovered a conspiracy involving Berkeley's predecessor as Lieutenant, Sir Michael Blount. It was planned that he should take control of the fortress on the queen's death, and hold it on behalf of the Earl of Hertford and his son Lord Beauchamp, against the Privy Council's orders. Hertford, the former husband of Katherine Grey, may have considered making a claim to the throne; the question of the succession was so sensitive that, as a result of the investigation, he found himself in the Tower once more, not in control but as a prisoner, and he was held there for almost three months. The stock of weapons and the gunpowder, kept chiefly in the White Tower, would be invaluable for those attempting to carry out a coup. Alarmingly, some gunpowder was also stored outside the Tower, as the Lieutenant had noted in 1586, when he drew the government's attention to a warehouse on Tower Hill, containing 800 barrels of powder.

Lupold von Wedel wrote that the Tower 'by tradition is said to have been erected by Julius Caesar' and Justus Zinzerling, around 1610, referred to 'Caesar's Tower'. Shakespeare included in *Richard II* a mention of 'Julius Caesar's ill-erected tower', using the phrase in the sense of the Tower having a malign function. He explained the attribution to Caesar in *Richard III*, during an exchange between the Prince of Wales and the Duke of Gloucester, as the prince is being taken there:

Prince: I do not like the Tower, of any place:–
Did Julius Caesar build that place, my lord?
Gloucester: He did, my gracious lord, begin that place;
Which, since, succeeding ages have re-edified.
Prince: Is it upon record, or else reported
Successively from age to age, he built it?
Gloucester: Upon record, my gracious lord.

The explanation for such a massive misdating may be civic pride; the White Tower was assumed to be the oldest building in the city, and so it must date from the beginning of recorded English history. Whatever its basis, the notion that it was begun by Julius had a wide currency in the sixteenth and seventeenth centuries. Pride in the Tower's venerability was accompanied by an awareness of its role in history, which those at the London playhouses who saw Shakespeare's history plays could not fail to be aware of. Elsewhere in *Richard III*, Lord Hastings explains that his horse had started when he saw the Tower, 'As loath to bear me to the slaughter-house.'

Interest in the Tower should have been tempered by concern about its condition. Waldstein described the great hall of the palace as 'an ancient dining-hall, almost falling to pieces with age'. That applied to other buildings within the palace, according to 'A declaracon of the state of your Highnes Tower of London' of 1597, by Sir John Peyton, who had replaced Berkeley as Lieutenant. He reported that 'your Majesties lodgings and manie other buildings within the Tower are in decaye'. These included the gates and the prisoners' lodgings, also described as 'in decaye', while the sluices that drew water from the Thames to maintain the moat were 'nowe utterly decayed'. The moat itself was 'in many parts decayed', and the walls were 'in some places easie to bee mounted'.

Within the Tower the spaces were overcrowded, so much so that Waldstein thought that 'it gives visitors the impression of a town'. Those senior officers of the crown who were entitled to occupy the lodgings within the walls no longer chose to live there, preferring houses in more salubrious surroundings. Instead, their former lodgings had come to be occupied by the Tower's own officers and their families. Overcrowding had been exacerbated by allowing a practice by which 'the warders, minters, & other inhabitants have usually lodged their friends & other strangers, within the Tower'. A similar practice of permitting prisoners with 'liberty of the Tower' to have their families with them during meal times and while services were being held at St Peter's, when the gates were closed and most of the warders were off duty, was recognised as a potential security risk.

Of the thirty warders, just four were on duty overnight. Not all of them were reliable:

> Ther bee amongst ye warders divers unfitt for the place; some
> of them utterly neglectinge their duties in service, others given to

druncknes, disorders and quarrells, other for debilitie of bodye unable to performe their duties, others double officed and cannot attend in two places.

There were also 140 gunners and twenty labourers within the Tower, who should have taken their turns at the watch, but did not. Even worse, among the Mint's buildings was a common brewhouse, and the Tower also contained a hackney stable, with horses for hire 'whoe have had their contynuall passage, with their Carriages and horses in & out of the great gates'. Put simply, it was not possible with the resources available 'to restrayne the trayterous prisoners from intelligence & practice'.

Security problems were not eased by low wages and the corrosive impact of inflation, which could adversely affect morale and even loyalty. Warders were paid 8*d* per day, which Peyton recognised was 'smale wages regardinge the deernes of theis tymes, when the prices of all things and all mens labours are increased they are growne to exceedinge povertie'. They could be given money by the wealthier prisoners, which would supplement their wages, but such arrangements created a fine line between tips legitimately made for help provided, and payments which were inducements to break the regulations, such as those paid to Gerard's warder. A prisoner's resources could be considerable, especially with gentry support. Gerard's friends had offered his warder a deal that consisted of a down payment and an annuity thereafter, for his connivance in Gerard's walking out of the Tower in disguise. That warder refused, but another one, on low pay, might have been tempted by a similar offer. The officers also benefited, quite legitimately, from fees and perquisites due from prisoners, and their incomes therefore fluctuated as the number and wealth of the prisoners varied.

The strain on the manpower available to the Lieutenant varied, but could be increased without warning, when a plot or other threat was uncovered and suspects were imprisoned in the Tower. That occurred in the aftermath of the failed coup by the queen's erstwhile favourite Robert Devereux, Earl of Essex, in February 1601, when many of his supporters were arrested. He was held in the Tower, where witnesses were examined. His presence must have added to the problems of security and control, given his standing and the support which he continued to attract. Essex was executed on Tower Green on 25 February and was buried in St Peter ad Vincula. The Earl of Southampton, Shakespeare's patron, who had taken part in the coup, was also held in the Tower and convicted of treason, but his life was spared.

Peyton's 'declaration' of 1597 contains the kind of observations that only someone new to a post can make, pointing up problems that could not be blamed on him at that stage. As well as the condition of the buildings and their administration, he was concerned about the long-running dispute with the City over the status and boundaries of the Liberties of the Tower. The City was accused of claiming the area of Tower Hill as being within its jurisdiction, and allegations were made that the boundary stones had been moved. Peyton suspected that the City would claim the whole area, up to the moat. This had become an increasingly pressing issue in recent years. During a riot in 1595 by 'unrulie youthes on the towerhill', the lord mayor had arrived with his officers to quell the disturbance, and in doing so in that area had exceeded his authority. A plan of the Tower and its environs drawn by William Haiward and John Gascoyne in the same year as Peyton's 'declaration' included a text stating the boundaries of the Liberties as given in a judgement by the court leet in 1536. Peyton was adamant that the area belonged to the crown.

As well as problems with the fabric of the buildings, not all of the items kept there were well maintained. At least that was the impression conveyed by Jacob Rathgeb, from Würtemberg, when he inspected the armoury in 1592. While he admitted that 'there are many fine cannon in it', he also observed that 'they are full of dust, and stand about in the greatest disorder'. Admittedly, he could have had only a superficial view of the many pieces in the fortress, which by 1603 numbered 155, not including those on Tower Wharf that were temporarily landed from ships undergoing refit.

Notwithstanding the revelations made in Peyton's 'declaration', comments such as Rathgeb's, the condition of the buildings and its grim reputation as the state prison, there was growing pride in the Tower. This was reflected by the historian John Stow's summary of its role, in his *Survey of London* of 1598. He described it as a citadel, a royal palace 'for assemblies or treaties', a prison of state, the 'only place of coinage for all England', an armoury, a treasury for the crown's 'ornaments and jewels', and the 'general conserver' of most of the records of the royal courts of justice. Twenty years later Thomas Gainsford, in *The Glory of England*, was even more approving, with his comment that 'instead of an old Bastille and ill-beseeming arsenal, thrust as it were into an outcast corner of the city, you have in London a building of the greatest antiquity and majestical form, serving to most uses of any citadel or magazine that ever you saw'.

The Earl of Southampton's response to imprisonment in the Tower was to sit for a portrait in the window of his lodgings there. The portrait has an inscription in Latin that translates as 'In chains unsubdued', and the painter included, as an inset, a view of the fortress. He also showed Southampton's black-and-white cat, sitting on the window sill, its gaze fixed upon the viewer. The cat became the subject of a Tower legend, as a emblem of loyalty, for it was said that he had missed his master, had tracked him to the Tower and reached him by descending a chimney.

Representations of the Tower were becoming more common, in a variety of forms. Haiward and Gascoyne's plan showed the buildings in perspective. A Delftware plate dated 1600 has the loyal inscription 'The rose is red the leaves are grene God save Elizabeth our queene' around its centrepiece, which is a polychrome landscape showing a group of buildings that resembles the Tower. From a dominating fortress built to overawe Londoners and representing state control, it was becoming a positive symbol of national as well as civic pride.

6

SCIENCE & CIVIL WAR

The problem of the succession, so long a major concern, was resolved before Elizabeth's death in March 1603. Sir Robert Cecil, Burghley's son, had worked steadily to become the queen's leading councillor, and he prepared for the untroubled accession of James VI of Scotland, the first of the Stuarts. Yet within forty years James's son and successor, Charles, had been engaged in two wars with his Scottish subjects, faced a rebellion in Ireland and become embroiled in a civil war in England and Wales. His political travails were to cost him both his throne and his head, and usher in a republic.

After news of Elizabeth's death reached James, he began a leisurely progress south. Doubtless in imitation of Elizabeth's arrival in London in 1558, James I also went directly to the Charterhouse when he reached the city in May, and held court there before going to the Tower. He was informed that artillery pieces were 'layde in readines on the Tower Wharfe to be shott off (in Princely Triumphe) at the first entrance of your Majestie into the same youre hignes most royall Towre of London'. James was not disappointed and watched from the royal barge 'to see the ordinance on the White Towre (commonly called Julius Caesar's Towre), being in number twenty peeces, with the great ordinance on Towre-wharfe, being in number 100, and chalmers [chambers] to the number 130, discharged and shot off'. So many pieces made an impressive display which was 'very acceptable to the King'. He inspected the Tower over the following two days, before going on to Greenwich by barge.

Following custom, the king returned to prepare for the coronation, appropriately fixed for St James's Day, 25 July. But the royal progress through the city and the displays and ceremonies usually associated with a coronation were omitted because of an outbreak of plague. James travelled from the Tower to Westminster by barge. That was an inauspicious beginning to the reign; the epidemic worsened during the summer and by the end of the year it had killed roughly one in five Londoners in the worst outbreak for forty years. The royal entry to the City was deferred until the following March, preceded by three days of royal residence at the Tower.

Even before the coronation, the first plots of the reign were being investigated. These were to be dubbed the Bye and Main plots. The Bye Plot was a response to disappointment with James's failure to ease the burden on Roman Catholics; it would have involved kidnapping the king and Henry, Prince of Wales, and imprisoning them in the Tower. The principal plotters were Sir Griffin Markham, George Brooke and a priest named William Watson, who were arrested and confined to the Tower themselves. The Main Plot was a separate scheme, partly hatched by George Brooke and by Lord Grey of Wilton, who vaguely planned to replace James with his cousin Arabella Stuart. As she was born in England, she could be held to have the stronger claim to the throne than he did. This led to Brooke's brother Henry, Lord Cobham, being questioned and also his friend Sir Walter Raleigh.

From a modest background in Devon, Raleigh had a brilliant

career as a favourite of the queen, soldier, sailor, explorer and founder of the colony of Virginia, talented writer and poet. But he was thought to harbour resentment against the new regime, for he had been deprived of the post of Captain of the Guard, which he had held since 1587, lost his income from wine duties and been ordered to hand over Durham House in the Strand forthwith to the Bishop of Durham. Raleigh had occupied the house by royal grant for almost twenty years and had spent £2,000 on improvements.

Raleigh and Cobham had both been excluded from James's new council. However bitter Raleigh's feelings may have been, it was Cobham's ill-judged and incriminatory comments, which he later withdrew, that landed them both in the Tower. They had, admittedly, held conversations with Lord Grey during which, it was alleged, Grey had spoken 'nothing but treason at every worde'. However feeble the plot and flimsy the case against them, all were tried in Winchester in November. When Raleigh was taken from the Tower on his way to the trial, fifty horsemen were required to escort him through the 'multitudes of unruly people', who had assembled to jeer the unpopular favourite of Elizabeth. All three men were convicted of treason and were sentenced to death, but the sentences were not carried out, and they were returned to the Tower. Grey spent the rest of his life there, dying in July 1614; Raleigh was released in March 1616 and Cobham in the summer of 1617.

In the early stages of his captivity Raleigh was accommodated in two rooms in the Bloody Tower and was allowed two servants, but he was not an easy prisoner. He became depressed and on one occasion when he was dining with the Lieutenant, Sir John Peyton, he stabbed himself in the chest with a table knife. With such a distinguished prisoner behaving in such a way, Peyton's request to resign was understandable and it was granted on 30 July 1603. He described his post as one 'only composed of trouble, danger, charge and vexation'.

The king's religious policies provoked a small group of Catholics to engage in another and more famous plot, which evolved during 1605 and was supposed to reach its climax with the mass murder of the king and the members of both houses of parliament. A cache of gunpowder was placed in a cellar below the chamber of the House of Lords, to be detonated during James's opening of the new sitting of parliament, when members of the Commons would also be in the chamber. Following a tip-off, a search was made of the buildings and when Guy Fawkes opened the door of the cellar he was apprehended. He carried a fuse and a tinder-box, and thirty-six barrels of gunpowder were found hidden beneath a stack of fuel. Fawkes was taken to the Tower and his accomplices were gradually rounded up and despatched there. The gunpowder from the cellar was also taken to the Tower. It weighed eighteen hundredweight and, although described as 'decaied', was still potent enough to have caused a massive explosion.

The king authorised the use of torture on Fawkes, with 'gentler tortures' to be used first and, if he did not co-operate, more brutal ones later. According to Nicolo Molin, 'for two successive days he underwent the most excruciating torture without saying anything, except that the conspirators were twelve in number, whose names he would not mention'. They were traced anyway, and it seems unlikely that any of them were tortured, for the government gradually pieced together the details of the conspiracy. Four of the conspirators were killed by the sheriff of Worcestershire's men at Holbeach House in south Staffordshire, and Francis Tresham died in the Tower, of natural causes, towards the end of December and was buried there. The other eight conspirators were tried in January at Westminster and executed in London. The plot was commemorated by a wall monument in the Lieutenant's Lodgings.

The Tower also received another long-term prisoner as a result of the conspiracy. That was Henry Percy, 9th Earl of Northumberland, son of the 8th Earl who had committed suicide in the Tower twenty years earlier. He was suspected of having knowledge of the background to the plot, rather than being implicated in it. Whatever the doubts about his involvement, he was tried in the Star Chamber court in 1606 and kept in the Tower for fifteen years. After his arrest, Molin speculated that he would never leave the Tower alive, basing this opinion on his impression that 'it is a most remarkable fact in this country that if a nobleman is put in the Tower he either loses his life or ends his days there'. Of course, that was not true, and he should have been aware of the Earl of Southampton's release at the outset of the new reign. But his comment did reflect the Tower's reputation.

Northumberland was housed in the Martin Tower and took his recreation by walking to and from the Brick Tower. The ground between them was paved and designated 'My Lord of Northumberland's Walk'. An iron plaque, which carried his arms, was fixed on the wall there. It contained holes into which a peg was placed each time someone taking exercise completed the walk, so that he would know how many times he had done it and so how far he had walked.

Those three prominent prisoners may have been the reason for the replacement in 1605 of Sir George Harvey by Sir William Waad as Lieutenant. Waad had served Sir Robert Cecil, now Earl of Salisbury, for many years, and perhaps he was put into the post to be a stricter gaoler for those prisoners than his predecessor had been. They did not give him an easy time, and soon after his appointment he complained to Salisbury that 'my Lord Cobham used me very sullenly ... [he] did forget himself toward me yesterday in the afternoon in such sort as I could do no less than shut him up into his lodging'. Evidently his lordship gave vent to his fury so loudly that 'it was heard into the court'. Waad commented in the same letter that 'Sir Walter Ralegh used some speech of his dislike of me the day before, yet since he acknowledges his error'. After that unpromising beginning Waad did have some successes and after a time managed to persuade Bess Raleigh to leave her coach outside the gates, rather than ride into the Tower in it, as she had been doing.

With Northumberland, Raleigh, Cobham and Grey as residents, the Tower attracted attention as a focus for science and literature during the first half of James's reign. Northumberland's epithet 'the wizard earl' referred to his interest and experiments in astrology and alchemy. Despite a massive fine, he remained a wealthy man, and continued to provide support for the mathematician Thomas Harriot at his mansion at Syon, near Brentford. Harriot's wide-ranging interests included the refraction of light, optics, mechanics, astronomy, navigation and cartography. He had been employed by Raleigh during the 1580s to teach navigational skills to his ship-captains, and had been sent by him in 1585 to survey Virginia.

Robert Hues, another mathematician, was a servant of Lord Grey and was permitted to remain in the Tower until Grey's death. He had also been employed by Raleigh for his navigational abilities in the 1580s and 1590s, and he, too, received support from Northumberland. The third mathematician in Northumberland's circle was Walter Warner, who had become a member of his household in 1590. While Northumberland was incarcerated in the Tower, Warner made it the base for his own studies, which included a treatise concerning the circulation of the blood. These men were described as Northumberland's 'three magi', and the belief developed that the Tower at the time resembled a kind of academy for scholarly activity, called the 'School of Night', although that implies more formality than may have existed. What is certain is that Northumberland, Raleigh and Grey were patrons of a circle of scholars, and maintained that role during their imprisonments.

The prisoners were also engaged in their own pursuits. Cobham continued with his translation of Seneca's works, and to aid that task he accumulated a library of roughly 1,000 volumes. Raleigh had customarily taken a stock of books with him wherever he went, although, as John Aubrey later pointed out, until his imprisonment he had been able to find little time for study 'but what he could spare in the morning'. Aubrey summarised his bright intellect with the comment, 'He was no Slug; without doubt he had a wonderful waking spirit, and a great judgement to guide it.' Raleigh was visited in the Tower by his wife, who took a house on Tower Hill, and by his family, and also courtiers, ladies and ambassadors, and by Prince Henry, whose admiration was expressed in the comment that 'no one but my father would keep such a bird in a cage'. James frowned on the prince's friendship with Raleigh and complained of 'the lawless liberty of the Tower'. Raleigh's earlier unpopularity had turned to respect, partly because of the shabby way he was treated and partly through nostalgia for the old Elizabethan days that he had come to represent. Visitors to the Tower now looked towards the Bloody Tower, hoping to catch a glimpse of the fortress's most distinguished prisoner.

Raleigh's enforced leisure gave him time to work on his chemistry experiments and preparation of medicines, for he was allowed to set up a laboratory, or 'stilhows': he converted a henhouse in the garden adjoining his rooms for the purpose. He also produced a flow of letters, essays and treatises on a range of topics, including naval matters, politics and foreign affairs. Most ambitiously, he undertook to write for Prince Henry a history of the world, the first volume of which was published in 1614. One of the great literary achievements of the seventeenth century, its preparation drew more figures into Raleigh's orbit, among them Ben Jonson. It took the history of the world from the Creation down to 150BC, and contained the author's opinions on a range of subjects and individuals. Few monarchs escaped his criticism, and so it may not have been a surprise that the king disapproved of the work and ordered that it should be suppressed. The London gossip John Chamberlain wrote that the order was made 'for diverse exceptions, but specially for being too saucy in censuring princes'. Because most copies already had been sold the king's order was largely ineffective, and by 1617 the proscription had been lifted.

Eleven editions of the work were issued during the century and the book was very influential. Yet the second volume was not begun; Prince Henry had died in 1612 and Raleigh was disappointed with the king's hostile response. In 1616 he was released and Chamberlain wrote, 'Sir Walter Raleigh was freed out of the Tower the last week, and goes up and down seeing sights and places built or bettered since his imprisonment.' He went on a futile expedition to discover the fabled El Dorado in the Orinoco region of South America, and on his return in 1618 he was again imprisoned in the Tower. He remained there for a few weeks, and then was executed at Westminster.

The king's own interest in the fortress was focused largely on the royal menagerie; his stay in the Tower before the royal entry into London in March 1604 included 'bull-baiting and other sports'. He took the queen, Anne of Denmark, Prince Henry and the Venetian ambassador to watch bear-baiting and a bout between three mastiffs and two lions. Other visitors taken to the Tower included the queen's brother Christian IV of Denmark in 1606, where he was shown around the buildings, was entertained at a feast and was even allowed to fire one of the cannon on the roof of the White Tower.

In 1604–5 the menagerie building was remodelled and the two storeys of pens were connected by a stairway for the animals' use. A part of the moat around the Lion Tower was drained and the area was surrounded by walls, to create a yard as a 'speciall place to baight the Lyons with dogges, beares, bulles, bores, etc.' A viewing platform was constructed 'for the kinges Matie to stande on to see the Lyons lett out'. In 1622 the platform was replaced by a more substantial gallery, ninety-two feet long and ten feet wide. A variety of animals were put into the ring, including bears, dogs, cocks, a horse, even a lamb. And the king was most interested when one of the lionesses gave birth; he was so fearful that the cubs might die that he sent a description of a nipple to be attached to a glass bottle, so that they could be fed. George Montgomery, one of his chaplains, described this as 'a new engine to give a beast suck'. As well as reporting on his prisoners, Sir William Waad also kept Salisbury informed about the lions, with such observations as, 'The lion's whelps were playing this morning and got out of their nest, which when they do, their dam carries them always in again.'

After Cecil's death, in 1613 Waad resigned, under pressure on a charge of negligence, protesting that 'the Tower was never kept in better order in any time than it was while I served his Majesty there'. His successor was Sir Gervase Elwes, who owed his appointment largely to Henry Howard, Earl of Northampton and Lord Privy Seal, to whom he paid £1,400 for his patronage. John Chamberlain knew Elwes and found it surprising that he had been chosen, if only because he was of 'too mild and gentle a disposition for such an office'. The Howards' influence at court had grown after Salisbury's death and they had a stroke of good fortune when Frances Howard, daughter of Thomas Howard, Earl of Suffolk, began an affair with the king's favourite, Robert Carr. From being a page to the Earl of Dunbar, this handsome young man had become a groom of the bedchamber and caught the eye of the king. In 1611 he was created Viscount Rochester. His marriage to Frances could only strengthen the Howards' position, but she was already married, to the Earl of Essex. An annulment of that marriage was necessary, but its true purpose, to allow her to marry Rochester, had to be concealed. It certainly would be opposed by those groups at court who favoured maintaining a pro-Protestant stance in Europe, and were aware that the Howards would use Rochester to promote pro-Spanish and pro-Catholic policies.

Among those who knew of Rochester's involvement with Frances Howard was Sir Thomas Overbury, his close friend and mentor, who assisted him with his affairs, including matters of state. Overbury was generally unpopular and regarded as being too proud, 'always over-valuing himself and under-valuing others', according to Sir Francis Bacon. He was disliked by the king and had offended the queen, so had little support other than that derived from Rochester. Aware that if the marriage went ahead he would lose his influence, he tried hard to dissuade Rochester from pursuing the match. Northampton decided to act against Overbury, fearful that his influence with Carr could damage the Howards' plans. The king was persuaded to offer Overbury an ambassadorship, at first in Moscow, and then in other capitals, closer to England. When he refused, and persisted in his refusals, he was sent to the Tower on 21 April 1613: refusing the king was stated in the warrant to be 'a matter of high contempt'. This may have seemed to be a case of using the Tower to take someone out of political circulation for a time. But he was treated as a close prisoner and kept incommunicado, for although his accommodation was placed where 'he might have the best air, and windows both to the water and within the Tower', he was not allowed to receive visitors. Sir Robert Killigrew, who had been visiting Raleigh, was even detained briefly for speaking to Overbury through his window as he left the Tower. Nor was Overbury allowed to have his servant to attend him, and as soon as Elwes took up his post Sir Thomas Monson, Master of the Armouries, requested that Overbury's gaoler should be changed to one Richard Weston. He later justified the request by saying that Northampton had asked him to make it. Meanwhile, according to a rather embittered Waad, the other prisoners were enjoying a more relaxed regime under the new Lieutenant, for 'liberty was given to the condemned men as they walked and talked together, playing at cards and other pastimes, which liberty never before was seen there'.

The Howards may have intended simply to neutralise Overbury and keep him away from Rochester until Frances

Howard's annulment and second marriage were achieved. But Overbury became ill, which was attributed to his close imprisonment. He was feverish, vomited, lacked appetite and was perpetually thirsty. Killigrew dabbled in chemistry and supplied Overbury with a white emetic, hoping to induce symptoms that would lead to his release on medical grounds. Overbury also took other medicines and received treatment from Theodore de Mayerne, the king's physician, as well as broths, pasties, tarts and jellies thoughtfully sent to him from Frances Howard's kitchen. His condition deteriorated to such an extent that before the end of August it was reported that he was 'likely to run a short course, being sick unto death'. On 14 September Elwes was so alarmed that he sent for de Mayerne, who despatched the apothecary Paul de Lobel to the Tower. He found Overbury weak and ordered that he be given one of de Mayerne's enemas. But early the following morning Overbury died in agony. Chamberlain wrote that 'the manner of his death is not known, for that there was nobody with him, not so much as his keeper; but the foulness of his corpse gave suspicion and leaves aspersion that he should die of the pox or somewhat worse'. Elwes hastily assembled a coroner's jury of people from within the Tower, which pronounced that Overbury had died a natural death, and because of its foul condition the emaciated body was quickly buried in St Peter ad Vincula, 'without knowledge or privity of his friends'.

The annulment of the Earl and Countess of Essex's marriage was approved by an ecclesiastical commission ten days after Overbury's death. Three months later she married Rochester, who had been created Earl of Somerset. The Howards' schemes had come to fruition and there was no reason to link members of the family to Overbury's demise. Even though the death of a prisoner of state, in such circumstances, after just four months in the Tower, was likely to arouse suspicions, almost two years passed before they were followed up.

In the meantime, Elwes had the custody of another important prisoner, Lady Arabella Stewart, incarcerated not as a potential claimant to the throne, but for her marriage in 1610 to William Seymour, a grandson of the Earl of Hertford, which had not been authorised by the king. During her imprisonment in the Tower she suffered a debilitating illness, exacerbated by her refusal to eat, and she died there in September 1615.

A month after Lady Arabella's death investigations into Overbury's death began and Elwes resigned his place as Lieutenant. His conscience had troubled him over his role in the affair. Shortly after his appointment he had discovered that Weston was taking poison to Overbury's chamber, but he had kept quiet. Yet in the summer of 1615 he admitted his knowledge to the Earl of Shrewsbury and Sir Ralph Winwood, one of the two secretaries of state, when they questioned him about the matter. Winwood's suspicions perhaps were aroused by a confession by William Reeve, who had been Lobel's assistant, that in September 1613 he had been given the considerable sum of £20 to take Overbury a dose of sublimate of mercury in a clyster (a liquid injection to the intestines applied up the rectum). Reeve was in Vlissingen when he made this confession, which may have been sent to Winwood. The appointment of Elwes, his approval of Weston as gaoler and Overbury's classification as a close prisoner now began to seem significant.

Winwood's enquiries troubled Elwes sufficiently for him to write his own version of the affair. The Earl of Northampton had died in the summer of 1614 and his correspondence was found to include phrases that implicated Elwes in a plot. He was put on trial and the supplier of the poison, James Franklin, testified to having seen a letter from Elwes to Frances Howard, which contained an incriminating comment. Elwes was found guilty of abetting the plot and was hanged on Tower Hill, outside the fortress of which he had been in charge. Weston was convicted of murder, Franklin for supplying the poison and Anne Turner, a member of Frances Howard's household and the widow of a physician, as the agent for procuring it. The case against them referred to the application of a poison called roseacre, mixed in the broth served to Overbury, and two other poisons administered to him: white arsenic and sublimate of mercury. All of them were hanged.

Despite their position, the Somersets could not escape trial also. The countess pleaded guilty and the earl was convicted by his peers in the House of Lords of being an accessory, despite his protestations. A royal favourite who had risen so high had been brought down by a sordid plot to silence his friend and secretary. The Howards' success had been short-lived; in any case their opponents had already responded by drawing the king's attention to George Villiers, an attractive young man in his mid-twenties from a Leicestershire gentry family. Villiers was to advance rapidly as James's new favourite, and retain his high offices and influence into the next reign.

The Earl and Countess of Somerset were both incarcerated in the Tower. She refused to be lodged in Overbury's former accommodation, and so the rooms recently vacated by Raleigh were allocated to her. In the Tower she socialised with Northumberland and quarrelled with her husband.

Northumberland was freed in 1621. Chamberlain saw him as he drove away from the Tower through the City in his coach, but his comment that 'in my judgement he is nothing altered from what he was more than fifteen years ago' probably was a superficial view of the effects of such a long incarceration. The Somersets were released in January 1622.

Despite some mellowing of public attitudes towards the Tower, being imprisoned there brought not only loss of freedom but also shame, even for high-ranking figures who found themselves wrong-footed in the political game. When Francis Bacon, Lord Verulam, the Lord Chancellor, was sent there in 1621 having been impeached for bribery, he wrote to Villiers, now Marquess of Buckingham, asking for his help to obtain his release. He included the sad comment that 'to die before the time of his Majesty's grace, and in this disgraceful place, is even the worst that could be'. He was freed within a week.

Like the Howards before him, Villiers used his influence in the appointment of the Lieutenant of the Tower, when Sir Allen Apsley was selected for the post in 1617. Their connection was through Apsley's third wife, Lucy StJohn, who was related to the Villiers family by marriage. The Apsleys' daughter, also Lucy, later recalled her parents' time at the Tower and wrote that Sir Allen was 'a father to all his prisoners, sweet'ning with such compassionate kindnesse their restraint that the afliction of a prison was not felt in his dayes'. She was even more praising of her mother's role. To all the prisoners she behaved

> as a mother ... if any were sick she made them broths and restoratives with her own hands, visited and took care of them, and provided them all necessaries; if any were aflicted she comforted

them, so that they felt not the inconvenience of a prison who were in that place.

Lucy's comments were those of a loyal daughter justifying her parents' role as gaolers, but despite her understandable partiality, they provide a sense of the regime in the Tower during the 1620s, until Apsley's death in 1630.

Villiers was created Duke of Buckingham by James in 1623, and as well as being the king's favourite he had also taken that role with his heir, Henry's brother Charles. In that year they travelled to Madrid together, nominally incognito, so that Charles could woo the Infanta Maria. The bizarre episode was not a success; the prince would need to look elsewhere for a bride, and in terms of foreign affairs, it began a drift towards war with Spain.

Charles came to the throne on his father's death in March 1625. Marriage negotiations with the French court had gone more smoothly than those with Spain and three months later his bride, Louis XIII's sister Henrietta Maria, arrived at Dover and was escorted by the king to London. But once again an outbreak of plague, which was to develop into a major epidemic, prevented the pageantry that had been planned, and they travelled to the Tower by barge. The outbreak delayed the coronation until the following February. Because of her Catholic faith, the queen did not take part. The Tower's role in the ceremonies was somewhat diminished, for the Knights of the Bath were now created at Westminster.

Buckingham reversed James's peaceful foreign policy and went to war, first with Spain and later with France, in support of the Huguenots besieged in La Rochelle. England's direct military involvement was limited to a raid on Cadiz late in 1625, a landing on the Île de Ré in 1627 to relieve pressure on the Huguenots' fortress of La Rochelle, and the subsequent despatch of a naval force to break the French blockade of the town. The Ordnance Office stores at the Tower should have been adequate for the campaigns. An inventory of 1620 showed that it contained 437 pieces of artillery, of which 141 were heavy pieces, rated as demi-culverin or above. The ammunition included 145,000 iron round shot, more than 16,000 stone shot and 8,600 bar shot. The total issue for the Cadiz and Île de Ré expeditions was thirty-two pieces of ordnance and 152 lasts of powder. Apsley held the post of Victualler to the Navy, as well as that of Lieutenant of the Tower; he faced problems in provisioning the fleet caused by the fragile state of the crown's finances, which were exacerbated in 1625 by the difficulty of collecting taxes during a plague epidemic.

Parliament was asked to vote additional revenues, but its relations with Charles, especially over taxation, were strained, to say the least, and it wanted its complaints addressed. Buckingham's policies and his pursuit of power and position were strongly criticised, while Charles was protective of his favourite and chief minister. In February 1626 the Venetian ambassador's opinion on the relations between the court and parliament was that the king would insist upon his prerogative rights if parliament did not provide adequate assistance. He had heard that 'in order to fortify the King's authority they speak of bringing the troops from the fleet to the Tower and its neighbourhood. This would be a very violent innovation, very ill adapted to the humour of the country, and it will probably all end in talk and nothing more.' How seriously the court considered using the Tower as a military base to intimidate the citizens is uncertain; as the ambassador pointed out, that would have been a drastic step.

All the military expeditions were failures, yet Buckingham planned another attempt to relieve La Rochelle in the summer of 1628, under his own command. He got no further than Portsmouth, where he was assassinated in an inn by John Felton, a soldier disappointed at having been passed over for promotion. Felton was taken to the Tower and questioned before being tried and hanged. The government was concerned that the attempt had been part of a wider conspiracy, but eventually accepted that the killer had acted alone. Felton believed that he was benefiting his country by murdering the duke, having read 'the remonstrance of the House of Parliament'. Buckingham's unpopularity was such that news of his death was received with widespread celebrations.

In the 1626 parliament and subsequently Sir John Eliot had been to the fore in the attacks on Buckingham. After Buckingham's death and the dissolution of parliament in 1629, Eliot and eight of his allies were arrested. Shortly afterwards he and six others were transferred from the custody of the marshal of the King's Bench prison and taken to the Tower. Eliot refused to admit his guilt, even after the others had submitted and been released. Apsley's successor as Lieutenant was Sir William Balfour, and he, too, permitted prisoners such as Eliot to receive visitors and allowed him pen, paper and ink. Eliot passed his time writing letters, his memoirs, and two substantial works of political theory, *The Monarchie of Man* and *De jure maiestatis*.

In the autumn of 1631 he was moved to a different room, and restrictions were placed on his visitors. He explained, 'I am now where candlelight may be suffered but scarce fire ... None but my servants, hardly my sons, may have admittance to me.' Before the end of the following winter he fell ill and petitioned the king 'to set me at liberty, that, for the recovery of my health, I may take some fresh air'. Charles refused his request and his condition worsened. Like Southampton, Eliot commissioned a portrait of himself in the Tower, although the background gives no indication of the location. He is wearing his laced nightgown, his gaze is fixed on the viewer and his right hand is placed on his hip, in a defiant gesture. His health continued to deteriorate and he died in his room in the Tower on 27 November 1632. His son requested that his body be released for burial at Port Eliot in his native Cornwall, but Charles wrote on the petition, 'Let Sir John Eliot's body be buried in the Church of that parish where he died.' That was St Peter ad Vincula, and, strictly speaking, the king was correct. But his refusal could be seen as an act of almost staggering vindictiveness; resentment of a political opponent pursued beyond death, frustrating his family's wishes.

A few months after Eliot's death, the Tower received another high-profile political prisoner. William Prynne had offended the queen with comments in his book *Histriomastix*. Encouraged by the increasingly influential Bishop of London, William Laud, who was appointed Archbishop of Canterbury that year, she pursued the matter and Prynne was put on trial for sedition. Although he made a robust defence, he was found guilty and sentenced to life imprisonment, to have his ears cropped and to pay a fine of £4,000. Despite his being restricted, a co-operative warder permitted him to smuggle his pamphlets out of the fortress for publication. Four years later he was again accused of sedition, with Henry Burton and John Bastwicke, again found guilty, and once more had his ears cropped, this time far more savagely than in 1633. He was moved from the Tower in July 1637, to continue his sentence in the Channel Islands.

After his release and triumphant return to London with Burton and Bastwicke in 1640, and with the political upheaval which followed, he was to return to the Tower, not as a prisoner, but as Keeper of the Records. He was later credited with having collected 'out of huge Heaps, covered with Dust and Cobwebs, Popes Bulls, Parliament Writs and Returns, and Letters, which he Printed'. But he was censured, too, because he 'took less Care to sort and digest them, and leave them in Order for the Use of others'.

Charles pursued a peaceful foreign policy during the 1630s and did not need to call parliament, although to pay for extra ships for the navy he levied ship money, an innovation that was challenged in the courts. By the middle of the decade the Ordnance Office had further expanded within the Tower. Many spaces were used for storage, including 'old' and 'new' powder rooms in the White Tower – where more than 2,100 barrels of gunpowder were stored in 1635 – and 'the vault under the Master of the Ordnance his lodgings', which contained, among other things, fifty pounds of sulphur. In the 'old mynt' were carriages for cannon, for both land and on ships, and the 'shott howse in the mynt' contained cannon-balls and grenades for cannon. Even the green was used by the office for keeping cannon and their carriages, and almost 26,000 cannon-balls, stacked in piles. On Tower Wharf were eighty-four unmounted cannon; Wenceslaus Hollar's depiction of the Tower shows them laid neatly side by side at right-angles to the river. The office had also expanded beyond the Tower. Some buildings of the dissolved convent of the Poor Clares in the Minories had been converted into armouries and workshops, and the district became the centre of the London gun trade.

In 1639 the Tower's military resources were drawn upon, not for a campaign overseas, but a war against the Scots. Charles and Archbishop Laud had attempted to enforce the use of the Book of Common Prayer in Scotland, which met with strong resistance. Political intransigence on both sides allowed the ensuing dispute to slip into armed conflict, with two short wars, in 1639 and 1640. Preparations for war produced a burst of activity at the Tower. An artillery train of sixty-two cannon was prepared and taken by ship to the ports in north-east England, with powder, shot and the many tools and other items needed to support it. Small arms, too, were issued and thousands more were acquired. Benjamin Stone had established a mill for manufacturing swords and blades on Hounslow Heath in 1629, and in December 1638 was permitted to use a shed in the Tower for grinding blades and fitting them with hilts. He became a major supplier for the campaigns against the Scots, sharing the larger orders with his rivals in London, such as one for 22,503 swords. Men as well as weapons were transported from Tower Wharf, the assembly place for troops enlisted in the London area, some of them reluctant and looking for an opportunity to desert.

In the changed circumstances created by the Bishops' Wars, attention was turned to the military readiness of the Tower. Lord Cottington was appointed Constable in May 1640 and, unusually, chose to live there while its military arrangements were overhauled. He brought the strength of the garrison up to 200 men and accumulated stocks of ammunition and provisions. The fourteen demi-culverins were still on the roof of the White Tower and Cottington now deployed other cannon so that they

61. William the Conqueror ordered the building of the White Tower, which was begun in 1078. It was overseen by Gundulf, Bishop of Rochester 1077–1108. In this diorama they are depicted looking on as the work progresses.

Above left: 62. The Duke of Clarence allegedly was killed in the Tower by being drowned in a butt of Malmsey wine, in 1478. This imagined reconstruction was drawn in the 1880s. *Above right*: 63. The White Tower drawn by Hanslip Fletcher in 1920, in what was assumed to be its original form, after the later accretions had been removed during the second half of the nineteenth century.

64. The Tower was given its familiar concentric form by the early fourteenth century and is shown on Anthonis van den Wyngaerde's pen-and-ink drawing of *c.* 1544.

Above left: 65. James Northcote's painting of the Princes in the Tower about to be murdered was executed in 1786 and drew attention to that dramatic incident. Other artists later followed his choice of subject. *Above right*: 66. Perkin Warbeck, a pretender to the throne during the 1490s, was imprisoned in the Tower after his surrender. His attempt to escape was thwarted and he was executed in 1499.

67. The chapel of St Peter ad Vincula, built in 1286–7 and rebuilt in 1519–20, is shown as preparation is being made to insert new windows, *c.* 1755.

Above left: 68. It was the practice for the monarch to spend some time in the Tower in the days preceding the coronation and then process through London to Westminster. The drawing shows the coronation procession of Edward VI, leaving the Tower, crossing Tower Hill and making its way along Cheapside. *Above right*: 69. A Victorian depiction of the execution of Lady Jane Grey, mistakenly located on the south side of the chapel of St Peter ad Vincula.

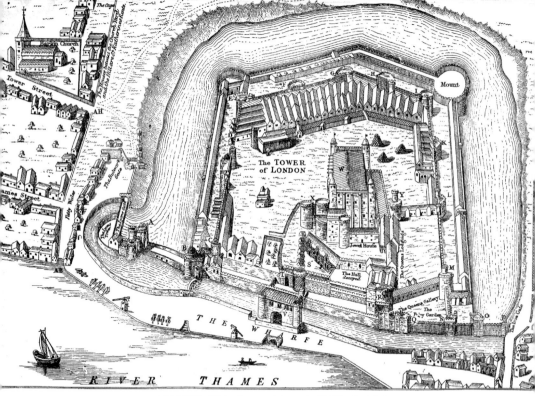

THE TOWER. (*From a Survey made in* 1597 *by W. Haiward and J. Gascoyne.*)

A Middle Tower.   B. Tower at the Gate.   C. Bell Tower.   D. Beauchamp Tower.   E. Devilin Tower.   F. Flint Tower.   G. Bowyer Tower.   H. Brick Tower.   I. Martin Tower.   K. Con
Tower.   L. Broad Arrow Tower.   M. Salt Tower.   N. Well Tower.   O. Tower leading to Iron Gate.   P. Tower above Iron Gate.   Q. Cradle Tower.   R. Lantern Tower.   S. Hall Tower.   T. B
Tower.   V. St. Thomas's Tower.   W. Cæsar's, or White Tower.   X. Cole Harbour.   Y. Wardrobe Tower.   A B. House at Water Gate, called the Ram's Head.   A H. End of Tower Street.

Above: 70. The Tower and the Tower Liberties, surveyed in 1597 by William Haiward and Joel Gascoyne on the direction of Sir John Peyton, the Lieutenant. *Left*: 71. The interior of the Beauchamp Tower, drawn in 1866. *Below left*: 72. This engraving depicting the execution of Lord Guilford Dudley on Tower Hill was used on the title page of a new edition by Edward Farr of *The History of England* by David Hume and Tobias Smollett, published in 1876.

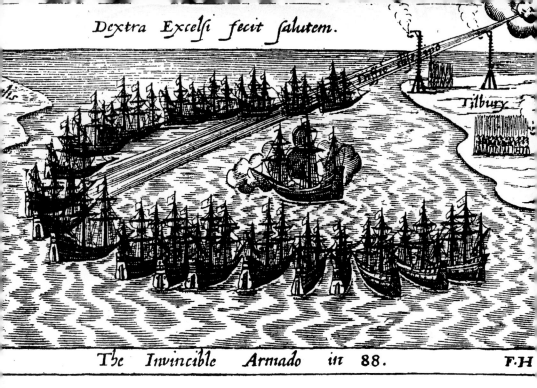

Dextra Excelſi fecit ſalutem.

Tilbury

The Invincible Armado in 88. F.H

73. The defeat of the Spanish Armada in 1588 was seen as a major national victory over Europe's strongest power and its commemoration became an important part of the displays in the Tower.

Above left: 74. Sir Thomas Wyatt led a rebellion against Mary in 1554, which was suppressed. He is shown going from the Tower to his execution. *Above right*: 75. Princess Elizabeth was imprisoned in the Tower by her sister Mary on suspicion of complicity in Sir Thomas Wyatt's rebellion in 1554, which, if successful, would have dethroned Mary and placed Elizabeth on the throne.

Robert Winter · Christopher Wright · John Wright · Thomas Percy · Guido Fawkes · Robert Catesby · Thomas Winter

76. The gunpowder plotters, from *The Gunpowder Plot Conspirators* (1605), who were imprisoned in the Tower. It is likely that Guy (Guido) Fawkes was the only one of them to be tortured, as the government unravelled the plot to blow up the royal family and the members of both Houses of Parliament.

Above left: 77. The Tower featured in a number of William Shakespeare's history plays; he depicted it as a place associated with majesty, terror and treason. In *Richard III* he repeated the widely held view that Julius Caesar built the White Tower, an opinion which endured for at least another two centuries. *Above right*: 78. James I, portrayed at the head of a Chancery decree of 1613. James enjoyed watching the lions in the menagerie, and other animals being baited there, and used the Tower for entertaining visiting royalty.

The portraicture of Robert Car Earle of Somerset: Vicount Rochester: Knight of the most noble order of the Garter &c. And of the Ladie Francis his wife.

79. James I's favourite the Earl of Somerset and the Countess of Somerset, who fell from favour and were imprisoned in the Tower for complicity in the poisoning of Sir Thomas Overbury in 1613, while he was held there.

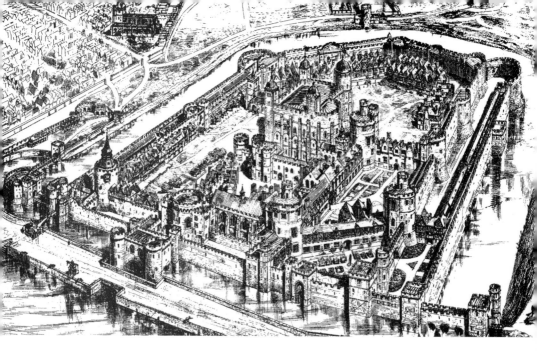

80. A bird's-eye reconstruction of the Tower of London *c.* 1600, by Henry William Brewer (1836–1903).

Above left: 81. Sir Walter Raleigh was allowed to carry out chemistry experiments during his imprisonment in the Tower in the early seventeenth century, as shown in this drawing from the 1880s. His wife Bess and their children look on. *Above right*: 82. Among the senior figures to be incarcerated in the Tower during the early seventeenth century was Sir Francis Bacon, the Lord Chancellor, in 1621.

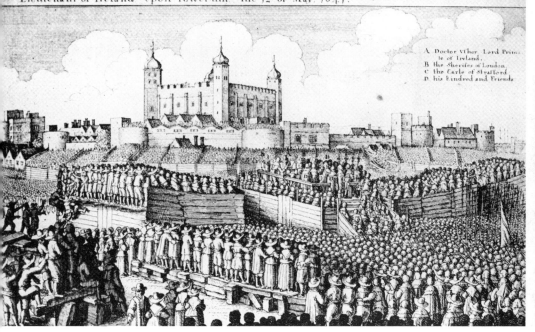

A Doctor Vsher Lord Prima
te of Ireland.
B the Sheriffes of London.
C the Earle of Strafford
D his kindred and Friends

83. Thomas Wentworth, Earl of Strafford, Charles I's leading advisor, was condemned to death by an Act of Attainder. He was immensely unpopular and his execution on Tower Hill in May 1641 was carried out before an enormous crowd, depicted by Wenceslaus Hollar.

Above left: 84. In May 1662 Samuel Pepys went with Sir Thomas Crewe's children to the Tower 'and showed them the lions and all that was to be shown'. The episode was depicted by Ernest Shepherd, in 1926. *Above right*: 85. In 1671 'Colonel' Thomas Blood and his accomplices almost succeeded in their audacious plan to steal a part of the regalia. When their intentions were known they fled from the Tower, but were quickly caught.

86. Lieven Vershcuur's painting of the Great Fire of London in 1666. The blaze did not reach the Tower and its stocks of gunpowder, but the opportunity was taken to create a fire-break by pulling down houses that had been built too close.

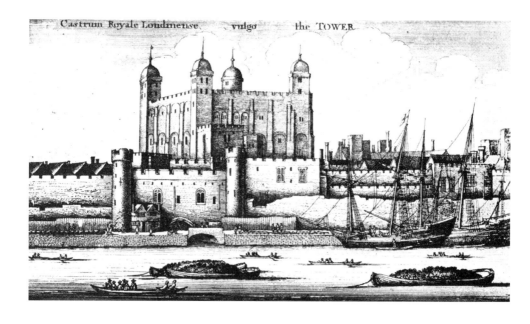

Castrum Royale Londinense, vulgo the TOWER.

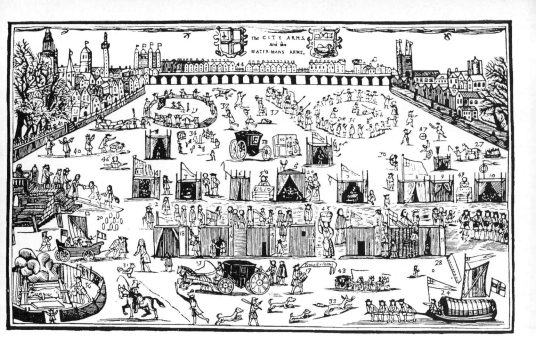

Above: 89. The Tower was a landmark at the eastern end of the City and was used as such on representations of London, such as this one depicting the frost-fair on the Thames in 1684. The White Tower is shown as a prominent feature beyond London Bridge. *Right*: 90. A plan-view of the Tower in 1688 by Holcroft Blood, son of Thomas Blood and a military engineer. The newly erected New Armouries building is shown in the south-east of the inner ward. *Opposite centre*: 87. Special occasions were marked by the firing of the ordnance at the Tower. On this occasion a royal procession is leaving the Tower and passing through triumphal arches, in 1696, as the cannon are being fired. *Opposite bottom*: 88. As a military store and arsenal, and a strong point from which the city could be overawed, control of the Tower was of great importance to Parliament's cause during the Civil War. This drawing by Wenceslaus Hollar probably was made during the early 1640s.

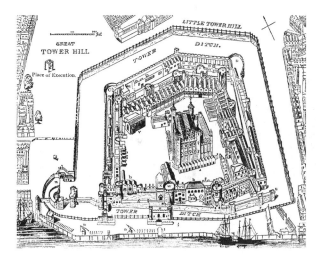

91. The execution of Lord Lovat in 1747, after he was convicted of involvement in the Jacobite rebellion of 1745–6. He was the last person to be executed on Tower Hill.

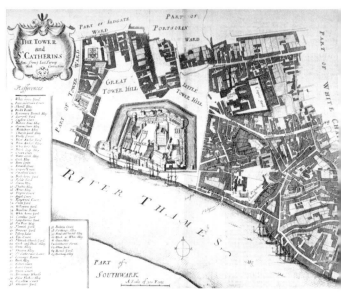

Above left: 92. Visitors were conducted around the Tower by a yeoman warder, and were likely to encounter members of the garrison, as in this illustration of the east end of St Peter ad Vincula. *Above right*: 93. Plan of the Tower and the densely built area of St Katherine's to the east *c*. 1700. Henry VI granted St Katherine's hospital a charter in 1445. Its buildings and much of the neighbourhood were demolished in 1825 for the building of St Katherine's Dock.

94. The rebuilding of the City to the west of the Tower after the Great Fire emphasised the contrast between the medieval fortress and the new brick buildings. This illustration from 1746 shows the varied skyline produced by the towers and spires of Wren's post-fire churches.

95. One of the most popular sites in the Tower was the menagerie, where the animals' cages were arranged on two storeys, shown on an illustration of 1779.

96. A workshop in the Mint c. 1800, before it was removed from the Tower.

97. The Tower from the river, which provided an increasingly busy and polluted neighbour, by William Clarkson Stanfield, 1827.

Above left: 98. Prisoners' inscriptions in the towers were uncovered in the late eighteenth century, as in the upper chamber of the Broad Arrow Tower, where they include the IHS symbol. *Above right*: 99. Visitors could be shown around only by a Yeoman Warder, here in a part of the White Tower.

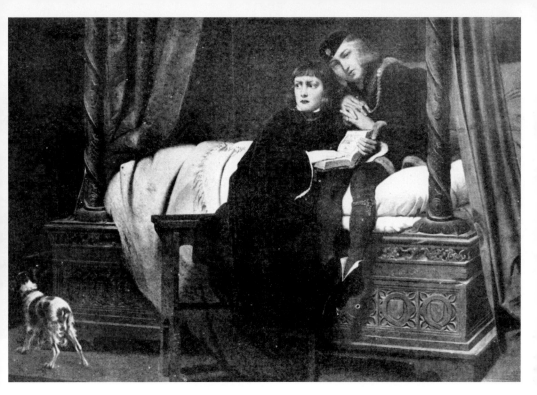

100. Paul Delaroche's treatment of the Princes in the Tower of 1831 was well known, as the Tower became an increasingly popular place to visit.

Above left: 101. A drawing of the executioner's block, axe and mask, part of the Tower's displays in the mid-nineteenth century. *Above right*: 102. The south aisle of St John's chapel, after the removal of the records in 1858.

103. The Horse Armoury in the Council Chamber on the topmost floor of the White Tower, drawn in 1885, with the comment, 'There is enormous difficulty in making out the features of the rooms in the White Tower, owing to the enormous accumulation of arms which has gradually grown up in them.'

Above: 104. This model of the rack was made for display, after the original was destroyed in the fire at the Grand Storehouse in 1841. *Left*: 105. Thumbscrews were a part of the exhibition in the Spanish Armoury. They were said to have been carried in the ships of the Spanish Armada, for torturing the English after the invasion had succeeded. *Opposite*: 106. This montage by William Henry Prior (1812–82) to promote the Tower uses a dozen images of the buildings and their associations. The name IANE copies the inscription uncovered in the Beauchamp Tower which was assumed to refer to Lady Jane Grey.

THE TOWER OF LONDON

WHITE TOWER

MIDDLE TOWER

BYWARD TOWER

STAIRCASE WHITE TOWER

PASSAGE IN BLOODY TOWER

St JOHN'S CHAPEL

JANE

BLOODY TOWER

BELL TOWER

TRAITOR'S GATE

107. The stands of arms in the Banqueting Room in the White Tower, *c.* 1885.

Above left: 108. The regalia in the Jewel House in the Wakefield Tower, where they were installed in 1870. *Above right*: 109. A drawing of the Grand State Salt Cellar, or Salt of State, made in the 1880s to illustrate the royal treasure. It is a representation in gold of the White Tower, and was presented to Charles II.

110. The Victorian restoration of the medieval fabric involved the removal of post-medieval fabric and the re-facing of much of the original walls. St Thomas's Tower and Traitor's Gate are shown in 1866, just as the process was coming to an end in that part of the fortress.

111. The context of the Tower continued to change. Sydney Jones's drawing of 1929 shows the Port of London Authority building in Trinity Square, erected in 1912–22, seen across the entrance to the medieval fortress.

112. Sydney Jones's view of the Tower from Hay's Wharf, drawn in 1932.

threatened the city. The Tower had become the secure place of deposit for the coin and other valuables of London's merchant community; it was indeed the strongest and therefore the safest group of buildings in the city. Acting on instructions from the king, in July Cottington seized the bullion deposited there as a loan on which interest would be paid. Such a high-handed action was bound to provoke an angry response and Charles climbed down to a certain extent, announcing that he would borrow only one-third of the treasure seized. Although Cottington had been acting on instructions, the affair was held against him, in the City and by parliament, and he resigned the office of Constable in November.

Despite the efforts to raise money and equip the troops, the English army failed in both of the Bishops' Wars, and in 1640, after a defeat at Newburn, it abandoned Newcastle to the Scots. The king's parsimony during the 1630s had hampered the supply of his forces. He now needed more money, which could be obtained only through extra taxation, and that meant calling a new parliament. It assembled on 17 April 1640 and was dissolved by the king three weeks later. Nothing had been resolved and so another was called, which met on 3 November 1640, and was to be designated the Long Parliament. The military crisis evolved into a political one, as the members gave vent to their opposition to the king's personal government, and endeavoured to grasp the political initiative from the court. Charles was unable to prevent parliament from imprisoning in the Tower his two leading counsellors, Archbishop Laud on 1 March and Thomas Wentworth, Earl of Strafford, on 25 November. Others were consigned there by parliament on suspicion of political wrongdoing, some for only a short time, such as the case recorded by the Worcestershire gentleman Henry Townshend: 'The sheriff of Warwickshire committed to the Tower and fined an £100 for his irregular proceedings, and return of knights of the said county, and released about 4 days after.'

Parliament regarded Strafford as a particularly dangerous opponent and brought him to trial, but he made a strong defence and so parliament had recourse to an Act of Attainder. He was beheaded on Tower Hill on 12 May 1641, before an enormous crowd. Sir William Balfour could not let him see his friend Laud for a final conversation without parliament's consent, but he allowed him to pause outside Laud's window on his way to the scaffold, to be blessed by the archbishop. Hollar's engraving of the execution shows dense crowds of spectators on all sides of the scaffold, many of them packed on to grandstands. In the foreground people are being helped to climb on to stands that appear to be full already. He chose to depict the scene from a viewpoint at the north-west of Tower Hill, so that the full extent of the Tower is shown beyond the execution scene. The symbol of royal authority had become a prison for the king's leading counsellors and the backdrop to the execution of his chief minister.

From that low point the court began to recover its position and by the late summer had growing support among members of parliament and in the country. That was despite a plot earlier that year to seize the Tower. Known as the first Army Plot, it involved a small and inept group of royalists. In the aftermath of the Second Bishops' War many officers went to London, agitating for their pay arrears and hoping for other employment. They formed a disorderly group, hanging around Whitehall, intimidating the king's opponents. A few of them planned to take over the fortress and release Strafford, with a force of just 100 men. They took hardly any care to conceal their intentions, and, in any case, Balfour would not co-operate. But the plot raised concern about the security of the Tower should a more determined force make an attempt to capture it.

That again became an issue when, at the beginning of November, news reached London of a widespread and bloody rebellion in Ireland, and subsequent reports included accounts of horrible brutalities. An army had to be sent, but who was to appoint its commanders? That was part of the royal prerogative and Charles would not compromise on his right, while parliament's leaders feared that he would restore his position by force, deploying the army against his critics before it left for Ireland. The possibility of a political settlement receded and tensions in London rose sharply during December.

The court may have doubted Balfour's loyalty, as a Scotsman in the wake of the Bishops' Wars, and so he was displaced as Lieutenant. On 22 December the king appointed Colonel Thomas Lunsford to the post. He could hardly have made a worse choice, for Lunsford was one of those ill-disciplined officers who were seen as a threat by the Londoners. Moreover, he had been convicted of killing a neighbour in Sussex, Sir Thomas Pelham, and was described as a man of 'desperate fortune'. Londoners reacted to the news of his appointment by mounting demonstrations around Whitehall, which continued for three days, and strong objections were raised in parliament. On the following day the merchants were reported to be taking their bullion from the Tower, 'because they will not trust their treasure under the command of the new lieutenant'.

Sir Ralph Hopton took a message from the Commons to the House of Lords which stressed the potential economic damage of Lunsford's appointment, with its impact on the merchant community, because 'the Tower of London is the great Magazine of the Kingdom, and the Place where the Bullion of the Kingdom is kept and coined; and, if a Person be there, in whom they may not confide, it would put a Stop to Trade'. Faced with such a range of opposition, the king backed down and cancelled Lunsford's appointment, compensating him with a knighthood. The battle for the Tower had been won in parliament, in the violent clashes around Whitehall and by the actions of the merchants.

Sir John Byron was then appointed as Lieutenant. He was less objectionable to the parliamentary leadership and the City, but a royalist nevertheless and soon found himself in a difficult position. The crisis deepened after the king's failed attempt on 4 January to arrest five members of the Commons, entering the chamber to do so, only to find that they had had been forewarned and had left. They took refuge in the City and on the following day Charles went to Guildhall to demand that they be handed over, but was rebuffed. Londoners heckled him in the streets as he passed. Then, on the night of 6 January, a rumour that royalist soldiers were on their way to attack the City and set it alight swept through London. That was a false alarm, but the citizens' anxieties had been raised and could be lessened only if the Tower was in the hands of the king's opponents.

On 12 January the Commons ordered the trained bands, the City's militia, under their commander Philip Skippon, to place a guard around the Tower, blockading it. When Byron was summoned to the House of Lords, Skippon attempted to exploit his temporary absence by seizing the fortress with a force of 500 men. They took their positions 'very privately when it was dark', but failed to force an entry. Evidently, it was not as vulnerable to being captured as had been feared. But the attempt helped to convince Byron of the hopelessness of his position, and he requested the king to release him 'from the vexation and agony of that place'. Charles had left London, and on 11 February agreed to the replacement of Byron with Sir John Conyers, who had been the Commons' preferred candidate in December. Parliament had secured control of the Tower and removed the major threat to its authority in London.

Byron claimed that the loss of the Tower was not as serious to the king's cause as might have been thought. Writing towards the end of January he pointed out that

> very shortly there will be little cause to stand in awe of the Tower, for almost all the arms are already issued out for Ireland, and none are brought in to replenish the magazine. The powder likewise decreases apace, and by that time the navy, which the parliament is to set forth this year, is furnished there will be little or none left.

His summary was correct at the time, and in April the store at the Tower contained only 1,367 muskets and 354 pikes. But this did not apply for long, for in May parliament ordered that the magazine at Hull, which included the artillery train from the Second Bishops' War, should be brought to London. And it set about acquiring arms, armour and equipment to build up the stock in its arsenals and equip the armies which it began to raise as the threat of war loomed. In early August the ordnance officers were imprisoned by the House of Lords for refusing to issue munitions without the king's warrant, and, although released, they did not regain their positions.

War duly came in the summer of 1642. By the autumn, as the king's army advanced towards London, the Commons sent five MPs to inspect the security arrangements in the Tower, which was garrisoned by 200 men of the trained bands. They found that only sixteen warders and few of the officers lodged there, guarding fourteen prisoners who were accommodated in the warders' houses. That was a time of acute tension and parliament had imprisoned those leading royalists left in the capital, yet only three were classified as 'close' prisoners, and together they had just eighteen servants. Even so, the MPs were afraid that they might collude and plan a coup, especially as the houses were large enough to hold twenty men, who could be infiltrated into the fortress and concealed there. To tighten security, the MPs ordered that no horses could be kept within the fortress, that the prisoners' servants should not be allowed to come and go freely or to converse with anyone, and that the prisoners' families should speak to the prisoners only in the Lieutenant's presence.

In July 1643 Isaac Pennington was appointed Lieutenant. A leader of the parliamentarians in City politics, he had been elected lord mayor in August 1642, for the remainder of the current mayoral year, and he then served the full term of the following year. Among the prisoners in his charge were Archbishop Laud, until his execution on Tower Hill in January 1645, and Matthew Wren, Bishop of Ely, who was imprisoned there for almost eighteen years. Prisoners from across the political spectrum were incarcerated in the Tower, including the royalist former lord mayor, Sir Richard Gurney, from the summer of 1642 until his death in 1647, and the republican MP Henry Marten, for saying in the Commons that 'it were better one family be destroyed than many', which was assumed to be a reference to the royal family. Marten was released after two weeks. Also incarcerated was the poet Edmund Waller, who was a key figure in a plot in the spring of 1643 concerning a royalist coup in London for which his brother-in-law Nathaniel Tompkins and another man were executed. Waller was held for a year and a half until he agreed to pay the enormous fine of £10,000 and go into exile.

The Tower also retained its importance as an arsenal and centre of military distribution, with the arms and equipment sent to the garrisons and armies. It was the logical place to serve as the magazine for the New Model Army, which was established early in 1645 under parliament's direct control.

The war lasted for four years, during which the political situation became increasingly complex. This was reflected in the career of John Lilburne, who was an outspoken opponent of Charles's government before the war, played a prominent part at the Battle of Brentford in November 1642, where he was captured, taken to the royalist headquarters at Oxford and threatened with execution. Following his release he fought with the parliamentarian armies until 1645. An avid pamphleteer and supporter of the Independents, he became a spokesman for the Leveller movement later in the decade. In 1646 the House of Lords committed him to the Tower, where he was detained for sixteen months. Once there Lilburne asserted his rights 'to enjoy any priviledge within the Tower, as any prisoner in it'. And his reaction to the rules was, 'I am a free-born Englishman ... and I am not to be subject ... in the Tower unto any other orders, but what are consonant and agreeable to the fundamental Laws of the Kingdome.' He became friendly with the royalist prisoners and together they pulled off a stunt in which the chief warder, John White, 'an old tall man in black, with a great staffe in his hand', was made to sign a document stating that Lilburne was not the author of the pamphlets for which he was imprisoned. He continued to write while in the Tower and turned his attention to the reform of the City's government and widening of the franchise, stressing that the commoners of London, regardless of their wealth or lack of wealth, had the right to choose the lord mayor and other senior officers. In the Tower, he was in the ideal place, for the City's charters and related documents were stored among the Tower records. He obtained copies from the record keeper, for £3 or £4, which he then published.

While Lilburne was incarcerated a royalist counter-revolution against the growing influence of the Independents was planned in London. The New Model Army crushed it without difficulty and occupied the capital, in July 1647. A month later Oliver Cromwell visited the Tower, to inspect the ordnance. He dined with the Lieutenant and Lilburne and then chatted to some of the other prisoners. That the army's second-in-command, and one of the most powerful men in the country, found time to do so reflected both the prisoners' standing and the relaxed regime at the Tower. Lilburne was released on bail later that year.

Lilburne's conversations in the Tower with the royalists held there gave him hopes that a political settlement was possible. But these were dashed in 1648, when the king's plans to gain the support of the Scots and foment an uprising in England came to fruition. The Second Civil War that ensued was won by the parliamentarian army, and a new batch of royalist prisoners arrived at the Tower. They included Lord Capel, who had been captured at Colchester. Proceedings against him were delayed, and he escaped, helped by friends outside the fortress. According to the royalist statesman and historian Edward Hyde, later Earl of Clarendon, they supplied him with 'a cord and all things necessary'. One night he 'let himself down out of the window of his chamber' and then 'over the wall of the Tower'. His friends had told him the easiest spot to cross the moat. Perhaps he missed the place, because 'he found the water and the mud so deep, that, if he had not been by the head taller than other men, he must have perished, since the water came up to his chin'. He was exhausted by the time that he reached the other side, but his friends got him away, only for him to be betrayed subsequently and returned to the Tower. Capel was later executed, while Lilburne, who had again been imprisoned there, was tried, acquitted and freed in November 1649.

The Second Civil War and the king's lack of sincerity in negotiations so exasperated the senior army officers and their allies in parliament that, in January 1649, he was put on trial in Westminster Hall. Refusing to enter a plea, he was condemned to death and was executed on 30 January. At no time during his period in the custody of parliament was Charles held at the Tower, and he was beheaded outside the Banqueting House of Whitehall Palace. Previous monarchs deposed since the Tower was built had lost their throne there, and some of them their lives, with the exception of Edward II, who surrendered his crown at Kenilworth, and Richard III, who was killed on the battlefield.

After Charles's execution the monarchy was abolished and the Tower, with the other royal palaces, passed to the control of parliament. The contents of the wardrobe at the Tower were valued and removed, bringing that department to an end.

7

FROM THE REPUBLIC TO QUEEN ANNE

The republic maintained a large army during the 1650s, which was disbanded when the monarchy was restored in 1660. After the political experience of the 1640s and 1650s, such a standing army was widely regarded with suspicion, and there was strong opposition to the expansion of Charles II's much smaller forces. His brother James did increase their size, but it was under his successors, William and Mary, and then Anne, that the military establishment was greatly increased, to fight two prolonged wars against France. As the principal arsenal, the Tower was directly affected by the size of the military establishment. And so fiercely fought were the political controversies during the second half of the century that quite a few of those engaged in them had some experience of life inside the fortress.

Descriptions by visitors provide an impression of the Tower in the mid-seventeenth century. Lodewijck Huygens arrived in London with ambassadors from The Hague in 1651 and when he visited the Tower he found it to be 'oddly enough not strong. Apart from the high square tower, it has no other beautiful building; for the rest it is like a small town.' The Dutch artist William Schellinks spent some time in the city in the early 1660s, and he and his companions were shown around the Tower. He, too, noted that the area enclosed was that of a small town, but his interest was in its role as an arsenal and depot for modern weapons and equipment. Within the walls he saw 'a lot of large and small cannons, mortars, grenades and other war materials lying around'. In the buildings Schellinks noted 'several rooms full of all kinds of strange, ancient arms' and others that were 'full of old and new shooting gear'. Among the older and more decorative pieces on show there he mentioned a display in 'a long room' that contained 'behind a rail the body armour of several Kings and their horses' armour'. Described as the Line of Kings, those figures had been moved from Greenwich only recently. In other rooms suits of armour, weapons and firearms from the fourteenth century onwards were exhibited. Schellinks commented on 'a peculiar relic', which was the Swansdown Coverlet that Henry VIII wore over his codpiece, 'into which the English girls and women as an obeisance stick a pin and remove it and take it with them as a titillating keepsake'. But sensitivities increased, so that during the eighteenth century the item was withdrawn from the displays as being too risqué.

In 1669 Lorenzo Magalotti, secretary to Cosmo III of Tuscany, accompanied his master on a visit to London, and they, too, inspected the Tower. He mentioned that in the outer ward near the Mint were 'many houses built there for the dwellings of the officers and soldiers of the garrison and other artificers'. A garrison had been stationed in the fortress during the crisis that preceded the Civil War and the practice had continued through the Interregnum and after the restoration of the monarchy in 1660. Cosmo's party was shown the royal regalia, which were 'along with certain other silver vessels, in a chest, secured by a strong grate'. Magalotti was less impressed by the decorative suits of armour than Schellinks had been and was dismissive of the menagerie as 'very small and without any beauty of structure'. Schellinks was interested enough to count the animals and remarked on the fact that in one cage a lion lived with a dog 'as a companion'. This seems to have been a common arrangement, for seventeen years later a Polish nobleman commented on it and marvelled that such a ferocious creature as a lion 'never wants to eat the dog, even when hungry'. Yet care was required: in 1686, as Mary Jenkinson, who lived with the lion keeper, was showing a friend their cages, one of the lions put out a paw, which she stroked, 'as she used to do'. However, on that occasion the lion grabbed her arm and mauled it so badly that she died from her injuries a few hours later.

The royalist writer James Howell, in his *Londinopolis*, published in 1657, based his account on that of John Stow which was written sixty years earlier. He could not resist taking a swipe at the parliamentarian regime, with the observation that 'in the reign of the long Parliament, and ever since, the Tower of London hath had more number of Prisoners, than it had in the compasse of a hundred years before'. They included literary figures. In 1649 parliament committed to the Tower Clement Walker, a pamphleteer whose writings were uncomfortably critical, and he died there two years later, not having been brought to trial. In the following year Sir William Davenant was also imprisoned there. Poet, playwright and theatrical impresario, Davenant had succeeded Ben Jonson as Poet Laureate in 1638, but following his involvement in the Civil War and a period of exile in Paris during the late 1640s, he was captured by parliamentary forces. At first imprisoned in Cowes Castle on the Isle of Wight, he was then transferred to the Tower, where he was held for two years. While he was held there two of the three books of his 'heroic poem' *Gondibert* were published in London.

Howell was writing in the aftermath of plots against the Protectorate, including plans by Miles Sindercombe and John Cecil to assassinate Cromwell and to set fire to Whitehall Palace. Both were captured and imprisoned in the Tower, where members of Sindercombe's family managed to smuggle in poison, with which he committed suicide the night before he was to be executed.

The Lieutenant from 1652 until 1659 was John Barkstead, a Londoner who had served as an officer with the parliamentarian armies. Barkstead was criticised for treating the prisoners harshly and taking excessive fees from them. Cromwell had faith in his abilities and once commented that 'there never was any design on foot but we could hear of it out of the Tower'.

In 1659 a period of political uncertainty followed the resignation of Richard Cromwell as Protector, during which royalists planned to capture the Tower. By that time Barkstead's successor as Lieutenant, Colonel Herbert Morley, was in charge. Although a parliamentarian officer, he apparently colluded with the plotters, but their plans were betrayed and the scheme collapsed. When General George Monck's army occupied London in February 1660, Morley and his garrison complied with his orders, and so there was no dramatic intervention from the Tower.

Barkstead slipped away at the Restoration, but was captured in Delft in 1662, with two fellow officers from the New Model Army, returned to England, tried as a regicide and was executed at Tyburn. Almost at once a rumour spread that he had secreted a hoard of £7,000 in the Tower from his gains as Lieutenant, and had not been able to recover the money. A search found nothing in the cellars or beneath the garden, nor did several subsequent ones over the years, including an investigation as late as 1958.

Thirteen regicides were executed in the aftermath of the Restoration. They included Thomas Harrison, who had been held in the Tower during the later stages of the Protectorate, suspected of plotting against the regime, and was also held there before his execution in October 1660. Isaac Pennington, the former Lieutenant, had been a member of the court that had tried Charles I and had attended some of its sittings. Although he did not sign the death warrant, he was arrested and incarcerated in the Tower, where he died in December 1661. John Lambert was not a regicide, but was imprisoned there in March 1660 for attempting to raise an army to oppose the Restoration. He escaped within a few weeks, was rearrested and returned to the Tower, before being imprisoned elsewhere until his death in 1684. His life had been spared by the king, but Sir Henry Vane did not attract Charles's clemency. He was imprisoned in the Tower in 1662, was tried and executed on Tower Hill.

The Lieutenant of the Tower who oversaw the imprisonment of the former parliamentarian leaders and commanders was Sir John Robinson, who was appointed to the post by Charles II in June 1660. He had been active in City politics during the late 1650s and served as sheriff in 1657–8. Robinson had been prominent in manipulating the City's support for the Restoration of the Monarchy and the king rewarded his services with a knighthood. By appointing him Lieutenant, Charles made a significant gesture to the City, in granting the post to a prominent London merchant, not a soldier or courtier. Robinson was lord mayor in 1662–3 and chose to have his portrait painted, by John Michael Wright, with the mayoral robes and chain of office by his side and the White Tower seen through a window in the background. Samuel Pepys encountered him as he was developing his own career as an administrator to the Navy Board, and found him irritating, for being 'a talking, bragging Bufflehead' who boasted too much about the part he had played at the Restoration and his influence over the Court of Aldermen, 'when I am confident there is no man almost in the City cares a turd for him, nor hath he brains to outwit any ordinary tradesman'.

Pepys dined at the Tower in 1664, with Robinson, his wife and officers from his regiment. After dinner Lady Robinson 'would needs see a boy which was represented to her to be an innocent country boy, brought up to town a day or two ago and left here to the wide world, and he losing his way, fell into the Tower'. Pepys heard the boy tell his story and from the way that he told it and his manner decided that 'for certain he is an arch rogue and bred in this town'. But the Lieutenant's wife would not believe that and ordered that he be given food, and was considering keeping him 'as a foot-boy for their eldest son'.

A less compassionate side of the regime at the Tower in the early 1660s was revealed by Lucy Hutchinson. Her husband John was a former parliamentarian officer who had been excused by the House of Lords for his participation in Charles I's trial. But he was arrested in October 1663 suspected of having knowledge of a planned uprising in Yorkshire and, although no evidence against him came to light, he was taken to the Tower. Lucy was the daughter of Sir Allen and Lucy Apsley, and her account of the conditions in which her husband was held perhaps was intended to contrast with those when her father had been Lieutenant. Classified as a close prisoner and housed in the Bloody Tower, 'he was kept with a greate deale of strictnesse ... and every night he had three doores shutt upon him, and a Centinell at the outmost'.

He had been there for some weeks before she was permitted to see him, and then their children would have had to wait outside, if Robinson had not allowed them to see their father, which he did 'in hope of a fee'. But he would not permit Lucy to live in the Tower, which, she complained, caused her 'greate toyle and inconvenience, besides excessive charge of providing his meate att the Tower, and her company in another place'. Her gloom was heightened by the tradition that her husband's room 'was where 'tis sayd the two young princes, King Edward the fifth and his brother, were murthered in former dayes', and that the windowless 'darke greate roome' which led to it was the one in which 'the Duke of Clarence was drown'd in a but of Malmsey'. Robinson would not allow the door between the two rooms to be left unlocked during the night, thereby preventing Hutchinson and his servant from using 'a little necessary house', which proved unpleasant when they developed 'fluxes with their bad accommodation and diet'.

Lucy wrote that most of the other prisoners were held in similarly strict conditions, and that the warders hated the Lieutenant and his assistant 'because they cheated them and had nothing of generosity or bounty to engage the hearts of their soldiers'. The warders therefore sympathised with the prisoners and offered to do favours for them, including carrying letters. As an experienced soldier, Hutchinson investigated the extent of Robinson's fraud. By 1664 the soldiers of his company were owed twenty-two months' pay, which had been paid to Robinson but withheld by him. When Hutchinson threatened to go public with the information, Robinson paid them for fifteen of the months due. He was also guilty of returning false musters for the warders, by leaving places unfilled when vacated and yet drawing pay for them. His financial practices were not unusual among the officers of Charles II's army, but the soldiers and warders, even if they had been aware of that, had no means of obtaining redress.

A list of rules was issued for the garrison. It covered such matters as the curfew, chapel attendance and the wearing of uniforms, and prohibition of soldiers leaving candles burning in their quarters, drinking on duty, firing a musket within the fortress and blaspheming. The garrison soldiers increased the number of people living and working in the Tower, and hygiene was an issue. One of the rules ordered that no officer or soldier should 'ease themselves in any other place than those appointed for that purpose', and they were not to 'make water within six paces of the Guard, nor empty any pot, nor throw water out of any window, but bring it down and carry it to the hog stalls, or such other places as appoint[ed] for the purpose'. Those public health orders may have improved conditions in the fortress, but were not enough to protect the soldiers during the Great Plague in 1665. During the spring the Privy Council became aware of the possibility of an outbreak and the number of plague deaths rose steadily during June, followed by several months of very high mortality in what became the worst plague epidemic ever experienced by Londoners.

Monck, now Duke of Albermarle, did not billet soldiers in the city during the outbreak, preferring to house them in a tented encampment in Hyde Park, but leaving the garrison in the Tower. A pest-house was established, with Charles Wilcox as its master and physician, to take the sick from Tower Hamlets and those soldiers who fell sick in the Tower. During the outbreak, fifty-eight soldiers were taken there and treated by Wilcox, who claimed that 'not many' subsequently died. He had to pay for medicines, food and drink, and for the funerals of the deceased, while Robinson, who received both the money collected on a special rate for the victims and other contributions, promised to repay him. Wilcox later complained that of the £403 which he claimed, he received only £33 for the soldiers' treatment and £35 for the other patients. Eventually Robinson dismissed him from his post, which was redundant when the epidemic ended.

The Great Fire followed the Great Plague. The blaze began in the bake-house of Thomas Farriner, in Pudding Lane, off Thames Street, early in the morning of Sunday 2 September 1666. It could not be contained on Farriner's premises and spread through the adjoining district, and then for four days across much of the City. Although the flames were fanned by an easterly gale, the fire made some progress upwind through the buildings and stocks of flammable materials, towards the Tower. Buildings erected along Tower Street and on Tower Hill posed a danger to the fortress, for if the fire reached them, burning debris could spread to the Tower itself, where much combustible material, fuel and gunpowder were stored. And so buildings close to the walls were destroyed. This began on the Tuesday, as the flames continued to spread remorselessly. Pepys wrote in his diary, 'Now begins the practice of blowing up of houses in Tower-street, those next the Tower, which at first did frighten people more than anything; but it stop[ped] the fire where it was done.' When the wind dropped, on the Wednesday, the fires were extinguished.

Robinson took the opportunity to clear more houses close to the Tower, and

a few Weeks after, he caused all these old Houses which stood between the Tower Dock and the Tower Wall to be pulled down;

and not only them, but also all those which were Built upon, or near the Tower Ditch, from the Bulwark Gate, along both the Tower Hills, and so to the Iron Gate; and caused strong Rails of Oak to be set upon the Wharf where those Houses stood, which were about 350 or 400.

Early in November Pepys took friends to Tower Hill 'to show them what houses were pulled down there since the fire'. The Lieutenant's action created an open space between the City and the Tower, which would be a fire-break should another blaze threaten the area; a clear field of fire for the defenders if the Tower was attacked; and, by making the White Tower and the outer walls 'visible to passengers', provided an aesthetic benefit, noted by John Strype in the early eighteenth century, because it made 'a fine prospect'.

This opportunity to demolish nearby houses occurred during a series of improvements carried out at the Tower after the Restoration. To remedy 'the great want of convenient Roomes in the Storehouses belonging to the office of our Ordnance', in 1663–4 the Great Store House was constructed against the curtain wall between the Lanthorn and Salt towers. It is a brick building of two storeys and attics, which Pepys saw in November 1664 when he described it as the 'new great Store house'. The 'Small Gunn Office' was transferred there from the White Tower. In 1663 the ditch was cleaned and its banks were rebuilt, and in 1669–70 a timber building for the garrison was erected in the outer ward, between the Salt and Broad Arrow towers. It became known as the Irish Barracks. Work on the creation of a safety zone around the White Tower, with its gunpowder magazines, began in 1669. An associated scheme was to connect the White Tower directly to the wharf by an unobstructed zone, to reduce the risks when gunpowder was being moved and to allow loading to be carried out more quickly. That was implemented during the Second Dutch War in 1665–7, but the zone was abandoned soon afterwards.

The magazines in the White Tower were protected by reducing the window openings to narrow slits, 'to keep fire and gunpowder at their proper distance', as Ned Ward wrote, at the end of the century. That was not enough to ensure its safety from detonation. A dismal example of the risk of gunpowder storage had occurred in 1650 in Tower Street, opposite All Hallows church, just 170 yards from the Tower's outer wall, when powder barrels in a shop exploded, wrecking five houses, badly damaging five more and killing sixty-seven people. In 1678 an order was issued that the stock in the White Tower should be reduced, because the quantity held there was a danger to the building should there be an accident. A serious incident in July 1691 underlined the risk, when 2,000 gunpowder barrels fell through a wooden floor in the White Tower. Either the powder did not spill out of the barrels, or there was no spark or flame to detonate it, and so a potentially devastating accident was avoided. The Tower continued to be used for the storage of gunpowder – 16,000 barrels were despatched from there in the space of two weeks in 1708 – but its relative importance declined as the military establishment was expanded.

Other work around the White Tower included the demolition of the Coldharbour Gate and the fore-building against its south side in 1674, and it was during this process that the bodies presumed to be those of the Princes in the Tower were uncovered. Another storehouse was then erected, against the wall of the inner ward, north of the Wakefield Tower, and described as the 'Little Store house in Cold Harbour'. New offices were provided for the senior officers of the ordnance in a building north of the Lanthorn Tower and occupying part of the royal palace, the great hall of which was used as a storehouse. The Ordnance Office had effectively taken over the royal palace. In 1671, with the decreasing use of soldiers' body armour, the Office of Armoury was abolished and its remaining functions were absorbed by the Ordnance Office.

In March 1675 John Flamsteed was appointed as the first 'astronomical observator', later designated Astronomer Royal. He moved into the Tower shortly afterwards, using the north-east turret of the White Tower to make his observations. His salary was paid by the Ordnance Office, and Sir Jonas Moore, Master-General of the Ordnance, had been instrumental in the creation of the post. Flamsteed remained in the Tower only until August, when he moved to Greenwich to oversee the building of the new Royal Observatory. The Ordnance Office gave him further support through the skilled work of its artificers, who made him a quadrant and probably also a sextant.

Meanwhile Robinson had to deal with the embarrassment of an attempt by 'Colonel' Thomas Blood to steal the regalia. Blood had been involved in a plot to seize Dublin Castle in 1663, which had been thwarted, and a plan to capture the Duke of Ormond, Lord Lieutenant of Ireland, in London, in 1670, which only narrowly failed. He and his associates then devised an even more audacious scheme. Describing himself as Dr Ayliffe, 'he came to the Tower in the Habit of a Parson, with a long Cloak, Cassock and Canonical Girdle, and brought a Woman with him whom he called Wife'. They ingratiated themselves with the assistant keeper of the regalia, Talbot Edwards, who was in his late seventies, and Blood played his part so well that Edwards agreed that his daughter should marry Blood's son, who was posing as his nephew. The wedding was set for 9 May 1671 and on that day Blood went to the Tower with three accomplices 'all Armed with Rapier Blades in their Canes, and every one a Dagger, and a pair of Pocket Pistols'. The unsuspecting Edwards agreed to show them the regalia, recently moved to the Martin Tower. Once there, they overpowered him, wounding him in the struggle, and took the crown and the globe, but were disturbed by Edwards's son, who just then had fortuitously returned home from abroad. They did not have time to file the sceptre in two, as they had planned, and so were obliged to leave it; also, they had not secured Edwards senior completely. He managed to get free and, with his son, raised the alarm as the thieves set off to return to their horses. They were able to rush past the sentries and reached the wharf, but were overtaken and captured before they could get away. Blood was imprisoned, yet he was subsequently set free and granted a pardon by the king. It may be that he was thought to have useful contacts with some of the leaders among the nonconformists, especially the Quakers, who had been persecuted after the Restoration, but for whom the government now wished to grant greater toleration.

The precious stones that had been detached from the crown during the struggle were found, the 'great Pearl' by 'a poor Sweeping Woman to one of the Warders'. The crown itself 'only was bruised and sent to repair'. The incident led to a consideration of the arrangements for displaying the regalia: visitors in future were locked in the room by the sentries. But strict restrictions on admission were not introduced, for towards the end of the century Henri Misson noted that 'Any Body may see them all for a Shilling'.

The Lieutenant received a number of high-profile prisoners in the 1660s and 1670s, among them Sir William Coventry, a privy councillor and member of the Treasury Board. In 1669 Coventry allowed himself to be provoked by the Duke of Buckingham's caricature of him in his play *The Country Gentleman* and he challenged the duke to a duel. The king chose to interpret his challenge as a felony and consigned him to the Tower. If Charles's intention in imprisoning Coventry there was to isolate him politically then he failed, for he received many visitors, including Pepys, who on one occasion found him with Sir Henry Jermyn

> and a great many more with him, and more, while I was there, came in; so that I do hear that there was not less than 60 coaches there yesterday and the other day – which I hear also, that there is great exception taken at by the King and the Duke of Buckingham, but it cannot be helped.

Coventry was released after just over two weeks.

William Penn was the son of Sir William Penn, Master of Trinity House and Navy Commissioner. The younger William became a Quaker and published an attack on Trinitarianism, for which he was imprisoned in the Tower. On the king's instruction, Edward Stillingfleet, rector of St Andrew's, Holborn, visited him there to persuade him to change his views. Stillingfleet had a growing reputation for his writings on theological matters and his persuasive preaching, and was to be appointed Dean of St Paul's in 1678 and Bishop of Worcester in 1689. Yet he failed to move Penn, who told him that 'the Tower was the worst argument in the world to convince me'. Penn was released and, after another spell in prison, obtained a grant from the crown in 1681 of a large tract of land in North America, where he founded Philadelphia.

The Duke of Buckingham also found himself held in the Tower on the king's orders, in 1677, having argued that Charles had prorogued parliament illegally. Imprisoned with him for the same offence were the Earl of Salisbury, Baron Wharton and Anthony Ashley Cooper, Earl of Shaftesbury. Of the four, Shaftesbury was detained the longest, probably on the king's wishes, for Charles regarded him as a dangerous opponent. Shaftesbury took a leading role in politics after the Restoration, especially during the turbulent years of the late 1670s and early 1680s. He was prominent among the court's opponents who attempted to exclude the king's brother and heir James, Duke of York, from the succession, on the grounds that he was a Roman Catholic.

Shaftesbury skilfully manipulated the opportunity offered by the spurious allegations of a Popish Plot, which were made in 1678 by Titus Oates and Israel Tonge. When the rather hysterical reaction to that crisis had died down, he continued in opposition to the court as a leading figure among the 'exclusionists', who were dubbed Whigs by their opponents. The swings in political fortunes during those years, between the Whigs and their adversaries, disparagingly referred to as Tories, saw many of the leading figures detained in the Tower for a time. Even government officials did not escape the experience. Pepys, now Secretary to the Navy, was held there for six weeks in 1679 on suspicion of being a Catholic and passing naval secrets to the French, as was his friend the shipbuilder Sir Anthony Deane on a similar charge. Writers and booksellers, too, could be confined there, including 'one Browne [who] was committed to the Tower for dispersing scandalous Papers and Pamphlets, and ... came out on a Habeus Corpus'.

King Charles rode out the political storms created by the Popish Plot and Exclusion Crisis and by the early 1680s the political tide was running in his favour. Between June and November 1681 Shaftesbury was again in the Tower: this provoked demonstrations in his support, with bonfires in the streets and passers by ordered to give money so that the crowd could drink his health. On one evening towards the end of May, as some officers from the Tower were returning there, they found Tower Street blocked by coaches that had been halted by the crowd. Because the officers refused to give the money demanded they were roughly handled before they could break away and make an undignified run for the Tower, with, as one of them wrote, the crowd 'at our heels, hallowing like mad'. Shaftesbury's supporters provocatively produced a medal, which depicted him on one side and the Tower on the other, and the word '*Laetamur*' which translates as 'let us rejoice'. But the political situation had become so unfavourable that he fled to the Netherlands in the following year.

Before he went into exile, Shaftesbury had been a leading figure among a group of senior Whigs who planned to raise an insurrection to ensure the Protestant succession. Another, perhaps related, plot had the more drastic objective of assassinating the king at the Rye House near Hoddesdon in Hertfordshire, as he returned from the races at Newmarket in March 1683. The king and James returned early after a fire had destroyed much of Newmarket, and so the plot miscarried; it was exposed three months later by Josias Keeling, a London oilman and nonconformist. The government investigated his allegations and arrested the leading figures, sending many of them to the Tower.

Not all of those consigned to the Tower arrived. Lord Grey was examined by the council, which ordered that he should be taken there. But it was too late that day because the Tower's gates were closed, so he was entrusted to parliament's messenger,

Serjeant Deerham. According to Gilbert Burnet, future Bishop of Salisbury, 'he plied the messenger so with wine that he made him dead drunk, and next morning, as they went to the Tower, the messenger falling asleep, he called himself at the Tower gate to bring the Lieutenant to receive a prisoner'. While he was waiting he had second thoughts and decided to make his escape, which he did by taking a boat on the river 'and went away, leaving the drunken messenger fast asleep'. Grey got away and spent the next two years in exile. Deerham did not do so well. Another account adds that when the king heard of Grey's escape, he was 'so displeased at the Negligence of the Officer that he caused him to be committed to the Tower, and, we are told, is put into the hole, where he may have leisure to repent his indiscretion'. What space 'hole' referred to was not explained, although the name is suggestive. Deerham's salutary experience could have been avoided if the Tower's rules had been applied more flexibly, so that he could have delivered his prisoner after the curfew, or if he had not been Grey's only guard. But it seems that those being escorted to the Tower sometimes were lightly guarded. When the City's two sheriffs were imprisoned there in the aftermath of the disputed elections in 1682 they were taken through the streets with only two guards.

The repercussions of the Rye House Plot cost three leading Whigs their lives. William, Lord Russell was imprisoned in the Tower and, after being convicted of treason, was executed in Lincoln's Inn Fields within a month. The courts' opponents subsequently elevated him to the status of a martyr for the Whig cause; Burnet remembered him as 'that great and good man'. Algernon Sidney, political theorist as well as politician, was also imprisoned in the Tower, but for a longer period than Russell, because the prosecution had difficulty producing the second witness required for a charge of treason. It was almost five months before his trial was held, when the prosecution presented the manuscript of the defendant's tract *Discourses Concerning Government* as the second witness. This was accepted by the Lord Chief Justice, George Jeffreys, on the basis that 'to write is to act'; despite a skilful defence, Sidney was condemned and executed on Tower Hill in December 1683. Jeffreys himself was to die in the Tower in April 1689, having been imprisoned there following the end of James's reign.

The third of the six leading figures involved in the Rye House Plot to lose his life was Arthur Capel, Earl of Essex. While Sidney was a republican, Capel was the son of the royalist Lord Capel executed in 1649 and had served Charles II as First Lord of the Treasury. By the early 1680s Essex had become so alarmed at the extent to which the king was increasing his powers that he joined with those Whigs who shared that view. He was arrested early in July 1683 and accommodated at the Gentleman Porter's house, actually in the room which his father had occupied before his execution. That may have contributed to his mood in the Tower, described by Burnet as 'a great depression of spirits'. Three days later the king and Duke of York were at the Tower to inspect some ordnance, and as they were returning to their barge the news spread that Essex was dead, 'his man, thinking he had stayed longer than ordinary in his closet, had the door broken open, and found him dead on the floor with his throat cut'. The verdict of the coroner's jury was suicide, which his wife and brother accepted. Burnet agreed, but admitted that the circumstances 'with the ill opinion that was generally had of the Court, inclined many to believe that he was murdered'. The length and depth of the cut to his throat supported the suspicion, for it seemed unlikely that he could have inflicted such a wound upon himself. A likely candidate for the murderer was a former servant of the Earl of Sunderland. Related to both Russell and Sidney, Sunderland was in the process of breaking with his former allies and ingratiating himself with the court. That did give him a motive, for Essex's apparent suicide seemed to confirm that the plot had been a serious one and strengthened the case against Russell, whose trial was then taking place.

Another event suggested that Essex's death had not been suicide. Edmond Halley, a yeoman warder, went missing early in the following March and his body was discovered some weeks later on the foreshore at Strood in Kent, perhaps washed up after being thrown overboard. The body was naked, apart from shoes and stockings, and, judging from the degree of decomposition, had been in the water for some time. The inquest concluded that he had been murdered, and the implication, according to the pamphleteers, was that he knew too much about the circumstances of Essex's death and had been killed to silence him. Whatever the cause, the earl's death showed once again that the Tower was not an entirely safe place to be imprisoned. (Halley's son, also Edmond, was to succeed Flamsteed as Astronomer Royal, in 1721.)

After the discovery of the Rye House Plot and the imprisonment of their leaders, the Whigs were in disarray. One of the senior figures involved in the plot was James Scott, Duke of Monmouth, the king's oldest illegitimate son and the Whig candidate for the throne if his uncle were to be excluded. Politically compromised, Monmouth fled abroad. Charles's political position was now stronger than it had been for much of his reign and was increased by the displacement of the Whigs from power at Guildhall. Furthermore, the City was weakened politically by the withdrawal of its charter by the king, in 1683.

The Tower's defences were improved during those years, with most of the work carried out during 1682–6. New gun platforms were constructed along the walls and on the towers, and in the winter of 1682–3 gun carriages were provided for those platforms. The work included 'makeing and building two great Plattformes for 13 Gunns in Leggs Mount (formerly called the Old Tower) in the Mint'. Provision was made for a total of ninety guns. George Legge, Baron Dartmouth, had a long association with the Tower. He became captain of a company within the garrison in 1669, was appointed Lieutenant-General of the Ordnance in 1672 and Constable in 1685. In 1683 he told Pepys that 'he found but nine mortarpieces when he came to be Master of the Ordnance', but had ordered the making of twenty more, and by 1683 the Tower's artillery included twenty-nine mortars. He also exploited an invention by John Tinker, a 'fireworker' in the Ordnance Office, who in 1681 devised a 'new way of shooting Handgranadoes out of a small mortar-peece'. In 1685, fifty were made, at a cost of £5 10s each. Accommodation for the garrison was extended partly by converting existing coach-houses and stables, and partly by erecting a new barrack block in the Mint. Three companies of guards could now be housed within the Tower.

By the time that the re-fortification was completed, James had taken the throne, without opposition, on Charles's death in February 1685. A little over four months later Monmouth landed in the West Country, accompanied by Grey, and just eighty-three men. They quickly raised a considerable force, but not one that was capable of resisting the royal army, and suffered a shattering defeat at Sedgemoor on 6 July. Monmouth was captured, taken to the Tower, and executed three days after his arrival, on 15 July. Despite his royal blood, he was not beheaded on the green but on Tower Hill, watched by a large crowd. The executioner was the same man who had bungled the beheading of Lord Russell, when 'It took three strokes with the axe ... and then a knife to make an end of the work.' Monmouth was understandably apprehensive and 'bid the fellow do his office better than to my late Lord Russell, & gave him gold', but it was the necessary skill rather than money which he lacked, for he now 'made five Chopps before he had his head off, which so incens'd the people, that had he not ben guarded & got away they would have torne him in pieces'. Just a few years earlier, Monmouth had been a protestant hero. He was buried at the east end of St Peter ad Vincula.

James pursued a policy that would diminish the power of the Anglican establishment, both nationally and locally, and ease the restrictions on both his fellow Catholics and the Protestant nonconformists. In 1687 a Declaration of Indulgence was issued, suspending the religious tests and penal laws against Catholics and dissenters. But the king encountered considerable resistance and so he issued a second declaration, in April 1688, and ordered the bishops to distribute copies to the parish clergy, instructing them to read it to their congregations. Most declined and William Sancroft, the Archbishop of Canterbury, and six bishops petitioned the king, explaining their reasons for not obeying the order. They repeated these in an audience with the king and were despatched to the Tower, pending trial, having been refused bail. The extent of their support then became apparent, as John Evelyn described: 'Wonderfull was the concerne of the people for them, infinite crowds of people on their knees, beging their blessing & praying for them as they passed out of the Barge; along the Tower wharfe'. According to Burnet, 'In the Tower the soldiers and officers did the same', and so many people wanted to visit them, or at least go into the Tower to show their support, 'that the soldiers are forced to keep all the gates shut'. Even so, when Lord Clarendon visited them, he found 'a vast concourse of people going in and out'. The bishops were treated 'very surlily' by the Lieutenant, Sir Edward Hales, a convert to Catholicism who had been appointed to the post in June 1687. While they were incarcerated there Evelyn noted on 10 June that 'we heard the Toure Ordnance discharge, & the Bells ringing; for the Birth of a Prince of Wales'. This raised the possibility that James would be succeeded by a Catholic and that the future lay with a Catholic dynasty and not a Protestant one.

On 30 June the bishops were tried and acquitted. Released from the Tower, they refused to pay Hales the fees that he demanded, 'denying any to be due' because their detention and his claim for fees were unlawful. Also on that day a letter from six peers and the Bishop of London was sent to William of Orange, inviting him to intervene, as the husband of James's elder daughter Mary, the heiress to the throne until the birth of James's son. Having alienated much support and accrued little, the king was unable to mount an effective resistance after William's army landed in Torbay on 5 November. James joined his army at Salisbury, but some of his senior officers defected to William and James would not advance to engage the Dutch forces. Meanwhile, Hales mounted mortars on the White Tower, in an obvious threat to the citizens, should they be tempted to rise in William's support. However, Hales's unpopularity was such that he became a political liability and James dismissed him from the post when he returned to London in late November. The replacement was Sir Bevil Skelton, who had earlier been a prisoner in the Tower, prompting someone to remark that Hales had committed Skelton to the Tower, only to commit the Tower to him. Skelton was apprehensive of William's arrival in London, writing on 4 December that 'Orange they say demands the Towre to be deliverd up to him, trusting in that more then a free Parliamt'. He should not have been surprised that William aimed at military security before negotiating a political settlement.

Without the possibility of a sustained military resistance and not having a political solution that was acceptable, James left London on the night of 10–11 December, accompanied by Hales, but was recognised near Faversham and returned to the capital. After some fruitless negotiations he departed again, on 18 December. The Tower's garrison acted with the other troops, and did not resist the entry of the Dutch regiments into London. Skelton followed James into exile, but Hales had been arrested and in January 1689 was returned to the Tower as a prisoner, where he remained until June of the following year.

William and Mary accepted the offer of the crown on 13 February 1689, ending the political upheaval that came to be known as the Glorious Revolution. A month later James landed in Ireland with a French army; the war with France, which was declared in May, was to last for nine years. After a pause, another general European conflict erupted in 1701 over the succession to the Spanish throne, with Britain fighting France once more. The war continued after William's death in 1702 and until 1713, through much of the reign of his successor, Anne. For his campaigns against France, William expanded the army to an average size of 76,000 men and the navy to an average of 40,000 men during the Nine Years' War. The average annual expenditure of the Ordnance Office was £113,800 during the 1670s, but £275,800 in the 1690s and £289,300 during the War of the Spanish Succession.

A new ordnance store within the Tower was begun before the end of James's reign, replacing the 'long house of ordnance' north of the White Tower built in the 1540s and now inadequate. Work began in April 1688 and was completed after William and Mary took the throne, so that the lower windows carried the insignia JR and the upper ones had WMR. The new Grand Storehouse was 345 feet long and 56 feet wide, of two storeys and an attic storey. Above the centrally placed main entrance was a large pediment, carved by John Young, with the royal arms flanked by horses, cannon, drums and other military equipment. The building is shown on a plan of the Tower in 1692, which has outlines of three proposed bastions on the north side of the outer wall, and a half-bastion at the western entrance. An earlier plan of around 1666 also showed proposals for adding bastions to the outer defences, but none was built. Despite the new artillery positions and other works, Misson was not impressed by its defensive capabilities, commenting that 'tho' it might, indeed, incommode the City, he that were Governor of it must expect to perish in it'. Such a situation never arose, and when the garrison was deployed in London, it was to help the civil authorities to suppress disorders rather than repel a military attack.

William appointed Lord Lucas to the Tower in March 1689, and he remained in post until 1702. Also appointed in 1689 was William Meekers, a Dutch artillery officer, who became Principal

Storekeeper of the Board of Ordnance. During their period, the number of iron cannon kept at the Tower dwindled away. In the early 1660s it had housed more than 2,600 iron pieces, by the end of the 1670s the number had fallen to 550, and an inventory taken after Meekers's death in 1701 listed more than 250 brass artillery pieces, but none of iron. That was despite a considerable increase in the number of iron cannon being cast during the later seventeenth century. Of course, during wartime the artillery pieces were deployed with the armies and at the garrisons, with many of them returned at the end of hostilities. But from the Nine Years' War onwards, that pattern came to an end and they were not taken back to the Tower; the storehouses at Deptford, Woolwich, Chatham and Portsmouth came to house much of the artillery, including all the heavier pieces. Thus the Tower had lost one of its major roles. Woolwich became the centre of artillery manufacture, as the foundry there was developed during the second decade of the eighteenth century.

From 1714 the Board of Ordnance no longer met at the Tower, but in Old Palace Yard at Westminster; but the Tower continued to serve as a military depot and artillery trains were assembled there before being sent to the armies. In April 1702 it was reported that 'they work day and night at the Tower, shipping off ammunition', and in the following month, on one day '200 artillery horses, with their harnesses, went from the Tower to the camp in the Isle of Wight'. For the campaign in 1703, 'a vast quantity of arms ammunition, &c. were ship't off at the Tower for Portugal', and two years later 'a great quantity of ammunition and other stores were shipt off at the Tower'. Other reports of the same kind confirm that the Tower was a hive of military activity during the wars.

Lucas did not have to make arrangements for the coronation of William and Mary. Charles II had gone to the Tower on the eve of his coronation, but James had not done so, and nor did they. And so that practice had come to an end and the royal apartments were no longer required, even for that short stay, although the Tower still had a formal role as the backdrop to the official reception of ambassadors. After newly arrived ambassadors were privately settled in London, they were taken by barge from Greenwich to Tower Wharf, where they were welcomed by a delegation from the court and the City, and an artillery salute by the fortress's guns. After the formal greetings were completed, they processed through London to Whitehall Palace.

From the 1690s the Lieutenants did not reside in the Tower and the oversight of prisoners was undertaken by a Deputy Lieutenant and a Major. Prisoners held there after the Glorious Revolution included those who continued to fight for James, some suspected of having communications with the exiled Stuart court, and would-be assassins of William III. Dartmouth, the former Constable, was imprisoned there in the summer of 1691 on suspicion of passing information on the fleet to the Jacobites in France. He died there three months later. Also detained for a time, suspected of having contacts with James's court, was John Churchill, Lord Marlborough, a rising star among the senior army officers, but one who was mistrusted by William. He was sent to the Tower in May 1692, when there were fears of a Jacobite invasion.

Churchill and his wife Sarah were great friends of Anne, Mary's sister, who was now the heir to the throne. She wrote to commiserate with Sarah, commenting 'methinks it is a dismal thing to have one's friends sent to that place'. Marlborough was released after six weeks, on bail of £6,000. More deeply involved in Jacobite plotting than Marlborough were Thomas Bruce, Earl of Ailesbury, and Sir John Fenwick, both of whom were also held in the Tower. Ailesbury attempted to keep fit by walking across his room, which was thirty-three feet wide, for five hours a day, completing fifteen 'London miles' daily and wearing out a pair of shoes every fortnight. He was released in February 1697 after ten months' imprisonment, but Fenwick was beheaded on Tower Hill. The baize which draped the scaffold cost £15, payable by his wife with the other funeral expenses, not by the state.

Two other prisoners at this period made their escape. The Earl of Clancarty took part in James's campaign in Ireland until he was captured at Cork and sent to the Tower. By leaving a 'periwig block' on his bed, dressed to resemble him, he deceived the warders into thinking he was in his room, while he made his way out of the fortress. Colonel John Parker was imprisoned there for raising troops for James's cause among the Catholics in Lancashire. He, too, escaped, by bribing rather than tricking the warders, allegedly with £300 he raised for the purpose.

Because of fears that security had been breached, in 1697 the garrison soldiers were ordered to search the Tower, acting on a specious report that James II had returned to London. The house of the Roettier family, the Mint's engravers, was searched and the main gate into the Mint was blocked by the soldiers. The Board of the Mint protested strongly against that encroachment on their privileges.

As the Jacobite threat receded, the prisoners were mostly those who had been outmanoeuvred politically and also, perhaps increasingly, those suspected of peculation. Bribery or other wrongdoing at a parliamentary election could land the suspects in the Tower, such as Samuel Shepherd, who was adjudged guilty of bribery by the Commons during the election for Newport, Isle of Wight, in 1701. The wars against the French required government expenditure on an unprecedented scale, and parliament's now regular sittings allowed its members to keep a keen eye open for those engaged in financial wrongdoing. In 1664 the Navy Committee appointed themselves as the commissioners for prize goods, to supervise the disposal of captured ships and goods, and two of the commissioners of the Prize Office, as it became known, were committed to the Tower in 1701, for not making up their accounts. When they had done so, they requested that they be released. Marlborough's brothers George and Charles Churchill, respectively naval and army officers, both had short spells there after the Glorious Revolution, suspected of corruption. That did not prevent Anne from appointing Charles Lieutenant of the Tower in 1702 and he held the post for four years.

Political ascendancy was still accompanied by enough rancour to bring with it the risk of imprisonment in the Tower. After the Tories came to power, in January 1712 Jonathan Swift wrote to Esther Johnson that 'I hope Walpool will be sent to the Tower, and expelled the House'. His wishes were gratified and Robert Walpole was consigned there for 'a high breach of trust and notorious corruption'. During his imprisonment of almost six months he was visited by his political allies and treated by the Whigs as a martyr to their cause. When they regained office under Anne's successor, George I, Elector of Hanover, Walpole re-established himself and his time as a prisoner in the Tower proved to be no bar to his emergence as a leader of the Whigs and ultimately as our first Prime Minister.

The search of the Mint's buildings did nothing to improve relations between its employees and the garrison, which had worsened in 1696, as preparations were made to undertake another recoinage. This was the second major operation undertaken by the Mint since the Restoration. Dunkirk had been captured in 1658, but sold to France by Charles II; the French government paid in coin, much of which was taken to the Tower in December 1662 and subsequently recoined into £336,773. The new silver coins issued under Elizabeth were now withdrawn and replaced by a new issue. Buildings were erected and others adapted, some to provide stables for the horses required to turn the extra machinery. This involved reclaiming buildings that the garrison had taken over, and their accommodation became so restricted that, the Lieutenant complained, the soldiers had to sleep three to a bed. Most of the machinery was in place by March 1696 and the recoinage continued until the end of 1698, when the Mint had issued new coins to the value of £5,030,678. Earlier in the process, Isaac Newton was appointed warden and brought his considerable organisational abilities to bear on the project. By that time the senior officers of the Mint lived elsewhere, and he took a house in Westminster.

Peter the Great, Czar of Russia, visited London in 1698 and was shown around the Mint by Charles Montagu, Chancellor of the Exchequer, who had advocated the recoinage and piloted the necessary legislation through the House of Commons. His tour included the armouries, where he was not shown the axe used to behead Charles I, 'as it was feared that he would throw it into the Thames' in his rage at such a relic of the regicide.

By the time of the czar's visit the armoury's displays had been greatly improved. The Spanish Armoury consisted of weapons and armour supposedly dating from the defeat of the Armada in 1588. When the Tudor storehouses were demolished the display was recreated in the storehouse north of the Wakefield Tower. In 1688 the Line of Kings was transferred to the new Grand Storehouse. It had been extended in 1685–6 with effigies of Charles I and Charles II, both mounted on life-sized carved horses, as were the other figures in the line. William III's effigy was added after his death. Designed to impress rather than convey historical accuracy, the display did contain some anachronisms, such as William the Conqueror holding a musket. On the first floor was set out a spectacular display of small arms, described in 1712 by Lord Lucas's nephew, Samuel Molyneux, as

> a most beautifully dispos'd Armory for above 70 thousand men … the walls cover'd with Swords, Pistolls, Carbines and Bayonetts, dispos'd into such odd figures so exactly and kept so close with flat Pillars made of Pikes set close to one another by which the Pannells are divided with Pistolls for their Chapiters, that nothing can be imagined more curious.

The patterns included the form of an organ and a 'seven-headed monster'. On the floor were racks of firearms with stands of pikes at the ends, with only narrow passageways between them, so that 'the Area of the room is entirely fill'd with arms'. The fourth element in the displays set out in the 1680s was the artillery, perhaps 200 pieces by 1712, which incorporated cannon, standards and colours captured by British troops, a measure of their military achievements under William and Marlborough. Ned Ward was so impressed that he described the displays as 'the most renown'd armoury in Christendom'. Molyneux's reaction to 'this mighty Arsenal' was rather different, for he found the 'furniture of War, of Pain & Torture' disquieting, and left with 'Reflections of Regret and Concern'. Not everyone admired martial displays symbolising the country's ability to wage war.

Improvements in the armouries had not been matched by the arrangements for seeing the regalia. In 1710 Zacharias von Uffenbach, from Frankfurt am Main, complained that the display in the Martin Tower was in 'a gloomy and cramped den', its doors bolted on both sides, with sentries outside. In the room, visitors sat on wooden benches and inspected the regalia through 'a trellis work of strong iron', although it was well lit and even 'sparkles charmingly'. Molyneux, too, was less than impressed by the setting, which he described as 'a small room which is divided by an Iron Grate; on one side you stand and on the other appears a Table Spread and two Candles to expose these precious Regalia'. After a while the keeper appeared, 'a very venerable person ... who seems to have no better recommendation to this Office than that he looks to despise the trifles'.

The yeomen warders showed visitors around most of the site, accepting a separate payment for each part. Ward described them as 'a parcel of bulky warders in old-fashion'd lac'd jackets, and velvet flat-caps hung round with divers coloured ribbons'. They could be seen as picturesque attendants, not gaolers, and the Tower had become a place visited not only by the curious and the privileged, but a destination suitable for a society outing. Its image as an arsenal and a grim prison for those who challenged the political status quo had begun to soften, and it now had displays designed to show off the collections to best effect. In 1710 Swift was one of a party of ladies, gentlemen and children which set out on a December morning in three coaches from Lord Shelburn's house in Piccadilly to the Tower, where they 'saw all the sights, lions etc'. Their visit was marred only because 'it was the rainiest day that ever dripped'.

The transformation of the Tower into a place to visit was symbolised by the fact that the rack was among the items shown, its role having been transformed from an instrument of torture to an object of curiosity. The yeomen warders were primarily guards still, yet were also guides, dispensing a fund of anecdotes, some of which no doubt provided the germs of the Tower's legends.

8

THE GEORGIAN TOWER

The eighteenth century saw the beginnings of major changes at the Tower. Its role as a military storehouse and supplier of small arms and munitions to the forces was continued, although the ordnance were kept elsewhere, and its weakness as a fortress was recognised and accepted, without further attempts to modernise it. Attention was still drawn to the prisoners despatched there, but political struggles no longer culminated in the dismissal of many of the vanquished to the Tower, facing trial and even execution.

The artillery at the Tower had come to consist of the royal artillery train of brass cannon, trophies taken from the enemy, obsolete pieces and distinctive ones and curiosities. Some of the trophies were drawn in triumph through the city to the Tower, and the number increased, as British forces fought successful campaigns in the wars of the later eighteenth century. Britain was engaged in war for almost a half of the 100 years after the accession of George I in 1714, mostly with France and her various allies, as diplomatic alignments shifted. As the repository for those artillery pieces and standards treated as the spoils of war, the Tower became the national museum of military mementoes.

Victories were also celebrated by salutes fired by the Tower's batteries, maintained for that purpose and for marking other special days. On Tower Wharf, from the early eighteenth century, were sixty-one cannon 'lying in a Range fast in the Ground, always ready to be discharged on any occasion of Victories, Coronations, Festivals, Days of Thanksgiving, Triumphs, etc.' Another line of guns was mounted within the walls, on a platform seventy yards long, parallel to the wharf and 'called the Ladies Line because much frequented by the ladies in the summer, as within it is shaded with a lofty row of trees and without it has a delightful prospect of the shipping'. The Ladies Line was under the control of the Ordnance Officer and those on the wharf were the responsibility of the governor, which generated a certain amount of rivalry. In 1774 the wharf guns were described as having recently been mounted on 'new and very elegant carriages' and placed on 'a long and beautiful platform'.

Not only did the Tower's importance as an artillery depot decline in the early eighteenth century, but so, too, did its military effectiveness. A report in 1714 pointed out that 'the greatest part of the Guns, can be reckoned no more than an appearance the wall not having breadth for them and a reasonable parapet'. In other words, the pieces mounted around the walls during the work undertaken in the 1680s were ineffective: 'All the Gunns of the Inner Line are intirely useless, and none of the Towers are Vaulted, the Weight of the Gunns are too much for such a wall and may be of Ill Consequence to the buildings which hang on it.' Many of the gun platforms built then were decayed, only forty cannon on four batteries on the outer line could be fired, and the other seventy-eight on that circuit were useless. In the light of the report, the number of guns in the batteries was reduced to forty-five. An account of 1753 mentions twenty-six nine-pounders, on three batteries.

As well as obsolete and unusable artillery pieces, other weapons and items of equipment accumulated, as they were no longer needed or were outdated. Pikes and body armour had gone out of use, for example, and other items were kept only for ceremonial purposes. The Ordnance Office's workshops were used chiefly for finishing and repairing firearms. In 1718 the Flint and Bowyer towers were fitted up 'one for stocking and one for lock hardening'. When Cesar de Saussure visited the Tower in 1725 he was told that the work force in the arsenal consisted of 200 men. The 'small guns' aspect of the office continued to expand; as the wars grew in scale so did the army, with a peacetime complement of around 30,000 men rising during the 1760s to 45,000 men. More space was required and an opportunity came following a fire in the Lanthorn Tower in 1774. The tower was demolished in 1776 and, soon afterwards, the remaining parts of the royal palace in that area, including the early-sixteenth-century gallery, were also pulled down. A new Ordnance Office and a storehouse replaced them, and the office was renovated and extended after another fire in the store houses in July 1788.

The military presence in the Tower continued to include a garrison, which consisted of at least one battalion of foot guards. Pressure on accommodation was such that the earlier running disputes with the Mint continued. Its officers routinely rented out their houses within the Tower, but the tenants found themselves billeting soldiers until an order in 1736 prohibited the troops from the Mint's buildings. A part of the problem was the deteriorating condition of the Irish Barracks building; when a survey showed it to be dilapidated beyond repair it was replaced, in 1755, by a new barracks of three storeys and attics.

The number of yeomen warders remained the same, at forty. By the mid-century their uniforms were so unusual that their coats could be described as 'of a peculiar make, but very becoming'. The warders' role continued to change during the century, with fewer prisoners to guard and increasing numbers of visitors to be guided around 'in regular Order to the several Places, where the Curiosities are shewn'.

The menagerie remained one of the most visited parts of the fortress, partly because it was the first of the places of interest that visitors came to. But it also had a genuine attraction. The author of *An Historical Description of the Tower of London and its Curiosities*, published in 1753, included short biographies of the lions and provided information on the other creatures, giving considerable attention to a golden eagle, an ostrich and a horned owl, and including a drawing of the owl. At that time the menagerie also contained bears, tigers, a raccoon, a baboon and a leopard. In Tobias Smollett's epistolary novel *The Expedition of Humphrey Clinker* (1771), the maid-servant of a gentry family from Wales wrote, 'Last week I went with mistress to the Tower, to see the crowns and wild beastis; and there was a monstracious lion, with teeth half a quarter long.' A gentleman warned her not to go near his cage if she was not a maiden, for it would 'roar, and tear, and play the dickens'. It did get excited when her mistress approached, confirming the maid's opinion that she was no longer a virgin, 'and the gentleman tittered forsooth'. That was a rather earthy inclusion of Smollett's.

Among the trophies that drew large crowds was the treasure captured by Commodore George Anson from a Spanish galleon, the *Nuestra Señora de Covadonga*, during his circumnavigation in 1740–4. This was drawn on wagons through London's streets to the Tower, watched by the cheering citizens. During the Seven Years' War, Cherbourg was captured in 1758 and held for a week, which was long enough to load twenty-one brass cannon and two mortars on to the Royal Navy's ships. Before being taken to the Tower they were displayed in Hyde Park 'to the great amusement of his Majesty's subjects who flock in vast numbers to see them daily'.

High-profile figures were still sometimes detained in the Tower in the eighteenth century, such as the Jacobite lords imprisoned after rebellions in 1715 and 1745–6. Some Jacobites responded to the accession of George I in 1714 by raising a rebellion in Scotland: plans for an uprising in England were forestalled. That attempt ended in military defeat, at Preston and Sheriffmuir, near Dunblane, in mid-November 1715. Leading Jacobites were imprisoned in the Tower and the Earl of Derwentwater and Viscount Kenmure were executed on Tower Hill in February 1716. Two other Jacobite lords who were condemned to death escaped, the Earl of Winton allegedly concealed in a hamper and the Earl of Nithsdale through a ruse arranged by his wife, Winifred. At first she was refused permission to visit her husband unless she stayed with him, which she would not do. But by bribing the yeomen warders she often saw him and was able to go to his room on the day before his execution, taking with her the woman with whom she was lodging. She then dressed her husband as that woman and as it grew dark led him out, holding his handkerchief to his face, and passed him on to her maid, telling him to fetch a Mrs Betty. The guards not only let him out thinking that it was her companion, but 'opened the doors' as he left, while his wife returned to mimic a conversation between the two of them in his room. Lord Nithsdale went to the Venetian embassy and from there escaped to France.

An invasion by a Spanish and Jacobite force in 1719 was much less well supported and it was defeated at Glenshiel. A subsequent conspiracy by Jacobite sympathisers and dissident Tories was uncovered by the government, and Francis Atterbury, Bishop of Rochester, was committed to the Tower, in August 1722. The plan involved seizing the Tower and the Bank of England, and capturing the king, offering him the opportunity of returning to Hanover. Atterbury was not put on trial, but proceeded against by a parliamentary Bill to deprive him of his posts and revenues. This duly passed and he went into exile, subsequently serving as secretary of state to James, the Old Pretender, son of James II.

The Jacobite cause revived in the 1740s, with French support, and in 1745 the Old Pretender's son Charles (Bonnie Prince Charlie) landed in Scotland and quickly assembled an army. After defeating the government's forces at Prestonpans and Falkirk, he advanced into England and reached Derby before turning back to Scotland, where his army was defeated at Culloden, on 16 April 1746. After such a scare, George II's government was not inclined to mercy and three Jacobite lords were taken to the Tower. According to a guide published a few years later, they 'were publickly admitted at the main Entrance', not through the Traitor's Gate 'thro' which it has been customary to convey Traitors and other State Prisoners to or from the Tower'. Lord Balmerino, the Earl of Kilmarnock and the Earl of Cromarty were tried for high treason and sentenced to death. Kilmarnock and Balmerino were beheaded in August 1746 on Tower Hill, but Cromarty was reprieved and was released from the Tower in February 1748. Simon Fraser, Lord Lovat, had been captured after Culloden and, then in his late seventies, taken to the Tower. Over his long and eventful life his loyalties had swayed between Whig and Jacobite, but his part in the rebellion was enough to secure his conviction for treason, and no clemency was shown, despite his age. He was executed on Tower Hill on 9 April 1747, before an enormous crowd, some of whom were killed when a stand collapsed. Lovat was the last person in Britain to be beheaded in public. Ned Ward had described the approach along Tower Hill, commenting on its 'emblem of destruction, the scaffold, from whence greatness, when too late, has oft beheld the happiness and security of the lower stations'. When another Tower prisoner, Earl Ferrers, was executed in 1760 for murdering his steward, he was hanged at Tyburn, having been denied his request to be executed within the Tower. Three members of the Black Watch regiment had been executed on the green by firing squad in 1743, for mutiny.

In the 1760s and 1770s the high-profile prisoners were those who challenged the government on freedom of publication. George III came to the throne in 1760 and two years later his favourite, John Stuart, Earl of Bute, replaced the Duke of Newcastle as Prime Minister. During Bute's government, the radical MP John Wilkes, assisted by the poet Charles Churchill, launched a newspaper entitled *The North Briton* which was critical of Bute and his circle. Its title was a satirical reference to the fact that Bute and some of his allies were Scotsmen, and its standpoint was declared in the opening phrase of the first issue, that 'the liberty of the press is the birthright of a Briton'. In No. 45 of the paper, published on 23 April 1763, Wilkes attacked aspects of the Treaty of Paris, signed two months earlier, which had brought the Seven Years' War to an end. His comment that, in the speech, the king had given 'sanction of his sacred name to the most odious measures and to the most unjustifiable public declarations from a throne ever renowned for truth, honour, and unsullied virtue' was treated by the king as a personal libel, not a criticism of his ministers' policy. Bute became so unpopular in the wake of the peace treaty, and a proposal to impose a cider tax, that, despite having the king's support, he resigned and was replaced by George Grenville in May.

The new government, rather than letting the matter drop, declared No. 45 to be a seditious libel, ordered it to be burned by the common hangman, and pursued those involved in printing it. Unable to obtain evidence against an individual, it issued a general warrant that did not name any author, printer or publisher, and among the forty-nine people arrested on that warrant was Wilkes. He was sent to the Tower and his papers were seized. That provoked popular demonstrations in his support and Wilkes's appeal, on the grounds of parliamentary privilege, was upheld by the Lord Chief Justice and he was released, though he was expelled from the Commons. One outcome of the affair was that general warrants were subsequently held to be illegal. Another developed after Wilkes returned from exile in 1768 and was elected as MP for Middlesex. The Commons refused to accept him, even when he was returned at three more polls. A major political controversy ensued, while Wilkes was serving two years imprisonment for earlier convictions relating to the offending issue of *The North Briton* and the *Essay on Woman*, which Wilkes had written in 1754 as a parody of Alexander Pope's *Essay on Man*, and was condemned as obscene. He served his sentence in the King's Bench prison, not the Tower. Reform followed, with disputed elections referred to a committee, not to the whole house.

Wilkes was also involved in City politics and the refusal to allow him to take his seat in the Commons prompted a delegation from the City to present a petition to the king on his behalf in March 1770. The delegation was led by the lord mayor, William Beckford, one of the City MPs during this period and an active campaigner for the reform of parliament. Dissatisfied with the king's unsympathetic response, a second delegation went to the king in May and, again meeting with an unfavourable reaction, Beckford spoke directly to the king, without having previously submitted his speech, which was a breach of etiquette. But he was regarded as having upheld the rights of the City and so, when he died a few weeks later, £1,000 was allocated for his statue in Guildhall. It is there today, with the text of his address to the king inscribed on the pedestal.

Brass Crosby was chosen as lord mayor for the mayoral year 1770–1: by then Wilkes was serving as an alderman. Press reporting of parliamentary debates had not been allowed, but the ban was challenged in the spring of 1771 when reports were published in the *Middlesex Journal* and *The Gazetteer*. The Commons chose to interpret this as a breach of privilege and ordered the printers to appear at the bar of the house. When they did not appear, it sent a messenger to arrest one of them, which he did, bringing the offender before the City magistrates. These were Crosby, Alderman Richard Oliver, both of whom were MPs, and Wilkes. They released the printer, and detained the messenger for violating the City's rights. The Commons responded by summoning Crosby and Oliver, preferring not to meddle with Wilkes, who was not then an MP. On the instance of the now Prime Minister, Lord North, the Commons voted to commit the two MPs to the Tower. They were accompanied by a large crowd of supporters and while they were held there they entertained many visitors, including leading members of the opposition. At the end of the parliamentary session six weeks later they were released and returned to Guildhall in a triumphal procession of coaches and crowds, to 'loud and universal hurrahs'. Their actions in what became known as the Printers' Case, no doubt orchestrated by Wilkes, established the right for parliamentary debates to be published. The Commons had been outmanoeuvred and had discredited their argument by committing two such senior figures from the City to the state's prison. Crosby was the first lord mayor to be imprisoned in the Tower since the Civil War.

The Society of Gentlemen Supporters of the Bill of Rights was formed in 1769 to support Wilkes. It was dissolved in 1775, but its former members continued with their political activities. They generally supported the American colonists in their dispute with the British government. The American War of Independence broke out in 1776 and widened into a conflict involving other European countries. Henry Laurens was President of the Continental Congress of the thirteen colonies at loggerheads with Britain, in 1777–8, and he set off to Holland in 1780, hoping to negotiate a loan of $10 million. The vessel in which he was travelling was intercepted and he was arrested. He had thrown his papers overboard, but they failed to sink and were recovered. As the British government did not recognise the Congress, Laurens was not entitled to diplomatic privileges and was committed to the Tower, as a close prisoner, where he remained for over fifteen months. Despite his pleas to be released on the grounds of ill health, his release came as a prisoner exchange, for Marquess Cornwallis, the British commander captured at Yorktown, and, ironically, Constable of the Tower since 1771.

Not all Londoners supported reform and change. London was a city of 675,000 people by the mid-century and continuing to expand, and its citizens held a range of political views. Anti-Catholic sentiment remained strong, as reflected in the contents of the Spanish Armoury and its description in *An Historical Description of the Tower of London and its Curiosities*. Of its sixty-eight pages, six were devoted to an account of the armada campaign in 1588. The tone of the account describing the exhibits was expressed in the comment that the 'Spanish Cravats' displayed were iron instruments of torture 'to Lock, the Feet, Arms, and Heads of English Hereticks together'. And in the section devoted to the thumb-screws displayed, its readers were informed that 'there were several Chests full on board the Spanish Fleet. The Use they were intended for is said to have been, to extort Confession from the English where their Money was hid, had that cruel People prevailed.' That section also explained that 'the most noted Heretics were to be put to death; those that survived were to be branded on the Forehead, with a hot iron and the whole form of government in both church and state was to be overturn'd'. John Noorthouck mentioned in 1773 that the collection contained

> fetters and engines of torture, with which the fleet was plentifully stored on the presumption formed of a certain conquest of this kingdom. Of this they entertained no doubt; for among other articles is shewn the consecrated banner with a crucifix on it, bestowed on the Spanish general by the pope.

If the museum in the Tower accurately reflected national sentiment, a hostile reaction to the proposed extension of Roman Catholics' civil rights, in the Catholic Relief Act of 1778, might have been anticipated. But neither the national pride verging on xenophobia reflected in the display at the armouries, nor the views of the London Protestant Association and its vociferous president Lord George Gordon, should have provoked the violent disorders which erupted in London in early June 1780. Gordon's opposition to the Act was to have culminated in a large-scale demonstration and protest march to parliament to present a petition. Yet crowds of demonstrators ran amok for several days; at one stage groups of them mounted three attacks on the Bank, but were driven off by a detachment of soldiers directed by Wilkes. By the time that order had been restored more than 200 demonstrators had been killed and three prisons and other buildings, including Catholic property, had been burned. Gordon was arrested and taken to the Tower; eight months later he was tried on a charge of high treason, and acquitted. During the disturbances a crowd wrecked the house of one Lebarty in St Katherine's Lane, east of the Tower, allegedly urged on by two women and a soldier named William MacDonald. All three were hanged on Tower Hill on 11 July 1780, the last of the 125 people known to have been executed on the site.

In contrast to the conservative London Protestant Association, societies promoting reform were established during the following years, but their activities were viewed with increased suspicion after the outbreak of the French Revolution in 1789 and war with France in 1793. Horne Tooke became prominent in the reform movement and the Society for Constitutional Information, and in May 1794 he was arrested and sent to the Tower, after government agents intercepted a letter to him which included the phrase, 'Is it possible to get ready by Thursday?' Among the six men who were kept in the Tower for five months at that time, on suspicion of high treason, were John Thelwall and Thomas Hardy, the secretary of the Corresponding Society. All were acquitted at their trial, Tooke showing that the offending phrase referred to the preparation of a pamphlet, not an insurrection. Tooke kept a diary while in the Tower and, like many before him, found that imprisonment provided him with 'time to review my life that is passed'. Stewart Kyd was one of those held on the same charge, and he spent his time in the Tower working on the second volume of his *Treatise on the Law of Corporations*. Most of those accused of political offences were held in the Cold Bath Fields prison, not the Tower. On the other hand, after the demolition of the Gatehouse Prison in Westminster in 1776, prisoners committed on parliament's authority were sent to the Tower.

Fears of the French revolutionary regime were satirised by James Gillray in 1801, following the Treaty of Amiens, which ended the war begun in 1793. William Windham had resigned as Secretary at War earlier in the year and was known to be concerned by the terms the treaty. Gillray depicted him on his bed, imagining the various disasters that could ensue, which include a French tricolour flying above one of the turrets on the White Tower, that symbol of national security. Anxieties about the Tower's defence also had a practical expression, for instance in the response to Richard Horwood's application for access to it as part of his survey of London between 1792 and 1799. He was refused and so on the plan left the area within the walls blank, with the inscription 'The Tower; the Internal Parts not distinguished, being refused permission to take the Survey'.

The Ordnance Office had been producing plans of its own at the Tower since the early eighteenth century. The Corps of Engineers was created within the Board of Ordnance in

1716, with responsibility for surveying, and a map room was established on the east side of the White Tower. Staffed by civilian draughtsmen, this produced large-scale plans from surveys of sites of military concern, such as forts and harbours. It was also responsible for training military surveyors and draughtsmen. After the Jacobite rebellion of 1745–6, the Scottish highlands were surveyed, for a military map. Such surveys could be extended to the whole of the British Isles, and a step towards that end was taken by Major-General William Roy in 1784, when he produced a trigonometrical survey of south-east England. In 1791 the Ordnance Survey was established, as a branch of the Board of Ordnance, still based in the Tower, where a survey of Sussex was converted into a map, published in 1795, at a scale of one inch to a mile. That work was extended and other parts of the country were mapped in the wake of the trigonometrical surveys. The first of the 'Ordnance Survey maps' was published in 1801 and covered the county of Kent, given priority for military reasons during the war against France. It was followed four years later by the one-inch map of Essex. The Ordnance Survey's drawing office and stores remained at the Tower after the end of the Napoleonic War, with its personnel reverting to civilian status, after being part of the military establishment during the conflict.

Security during the wars should have been especially tight for every area of the Tower, but it was breached in 1798 when a soldier of the garrison went into the press room of the Mint, threatened the staff with a pistol and made off with a bag containing 500 guineas. That incident would hardly have improved the fragile relations between the garrison and the Mint. Despite that lapse, the Tower itself remained a safe place for the deposit of bullion and valuables, but the context had changed since the seventeenth century. The Bank of England was established in 1694 and from 1734 occupied purpose-built premises, which were enlarged between 1765 and 1788. That became the place of deposit for the City's merchants and the holder of bullion. The goldsmiths had developed into bankers; London had twenty or thirty banks in the mid-eighteenth century and seventy by 1800, and the tower's role as the primary place for secure deposits had been reduced by this process.

Among those who campaigned in support of the prisoners incarcerated during the campaigns for political reform was Sir Francis Burdett, who, in 1810, was held in the Tower himself for more than two months on the vote of the House of Commons. This was a further step in the campaign for press freedom: the breach of privilege he was sent there for was his criticism of the exclusion of reporters from the debates held to discuss the abortive campaign on the island of Walcheren in 1809. His letter to the electors of Westminster on the subject had been published in William Cobbett's *Political Register*. When he initially refused to accept the Speaker's warrant, violent clashes erupted in London. He was eventually taken when listening to his son, a pupil at Eton, translating Magna Carta from Latin, no doubt a significant piece of stage-management on his part. His popularity did not extend across the political spectrum and a satirical print entitled *A New Cure for Jackobinism or a Peep in the Tower* depicted him as a caged exhibit in the menagerie, with a yeoman warder holding a roll advertising this 'New curiosity'. One onlooker explains to his companion that 'he is not very quiet at the appearance of any being Royal, but is particularly savage at the sight of a Prime Minister, or Speakers Wig ... he brings a power of people here, we never had so many since we shew'd wild Beasteses'. Whether the response of 'A great Curiosity indeed, keep him here! keep him here!' was a reaction to his dangerous politics, or advice on maintaining visitor numbers, was left unexplained. In fact, the menagerie was then in decline, with the twenty-three animals listed in 1805, including fifteen 'big cats', reduced to just eight by 1821.

The Ordnance Office's arms production was greatly increased during the wars, and an 'Arms Manufactory' was built on Tower Wharf, employing some hundreds of workers to produce the thousands of guns required. When the war finally came to an end in 1815, the factory was closed and small-arms manufacture was transferred away from the Tower, to Lewisham and Enfield. The Mint had been moved away earlier, in 1811–2, partly because the boiler fires of the steam plant that was being introduced were seen to be a fire danger to the fortress. A new building was erected for the Mint in East Smithfield, on the site of a tobacco warehouse which the government owned. After its removal its former 'scattered and inconvenient' buildings in the Tower were used as barracks and storehouses. The transfer of the Mint took away another of the Tower's major functions.

Within ten years the Tower had also ceased to be the state prison. The end of the war removed the threats of both Jacobinism and Napoleon, and so hopes for reform rose again. But the post-war period was one of difficult adjustment, economic hardship and social unrest. London's radical leadership organised three great meetings in Spa Fields, Islington, in November and December 1816, which were addressed by Henry Hunt, commonly known as Orator Hunt. Some of the radicals espoused the ideas of Thomas Spence, a London bookseller, who argued that private property had been acquired wrongfully and that land should be taken from its owners and returned to the people, as it belonged to everyone. One group of them, on its way to the Spa Fields meeting on 2 December, looted guns from the gunsmiths' shops. The Royal Exchange was defended by the lord mayor and some constables, and so the radicals moved on to the Tower and demanded its surrender. They were dispersed by a detachment of cavalry. Their intention of seizing the Tower was reminiscent of outbreaks of popular unrest in the past.

The leader of the demonstrators, Arthur Thistlewood, was charged with treason, along with James Watson and two others. They were acquitted. Thistlewood and his group then resumed their plans to destabilise the establishment, which culminated in a scheme to assassinate the cabinet as they dined together on 23 February 1820. Their group was known to the authorities and the advertisement which gave the details of the cabinet's dining arrangements, on which they based their plans, was a deception. On the day of the planned assassination, the conspirators were arrested at their base in a loft in Cato Street, close to the Edgware Road. During the struggle Thistlewood killed an officer and got away, but was captured the following day. He and some of his fellow conspirators were imprisoned in the Tower, before being convicted of treason. Thistlewood and four others of the Cato Street conspirators were executed. No prisoners were held in the Tower during the remainder of the nineteenth century. Visitors could no longer hope to catch a glimpse of some distinguished figure imprisoned there.

But the trophies from the wars were still an attraction. Among the finest of those pieces was a gun made in Italy in 1773 for the

Grand Master of the Order of St John. When the French captured Malta in 1798 they put the gun and eight standards on board a frigate, to be transported to France. But the ship was taken by an English frigate, the *Seahorse*, and the booty, including the gun, was sent to the Tower. It is a most ornate, exceptional piece, with the barrel, carriage and wheels covered in decoration in high relief, including the coats-of-arms of the Order and the Grand Master, trophies, banners and shields, and, on the carriage, the two furies grasping torches. Other pieces, too, may have attracted interest for the quality and appeal of the craftsmanship and design, or as tangible evidence of military success. That success culminated in the defeat of France and occupation of Paris, where items in the Museum of Artillery were appropriated by the victors, including cannon, antique weapons and armour.

The armouries and the regalia represented the success of the nation's forces, military strength and royal prestige. Some visitors were also aware of the significance of the setting. François de la Rochefoucauld visited London from Paris in 1784 and in his account wrote, 'The Tower of London has been of importance in every English revolution; such executions as have changed the political face of England have always taken place there.' He exaggerated somewhat, but the sense of the fortress as being close to the centre of political affairs for centuries was becoming an added attraction for those who toured the site.

The menagerie also provided more interest, as it was revived during the 1820s by the keeper appointed in 1822, Alfred Cops. He increased the number of animals and species, so that before the end of the decade the collection contained more than forty mammals, including four bears, fourteen birds and more than 100 reptiles, most of them rattlesnakes. Accidents did happen. In one incident a snake wound itself around Cops so tightly that he could not free himself, and it took two other keepers to force its teeth apart and release him. On another occasion a young man clearing the yard was attacked and badly mauled by a leopard that had got out of its cage because the door had not been properly secured. When a wolf escaped from its cage one Sunday morning, it set off across the drawbridge and chased a dog into the Sergeant's apartments, alarming his wife and two children. They got out unharmed while the 'large and furious wolf' chased the dog, until an under-keeper managed to get a rope around its neck and subdue it. Such incidents were reported in the press, and may have damaged the menagerie's reputation at a time of increasing public interest in collections of animals.

Another section of the Tower which was attracting interest was the record collection. This remained open to inspection, although records kept in the chapel 'commonly called Julius Cesar's Chapel in the White Tower' were described in 1720 as lying 'in Dust and Confusion'. In 1736 additional space was provided there, in an adjoining room. The other part of the fortress used for records was the Wakefield Tower, which had been repaired during Anne's reign, and there they were stored in three rooms 'one above another, besides the large round Room where the Rolls lye ... all beautifully wainscotted and pannelled'. Many of the records had been sorted and catalogued, so that by the mid-century the office there contained 'near a Thousand Folio Indexes'. They could be consulted for a fee of half a guinea and the office was open to those with legal and other historical enquiries for eight hours a day during most of the year, and for six hours in the winter months.

Among the junior clerks at the record office was John Bayley, who was promoted in 1819 to become chief clerk. He took advantage of his position to research the history of the Tower, which he published in 1821, having recovered from a near-disaster when part of the manuscript and first print-run were destroyed in a fire at the printers two years earlier. Published in two volumes, *The History and Antiquities of the Tower of London* was, according to the title page, 'deduced from Records, State-Papers, and Manuscripts, and from other original and authentic sources'. As Bayley pointed out in the preface, it was surprising that there was no history of 'a place of such real interest and importance as the Tower'. Subsequent historians have drawn upon Bayley's history, although Lord de Ros, the Lieutenant Governor, commented in 1866 that 'it is too bulky in form ... and gives too much dry detail, to suit the ordinary reader'. Bayley's contemporaries attacked both the editorial methods that he used in his other work and his high fees, and in 1832 he was described by Frederic Madden, then assistant keeper in the British Museum's department of manuscripts, as 'one of the greatest knaves breathing'. When his history of the Tower was published, Bayley was a Fellow of the Society of Antiquaries of London, but he was expelled in 1845 for not having paid his subscription for fourteen years.

When preparing his own *Memorials of the Tower of London*, Lord de Ros preferred John Britton and Edward Brayley's *Memoirs of the Tower of London*, published in 1830. They had been collaborating on topographical volumes for thirty years, and were not specialists on the Tower. In the introduction they explained that the publishers of a work on the menagerie had asked them to 'revise and prepare for the press, a mass of Manuscripts which had been designed for publication by a gentleman who has long been resident in the Tower', and from that material to publish a book on the fortress, 'of moderate size and price'. They had demurred at first, partly out of respect for Bayley's 'large and handsome publication', but eventually agreed and published a book of more than 370 pages, with twenty illustrations.

This burst of informed interest in the Tower's history, based on archival research, did help to correct some popular errors. Despite Thomas Gray's lines, written in the 1750s, describing the Tower as 'Ye towers of Julius! London's lasting shame; With many a foul and midnight murder fed!', confidence in the attribution of the White Tower to Julius Caesar had been faltering for some time, and could now confidently be dismissed: 'it is certain that the Roman general did not remain long enough in this part of the island to have erected any permanent edifice of defence'. Britton and Brayley also raised the question of nomenclature. The names of the towers had been subject to change before the late sixteenth century, but thereafter became more settled. They noted that the Garden Tower in Henry VIII's reign was designated the Bloody Tower in 1597, and speculated why that change should have been made. Perhaps one reason was 'the legend' that placed the death of the Princes in the Tower there. Yet, as they pointed out, the bones found in 1674 had been discovered within the White Tower. Their comment was that 'the propriety of assigning those remains to the young Princes, was, in the highest degree, questionable'. Not all of the Tower's legends could be resolved by evidence from the records, and so would remain a matter of conjecture and opinion. One tale related that during the Civil War a parliamentarian soldier was chasing a royalist up the north stairs of the White Tower. Finding that he could not escape, the royalist dropped to his knees close to a window with a low sill, and as his pursuer rushed up to him he tripped him up by the heels and pitched him headlong through the window and into the yard. His neck was broken in the fall.

The research into the history of both the buildings and the institutions within them was timely, as it came at a period of change and could be drawn upon to inform the debate on the Tower's future. The Zoological Society of London was founded in 1826 and in 1828 opened its collection of animals at a new zoo in Regent's Park. After the death of George IV in 1830 it was decided that the royal collections should be moved there. The menagerie at Windsor was transferred soon afterwards, and part of that at the Tower in 1831, although some animals remained until 1835. With its closure in that year, the possibility arose that the displays in the armouries and the regalia could also be shown elsewhere. That would allow the Tower to be used exclusively as a military storehouse and garrison. Alternatively, those collections could be developed and arranged to provide a modern museum of national interest.

9

THE TOWER TRANSFORMED

From the mid-nineteenth century the Tower gradually underwent a major change, as those functions remaining from earlier centuries continued to decline and its appeal as a visitor attraction greatly increased. That process was not a steady one, for it retained a garrison and its military role was resumed during the two world wars. Identified by Victorian architects as primarily a set of medieval buildings, its fabric was both modified and renovated according to their vision. The Tower's symbolic significance as an historic complex linked to crown and state was recognised and this gave it an appeal, as well as making it a target for terrorists. By the end of the twentieth century what had been a fortress on the edge of the capital city of medieval England through changing times had become a site of widespread interest and fascination.

The transfer of the menagerie in the mid-1830s removed one of the Tower's major attractions; indeed, a visit had become equated with viewing the menagerie, so that the phrase 'seeing the lions' had come to mean going to the Tower. On the other hand, its closure came at a time of increasing demands for public buildings to be accessible to all, preferably free of charge. Those connected with national history, housing collections of art and sculpture or having a literary association should be open as improving forces, especially for the growing educated working classes. The Tower clearly fell within those categories and from the late eighteenth century its history and its role as a prison for the famous had attracted increasing interest, as well as its collections. In 1796 the panels and graffiti in the Beauchamp Tower were uncovered, providing tangible connections with such as Lady Jane Grey and the Dudleys. The collections, too, were being treated in a more professional manner, as informed interest in the history of armour exposed some of the anachronisms in the armouries' displays. In 1825 Sir Samuel Rush Meyrick was authorised to rearrange the Horse and Spanish Armouries. His stated aim was to establish a chronology of armour, hitherto imperfectly understood, even by those artists who used the Tower displays as a source for the armour of characters in their paintings. Meyrick pursued his objective, although he was 'compelled by ignorant officials to appropriate every suit (right or wrong) to some great personage of the period'. New items were acquired and others received from unexpected sources, such as the wreck of Henry VIII's ship, the *Mary Rose*, which had sunk off Spithead in 1545 and was found in 1836.

Popular interest in the Tower's history and its connections with the famous was increased by works of art and the growing genre of historical fiction. During the late eighteenth century artists developed an interest in depicting scenes from English history, including the fate of the Princes in the Tower. The subject was treated by Joseph Highmore, twice by Samuel Wale, Henry Singleton and by James Northcote, whose painting was executed in 1786. Northcote showed the two boys asleep in each other's arms, about to be smothered by a man in armour whose accomplice holds a lamp. He later depicted the scene of *The Burial of the Young Princes*. History painting of that kind enjoyed another burst of interest from the 1820s, when Northcote's treatment of the Princes in the Tower was surpassed in popularity by the French artist Paul Delaroche's depiction of the subject in 1830. Delaroche also achieved great success with his pictures *The Execution of Lady Jane Grey* (1836), and of the Earl of Strafford being blessed by Archbishop Laud on his way to the scaffold (1837). These caught the Romantic mood of the time, were widely reproduced and were greatly admired.

Sir Walter Scott, pre-eminent among historical novelists, included the Tower in *The Fortunes of Nigel* (1822). When Nigel was imprisoned in the Beauchamp Tower he set himself to decipher the graffiti on the walls and so found himself inspecting 'the names of many a forgotten sufferer mingled with others which will continue in remembrance until English history shall perish'. Scott also set some scenes of *Peveril of the Peak* (1823) in the Tower, which again features as a prison. The eponymous hero Julian Peveril and his father are accused of involvement in the Popish Plot; when his father is imprisoned in the Tower Julian also wishes to be incarcerated there, to be with him, only to be told that 'the Tower is for lords and knights, and not for squires of low degree – for high treason, and not for ruffling on the streets with rapier and dagger; and there must go a secretary's warrant to send you there'. Despite that rebuff Julian does receive notification that he is to be transferred to the Tower, to which his reaction is,

The Tower! – it was a word of terror, even more so than a civil prison; for how many passages to death did that stark structure present! The severe executions which it had witnessed in preceding reigns, were not perhaps more numerous than the secret murders which had taken place within its walls.

Scott's representation of a prison with a distinctive social cachet and a sinister and frightening history was bound to encourage visitors to go to the Tower, as a mute but evocative witness of the events which he described.

Scott's practice in his historical novels was to set a story at a specific period, using an authentic context and locations, and with well-known historical figures among the characters. That technique was also used by Harrison Ainsworth, who, almost twenty years after the publication of *Peveril of the Peak*, set a novel in the time of Lady Jane Grey's brief reign, and located the action at the Tower, which he visited before writing each of the sections. Entitled simply *The Tower of London*, the book was published in 1841, with illustrations by George Cruikshank. In the preface Ainsworth wrote that 'it has been, for years, the cherished wish of the writer ... to make the Tower of London – the proudest monument of antiquity, considered with reference to its historical associations, which this country or any other country possesses – the groundwork of a Romance'. He explained that the novel was partly intended as an introduction to readers to those parts of the complex which they were not allowed to enter. In his view these were 'the property of the nation, and should be open to national inspection'. Within the text he included a history and description of the Tower; his depiction of historical characters and their setting had much appeal and drew a large readership, at a time when the debate on the fortress's future was attracting widespread attention. Also in 1841, Charles Dickens's novel *Barnaby Rudge* was published, which is set during the Gordon Riots of 1780. Dickens described Gordon's imprisonment in the Tower 'in a dreary room, whose thick stone walls shut out the hum of life, and made a stillness which the records left by former prisoners with those silent witnesses seemed to deepen and intensify'. These novels by such popular authors were certain to arouse interest in the fortress.

Yet there was opposition to making access to the Tower easier. An influential figure in that respect was the Duke of Wellington, Constable from 1826 until his death in 1852, who would have preferred it to be retained as a military store, not open to the public. He thought that the collections could be taken away and shown elsewhere, freeing up for military use the buildings in which they were housed. The Governor of the Tower, Major Elrington, put that point of view succinctly in 1837, when he described it as 'a Royal Fortress and not a public exhibition'. And, besides, allowing the public in at a reduced charge, perhaps even with some free days, was potentially dangerous. Uprisings in France, Brussels and Warsaw in 1830 and the agitation over the Great Reform Bill in 1832 were alarming and showed that popular unrest was not a thing of the past. Wellington feared that to admit the public indiscriminately was to risk an insurrection, with many people paying their admission fee and entering without question, then assembling within and seizing the fortress. As Lord de Ros put it, a generation later, 'there has never been any riot or serious disturbance in London, without some plan being laid by the ringleaders, for the attack and seizure of the Tower'. More mundanely, the danger of pilfering from the stores and the risk of fire had to be guarded against, and Wellington arranged that a force of twelve constables from the newly formed Metropolitan Police should be allocated to the Tower.

The yeomen warders had a financial stake in the existing arrangements and so were opposed to change. In 1830 the charges were two shillings per person to visit the armouries, another two shillings to see the regalia and one shilling to view the menagerie. Fees to the yeomen warders had to be added, which were one shilling per person at the armouries and one shilling for each company at the Jewel House. The fortress could be seen only in groups of twelve, each group accompanied by a yeomen warder, which in itself limited the numbers who could visit. When new charges and arrangements were introduced, a set of rules was issued, which included the unequivocal statement that 'No Fees are allowed to be taken by the Warder, or by any other person'. The warders were compensated by a fixed payment. The Duke of Wellington had introduced another reform by abolishing the practice whereby the positions of yeomen warder were purchased, or passed on within families, replacing it by appointing non-commissioned officers who had recommendations from the regiments of their 'merit and good service'.

The author and publisher Charles Knight was firmly in favour of greater accessibility. In *London*, published in 1842, he referred to the 'the surpassing historical associations which belong to this fortress' and commented that 'the Tower ought to be as a great national monument'. He praised the rearrangement of the armouries' displays and saw the Tower as an educational resource. He advocated the restoration of the buildings, so that they could appeal to visitors, who would 'be instructed in the domestic history of their country, by walking under the same roof beneath which their old kings sate, surrounded with the same rude magnificence, the same mixture of grandeur and meanness, arras on the walls and dirty rushes on the floor'. He argued for the renovation of the White Tower and the Beauchamp Tower, and of St Peter ad Vincula, which he regarded as 'perhaps, altogether, the place in all England most interesting in its associations' because it was 'the burial-place of the most renowned victims of their own ambition, the jealousies of power, or the sad necessities of state, that have fallen beneath the axe'. It should be restored as a 'Temple of Toleration', containing monuments to 'every illustrious sufferer, whether Protestant or Catholic, Republican or Jacobite!' He regretted that the menagerie animals had been taken away, for they were 'a part of the ancient regal magnificence, and we think they ought not to have been removed'.

The policy on admission already had changed, to attract more visitors from wider backgrounds. In 1838–9 the price of entry to the armouries was halved, to one shilling, and in 1839–40 was halved again. By 1840–1 visitor numbers had risen more than eightfold and, despite the reduced price, revenue was up by almost fifty per cent. The price of admission to the Jewel House was also reduced and in 1840 the regalia were seen by 94,973 visitors. And, as the advocates of accessible national monuments had predicted, the social range of visitors was widening, encouraged by the expansion of London and the growing railway network. Knight wrote that 'the poorest class of persons who now visit London, if they are animated by the least spark of curiosity or intelligence, had begun to regard the Armouries and Storehouse as one of the sights they would feel ashamed of having left London without having seen'.

Not everything in the Tower was appealing, however, at least according to Ainsworth, who objected to the architecture of the late-seventeenth-century Grand Storehouse, to the north of the White Tower. He condemned it as 'that frightful architectural abomination' which was 'ugly and incongruous'. Even so, he thought that it might not be possible to remove it. Yet soon after his book was published, in October 1841 the building burned down. Some of its contents were removed ahead of the flames, but only 4,000 stands of arms were saved, out of approximately 100,000. The rack had been discovered in 1799 among the stores in the Tower and it was among the items destroyed. The blaze gutted the Ordnance Survey's map office, from which most of the contents were removed in time, although there were some losses. Within a short time it had been found new quarters, at Southampton, and never returned to the Tower.

The record office was not affected and so remained, as a cause of complaint for those who were keen to promote the Tower as a national monument. They objected to parts of the buildings, especially the White Tower, being used for such storage. Bayley recognised that the chapel there was 'one of the finest and most perfect specimens of the Norman style of architecture now extant in this country' and yet, as Knight pointed out, it was 'fitted up as a depository of Records'. They were removed in 1858 to the new Public Record Office in Chancery Lane. The chapel could then be restored, but a proposal to use it as a clothing store was made by the War Office, which had been formed in 1855 by the amalgamation of departments, including the Ordnance Office. That plan was only narrowly defeated.

The Grand Storehouse was replaced by a large barracks building, which could house almost 1,000 men. Its foundation stone was laid by the Duke of Wellington on 14 June 1845, and the building was designated the Waterloo Barracks. Another building was adapted for the garrison in 1846, when the storehouse of the 1660s was taken over, enlarged and adapted as the new Main Guard. The large garrison was maintained at the Tower partly because of the continued fear of disturbances by radicals. The artillery for defending the Tower consisted of thirty-two cannon, in addition to those used for ceremonial purposes. Much of the impetus for electoral and parliamentary reform had become focused in the Chartist movement, and when, in 1848, another year of insurrections across Europe, the Chartists organised a rally in London, the government was alarmed. Its preparations included stationing 8,000 soldiers, 4,000 policemen and thousands more special constables in the capital, and so, although the crowd assembled on Kennington Common, its leaders did not proceed with their plan to march to Westminster. Wellington's anxieties had again been aroused and the Tower's outer defences were overhauled between 1848 and 1852. Further work in the 1850s included the construction of the north bastion, projecting into the moat, which had been drained in 1843 and was now a dry ditch and parade ground. The bastion's embrasures on three floors allowed the defenders to fire along the line of the ditch.

An important part of the Tower's security was the barring and locking of the gates at curfew. By the time that John Noorthouck had described the process in 1773 the gates were 'opened and shut every morning and night with great formality', with a set routine and dialogue. This process became known as the Ceremony of the Keys and was recognised as one of the Tower's traditions. Those officers of the garrison who wanted to come and go during the curfew used a small 'wicket gate', and to do so they had to leave their name and expected time of return. The tale was told of an incident during the 1860s involving an officer's wife 'who gave herself considerable airs'. She returned five minutes late and was challenged by the sentry with the call 'Who goes there?', to which she replied that she was 'the Major's lady', only to be informed by the sentry, 'Divil a bit do I care if ye were the Major's wife, you'll not get in till the wicket is open agin.'

The teller of the tale explained that the district around the Tower was unsafe, because

> tortuous alleys and dingy, narrow streets had to be traversed, and the garrotter was very much in evidence. Officers returning late carried knuckle-dusters and short blades in their right-hand overcoat pockets ready to job any footpad who attempted to seize them from behind.

The men commonly returned in twos and threes for their own security, and so the sentry was being particularly malicious when he forced the major's lady 'to hug the walls of the grim old fortress during the early hours'.

The Ceremony of the Keys was described as centuries old, and the history of the medieval period and its buildings was attracting increased attention. With little regard for the later structures, whatever their merits, both Ainsworth and Knight advocated the restoration of the Tower as it had been in the Middle Ages. Knight wrote that 'there is no building which can be shown to the people as so complete a monument of the feudal times, or which could be so easily restored to its former conditions', so that it should be returned 'as far as possible to the condition in which it was at some given period of our history – in the time of Richard II. for example'. That would allow visitors to see 'what royal state was, three, four, or five centuries ago. Let one room be fitted up as in the days of Henry III.; another as in the times of the Wars of the Roses; and another as in the reigns of Mary and Elizabeth.'

To achieve what could be an acceptable 'medieval' appearance, Knight believed that it would be 'a wise thing in the Government to sweep away all that encumbers and destroys the interior of this edifice'. The removal of what could be regarded as later accretions would be required and was indeed undertaken in the second half of the nineteenth century, under the direction of the architect Anthony Salvin and his successor John Taylor. Not only were buildings pulled down, but plaster was removed from the walls to expose the stonework, in the mistaken belief that by doing so the original appearance could be recovered. Architects who adopted that approach to restoration work came to be expressively designated as 'scrapers', and for a time their approach was much in vogue. Although Ainsworth had condemned 'the progress of destruction' and hoped that 'further mutilation and desecration' could be prevented, to achieve the medieval appearance that he wished for further destruction and defacement were required.

Among the buildings pulled down was the Lion Tower, demolished in 1853 after the death of Alfred Cops, the former keeper of the menagerie. Other structures in that area were cleared, and so the approach through the outer buildings, including the right-angled turn within them, was destroyed and access was arranged directly from Tower Hill through the Middle Tower. Also demolished was the stone building adjoining the east side of the White Tower, the fabric of which was medieval, albeit with a top storey added in the early nineteenth century which was criticised for further concealing that side of the White Tower.

Not all of the late-nineteenth-century work was destructive and some was necessary restoration. A hydraulic engine in St Thomas's Tower produced so much vibration that in 1862 part of the south-east turret collapsed. The engine had been placed there to pump water for the Tower's water supply, and was later used for boring gun-barrels. After the accident it was moved to a new building and the tower was restored. New houses for the yeomen warders were built west of the Bloody Tower to replace buildings pulled down in 1866. The upper stages of the Cradle Tower on the outer curtain wall, removed in 1777, were reconstructed in 1878–9, and the same process was then followed on the Devlin Tower.

A larger rebuilding was undertaken by Taylor in the mid-1880s, when the wall along the south side of the inmost ward was being rebuilt, destroying what was left of the medieval wall in that sector. As part of the scheme he constructed a new Lanthorn Tower, on a slightly different site from its thirteenth-century predecessor. On the other hand, the Ordnance Office buildings of the late eighteenth century and the record building adjoining the Wakefield Tower were demolished, despite cogent arguments for retaining them which were put forward by the recently formed Society for the Preservation of Ancient Buildings.

Changes were also taking place to the displays. In 1869 the War Office asked James Robertson Planché to look again at the arrangement of the armoury. Planché was a playwright, who also had an informed interest in history. He was elected a fellow of the Society of Antiquaries when he was in his early thirties, was active in the foundation of the British Archaeological Association in 1843 and in 1854 was appointed Rouge Croix Pursuivant at the College of Arms. He had previously arranged armour for display in Manchester and at the South Kensington museum and for some years had advocated organising the armour shown at the Tower in chronological order. This he proceeded to do, so that within ten years Walter Thornbury, an enthusiastic supporter of his efforts, could write that 'the Tower Armoury can now be studied in sequence, and with intellectual advantage. The blunders of former days have been rectified, and order once more prevails, where formerly all was confusion and jumble.'

That approach allowed the collections to be used more easily for an appreciation of the evolution of armour and for research, not simply as a display to please the public. Even so, the emphasis on the associations of the items remained, and Thornbury pointed out that they included 'breastplates ... on which Montfort's spear had splintered, and cuirasses on which English swords struck fire at Waterloo'. He noted that the collections contained

> trophies from all our wars, from Cressy and Poictiers to Blenheim and Inkermann, spoils of the Armada, relics of the early Crusade wars, muskets that were discharged at Minden, swords of Marlborough's troopers, shields carried at Agincourt, suits of steel that Elizabeth's champions wore at Cadiz, flags that have been scorched by Napoleon's powder, blades that have shared in struggles with Dane and Indian, Spaniard and Russian.

The instruments of torture retained a fascination and the destruction of the rack in the fire of 1841 was remedied by the construction of a model, with a figure representing Anne Askew being tortured.

There were changes, too, in the display of the regalia. With the removal of the records the Wakefield Tower became available and in 1868 work began to adapt it as a Jewel House. Colonel Blood's attempt to steal the crown jewels had become one of the best-known incidents in English history, and when the new display opened in 1870, the regalia were shown in a newly made iron cage. Even that came to be regarded as providing inadequate security and a screen of iron mesh was added, and, in 1910–11, the cage was replaced by a metal structure resembling a huge safe, with windows through which visitors could peer at the items.

Some of the misinformation that had been passed on to visitors was also slowly being corrected. Even de Ros included associations of places within the Tower with famous people which were not borne out by Bayley's research. William Hepworth Dixon's *Her Majesty's Tower*, published in 1869, was the outcome of his own work on the state papers and published books. He described the Tower as 'a mass of ramparts, walls, and gates, the most ancient and most poetic pile in Europe ... white with age and wrinkled by remorse'. He was aware that the majority of visitors wanted to see the places associated with the well-known prisoners: 'the chamber in which Lady Jane Grey was lodged, the cell in which Sir Walter Raleigh wrote, the tower from which Sir John Oldcastle escaped'. Hepworth arranged his book chronologically, with chapters based on episodes and individuals, using the findings of his research to correct some earlier assumptions. In the case of Sir Walter Raleigh, he had evidence that his imprisonment was spent in the Bloody Tower and 'adjoining Garden house', yet admitted that 'many other vaults and cells in the Tower assume the glory of having been Raleigh's home; the hole in Little Ease, the recess in the crypt, Martin Tower, Beauchamp Tower; but these assumptions find no warrant in fact'. Other associations continued to be repeated, including that in W. J. Loftie's *Authorised Guide* of 1904, which described the route into the Tower and the houses between the Beauchamp and Salt towers, adding, 'From one of these windows Lady Jane Grey saw her husband's headless body brought in from Tower Hill, by the route we now traverse; and the leads are still called Queen Elizabeth's Walk, as she used them during her captivity in 1554.' Gradually, some of those connections were disproved, and the new findings were incorporated into the guidebooks.

A link which did endure was that between a room in the Wakefield Tower and Henry VI's supposed murder in 1471. The room came to be shown as such and in 1923 the annual 'Ceremony of the Lilies and Roses' was inaugurated; lilies were part of his arms and in the twentieth century they were strewn on the spot, by a bequest from an anonymous benefactor. The ceremony has continued to be held there on the anniversary of Henry's death, attended by representatives of his two foundations, Eton College and King's College, Cambridge.

In 1866 a spot on Tower Green to the south of St Peter ad Vincula was marked as the site of the scaffold, on Queen Victoria's instructions. Even though it came to be recognised that there had not been a permanent site for a scaffold, and that some of the seven executions recorded as being carried out within the walls took place to the north of the White Tower, the site is still marked in that way. A stone set in the pavement of the garden of Trinity Square marks the location of the Tower Hill scaffold.

While some of the long-held misunderstandings were being investigated and corrected, other tales were springing into bud. When Natsume Soseki returned to his lodgings after visiting the Tower, in 1900, his landlord startled him by saying, 'There were five ravens there, I suppose.' He went on to explain that 'they're sacred ravens. They've been keeping them there since ancient times, and, even if they become one short, they immediately make up the numbers again. There are always five ravens there.' Not only had a belief become common that the ravens had been living at the Tower for centuries, but also a fear that if they disappeared the monarchy and state would fall, a comment attributed to Charles II. In fact, they had begun to visit the Tower in the mid-nineteenth century, as their previous nesting sites in London had been cleared for building. Some had been domesticated by the residents and kept in captivity, and those who died or escaped were replaced, so that there were indeed always five ravens at the Tower. The explanation which Soseki was given was a 'tradition' which had grown up relatively recently.

Reported sightings of ghosts perhaps were inevitable in such an old complex of buildings so strongly associated with imprisonment, murder and execution, and they gave a pang of apprehension to visitors sensitive to such matters. By the early twentieth century ghosts and rumours of ghosts were numerous enough for Walter George Bell to write an essay on the subject. Bell was sceptical, while acknowledging that, if ghosts exist, 'assuredly upon no spot on earth do they congregate more thickly than here. Eight centuries of England's story in tragedy and suffering are isolated within the Tower's encircling walls.' One tradition that he mentioned was that of the 'dark shadow of an axe' falling upon Tower Green. Then there was the ghost of Anne Boleyn, the presence of which was supported by the frightening experience of a sentry in 1864, who was found prostrate on the ground while he was on guard outside the window of the room which she was then thought to have occupied before her execution. Court-martialled for being asleep on duty, he claimed that a figure in white had approached him and continued to approach when he challenged it. He thrust his bayonet into the figure, meeting no resistance, and he then fell down in a faint, where the duty officer found him. He was able to produce two witnesses who corroborated his account and was acquitted. According to Sir George Younghusband, Keeper of the Crown Jewels, the same figure was reported to have been seen on that spot by other sentries 'for several years afterwards'. The spot thereby became one of 'evil repute' that was unpopular among the soldiers, who tried to avoid being placed on duty there. Perhaps their fears would have been lessened had they known that it was not outside the rooms where Anne Boleyn was imprisoned. Bell could identify only two more possible ghostly sightings and found both of them to be 'somewhat ridiculous'. Nevertheless, to some, ghosts were part of the Tower's imagined character.

Pictures of the Tower and its associations became increasingly common, as the number of printed images generally increased, on posters, the sides of omnibuses and trams, on hoardings, and on tins, bottles and other containers. The figure of the beefeater, as the yeomen warders were becoming known, came to be one of them. The term 'Beef-eaters o' the Guard' was used by John Crowne in 1671, in his play *Juliana: The History of Charles the Eighth of France*, and in 1864 Herbert Spencer linked the term specifically with the Tower, in the phrase 'the Beefeaters at the Tower wear the costume of Henry VIIth's body-guard'. The designation and image were taken up by James Burrough for his Beefeater Gin, first made at a distillery in Chelsea, which proved to be an enduringly popular brand. An advertisement for the Tower Furnishing and Finance Company which W. S. Gilbert saw while waiting for a train gave him the idea for setting an operetta in the Tower, although the title *The Yeomen of the Guard* confused the yeomen of the guard with the yeomen warders and was the source of misunderstanding thereafter. Gilbert set the story in the Tower in the early sixteenth century, and his collaboration with Arthur Sullivan was another of their great successes. The operetta was first produced in 1888 and its designs emphasised the link with the Tower. As described by Henry Lytton, the curtain rose on a faithful picture of the Tower of London, that picturesque and historic old fortress indissolubly connected with some of the brightest, and the darkest, annals of England. Soon we see the Yeomen of the Guard, clad in their traditional garb and carrying their halberds.

The link was perpetuated in later productions: for instance, the design for a drop-curtain for a production in 1939 showed a plan-view of the fortress in the Tudor period.

Images of the Tower and the beefeater were also used to promote London as a visitor attraction. In 1894 Tower Bridge was completed; with its twin Gothic towers it provided a new and dominant landmark so close to the Tower that it inevitably changed its context and illustrations tended to show Tower and bridge together. As the Tower was still regarded as a defensible fortress by the army, it was pointed out when the bridge was being constructed that it could be used as a platform from which to fire on the Tower. The building of an additional position in the fortress from which fire could be directed at the bridge was considered, but rejected. Military considerations apart, those who approached along the river were now confronted with the two strong images of modern bridge and historic fortress. H. G. Wells noted the contrast in *Tono-Bungay* (1909), writing of 'the dear neat little sunlit ancient Tower of London ... overshadowed by the vulgarest, most typical exploit of modern England, the sham Gothic casings to the ironwork of the Tower Bridge'.

Official guidebooks, the first of which was published in 1841, acknowledged the Tower's growing popularity and the need for a succinct and accurate description. Visitor numbers fluctuated during the nineteenth century, but the trend was for them to increase, especially after free admission on Mondays, Saturdays and public holidays was introduced in 1875. London's population continued to grow, people had more leisure time and steamships made travel easier, bringing international tourists. An underground station was opened at the north-west corner of Tower Hill in 1882, designated Tower Hill station, and it was replaced by the Mark Lane station close by two years later.

A terrorist bomb explosion on the first floor of the White Tower on a Saturday afternoon in January 1885 was one in a campaign of bombings by the Fenians which had begun the previous February. It was timed to coincide with other devices in Westminster Hall and the House of Commons. The explosion in the Tower started a fire, which was soon quenched, and caused some injuries, but no fatalities. It did not prove to be a long-term deterrent to visitors. The arms and armour displays had been moved into the White Tower a few years previously, although the arrangement was less than satisfactory, according to Loftie: 'the lighting of the rooms and their shape, with various other causes, prevent any strictly chronological arrangements of the collection, many objects of which also belong to long periods of time'. New pieces were acquired to enhance the collections and additional attractions were displayed from time to time. In 1893 the War Office unsuccessfully attempted to transfer responsibility for the armouries to the British Museum, and did manage to assign them to the Office of Works. A curator was appointed in that year, Viscount Dillon.

By 1900 the annual number of visitors was approximately half a million. To visit the Tower had become almost obligatory. Shortly after the First World War, Walter George Bell could write, 'Never yet have I met the man who has made open confession that he does not know The Tower. There would be a sense of shame in it.' The *Daily Telegraph* carried a series of ten articles by Bell, each one describing a part of the Tower. That a national title was prepared to give space to what effectively was a guide to the complex indicates how popular the Tower had become. The guide was timely, because the crypt of the White Tower, the Bloody Tower and St Peter ad Vincula had been newly opened to the public in recent years. Even so, Bell had to admit that it remained a 'military fortress' and that it was 'not practicable at present to convert it into a great national museum'.

Viscount Dillon's successor in 1912 was Charles Ffoulkes, who enthusiastically set about bringing order to the mass of weapons and armour in the galleries and storehouses around the Tower, as well as acquiring new items, such as two sixteenth-century cannon recovered from Dover harbour. He compiled, and in 1916 published, an inventory of the armouries at the Tower. After the First World War he managed to bring all 'Trophy Arms and Armour held by the Army' under the control of the armouries, although his predilection for order and tidiness led him to dispose of some broken and decaying pieces, to the public and to scrap metal dealers. On the other hand, he accumulated more items and developed an interest in relatively recent weapons, so that by the time that he retired in 1938 he had gathered together a large collection of nineteenth-century firearms. In his memoirs, which appeared in 1939, he described the Tower armouries as having 'a strange and varied history'.

The two World Wars in the twentieth century inevitably interrupted the development of the Tower as primarily a visitor attraction. It had remained a military base with a garrison several hundred strong, and was used for drilling civilian reservists. The garrison had been called upon during the Siege of Sidney Street in January 1911. Following the attempted burglary and murder of three policemen at Houndsditch, police surrounded a house in Sidney Street, where members of the group of Latvian anarchists who had carried out those crimes were reported to be staying. The police were fired on and a sergeant was seriously wounded. They were reinforced by a detachment of Scots Guards from the Tower, who directed their fire at the windows and roof, driving the anarchists from the upper floor. The house caught fire and eventually collapsed; the bodies of two of the gang were later recovered from the ruins, but its other members were never arrested. The incident attracted much attention because the offenders were political refugees, and because of the use of firearms by them and the police, the deployment of troops and the presence on the scene of the Home Secretary, Winston Churchill.

During the First World War a miniature rifle range was built in the outer ward, between the Constable and Martin towers. The building was probably where at least some of the eleven prisoners executed in the Tower during the war were shot. These included Fernando Buschman, a German-Brazilian engineer, who had been in the country for a few weeks when he was arrested and accused of spying on the Royal Navy. A virtuoso violinist, he was given permission to play his violin in his cell before his execution in October 1915. Other condemned prisoners were executed in the moat.

The years of war did not necessarily change the image of the Tower after the end of hostilities. It continued to attract visitors and the interest of those who wrote on the history of London. In 1923 Elizabeth Montizambert described it as the storehouse of mistakes – a place redolent with the memory of bygone blunders – where the great men of the nation like Sir Thomas More, Archbishop Cranmer and Sir Walter Raleigh, and innocent, beautiful things like the little Princes and Lady Jane Grey, were done to death.

Her contemporary Helen Henderson referred to the Tower as a place of 'tragic happenings', and a few years later Virginia Woolf also expressed a traditional view in describing it as 'that thick and formidable circle of ancient stone, where so many drums have beaten and heads have fallen, the Tower of London itself'.

The area around the Tower was developed for recreation, with the clearance of buildings on Tower Wharf and the setting out of gardens. In 1935 an artificial beach was created on the foreshore in front of the wharf for residents of the City and the East End. It proved to be very popular and remained in use for thirty years.

During the Second World War the Tower was again used for military purposes. It served as a collection point for prisoners-of-war before they were moved elsewhere and among the roughly 180 prisoners who passed through the fortress was Rudolf Hess, the German Deputy Führer, who was held there for four days. The final execution in the Tower took place in August 1941 when Josef Jakobs, a convicted spy, faced a firing squad in the miniature rifle range. Damage inflicted during bombing raids included the destruction of the North Bastion, a part of the range built in the early eighteenth century for the Ordnance Office staff, some of the former Mint buildings in the outer ward, and the late-nineteenth-century Main Guard, close to the south-west corner of the White Tower.

The Tower was reopened to the public in January 1946 and, as tourism developed in the second half of the twentieth century, so the numbers visiting the Tower grew. The demolitions in the nineteenth century and the destruction during the Second World War made some hitherto unavailable areas open to archaeological exploration, and the findings were displayed by leaving the wall lines open to view. Within the buildings, changing displays of the armouries and regalia continued to attract attention, and visitors still showed great interest in the prisoners held there over the centuries. Queries from the public prompted the Chief Yeoman Warder, A. H. Cook, to compile a list and brief biographies of those whom he could establish had been imprisoned there. His manuscript was prepared while he was serving at the Tower, between 1934 and 1954, and contains 1,826 names. Brian Harrison, another yeoman warder, subsequently took up the work and added to Cook's list, so that by 1995 it had grown to 8,000 names. Their work emphasised the Tower's role as a prison.

Those engaged in the renovation and presentation of the fortress during the second half of the twentieth century regretted the 're-medievalisation' process of the Victorian era, stressing the value of buildings of all periods and aiming to achieve a better perception of the Tower. From the 1960s the buildings were cleaned, beginning with the White Tower. The removal of grime and soot from the exterior surfaces exposed the limestone and bricks beneath and gave the whole complex a lighter look, altering perceptions of a dark, and hence grim, fortress. In 1973 the south door of the White Tower was brought back into use, approached from a wooden stairway from the inner ward: that had been the arrangement in the Tower's early years, before the fore-building was constructed. With the reduction of the numbers of garrison troops, the Waterloo Barracks became available, and the regalia were displayed there, from 1967. Another break with the Tower's past as an ordnance supply depot came in 1994, when the Royal Logistic Corps was moved away.

The fortress was again a terrorist target in July 1974, when a bomb planted by the IRA exploded in the White Tower, killing one person and injuring forty others. As with the Fenian bomb in 1885 it was part of a campaign across London. The bomb had been placed in the Mortar Room of the armouries' displays, but the incident did not discourage subsequent visitors. Considerable changes came in 1984, when some of the staff and a part of the armouries' collection were transferred to Leeds. In the following year the organisation was designated the Royal Armouries, described as the National Museum of Arms and Armour. That part of the historic collection retained and displayed in the White Tower was reorganised in 1996.

In recent decades London has attracted increasing numbers of visitors and its fortress has shared that popularity. It has become an international attraction for its 900-year-long connection with English, and then British, history, and its status as a royal castle. During the early twenty-first century, the Tower continued to attract increasing numbers, with over two million visitors annually, the majority of them from overseas.

The objective of those who campaigned in the early years of Victoria's reign for greater access has been achieved, albeit over a period of 100 years and more, but their conviction that sites of national importance should be accessible free of charge has not been accepted. Of course, they could not have thought in terms of the number of people who visit the Tower in the early twenty-first century, which in one year is roughly equivalent to the population of the whole of London when they themselves were campaigning.

The situation has also changed in terms of technological advances affecting travel and communication, the proliferation of images, economic prosperity, the provision of education and the dissemination of knowledge. And so the Tower's loss of functions has not led to neglect and decay, but to a new role and iconic status, as one of the world's major visitor attractions.

BIBLIOGRAPHY

Anon., *Chronicle of London, from 1089 to 1483* (London: 1827, reprinted, Felinfach: Llanerch, 1995).

Anon., *London in the Sixties* (London: Everett, 1908).

Ashbee, Jeremy, 'The Tower of London and the Jewish expulsion of 1290', *Trans. of the London & Middlesex Archaeological Soc.*, 55 (2004).

Bacon, Francis, *The History of the Reign of King Henry the Seventh*, ed. Roger Lockyer, (London: Folio Society, 1971).

Barber, Richard, and Barker, Juliet, *Tournaments: Jousts, Chivalry and Pageants in the Middle Ages* (Woodbridge: Boydell, 1989).

Barker, Juliet, *The Tournament in England, 1100–1400* (Woodbridge: Boydell, 1987).

Bayley, John Whitcomb, *The History and Antiquities of the Tower of London* (London: 1820).

Bell, Walter George, *The Tower of London* (London: Bodley Head, 1921).

Bell, Walter George, *The Great Plague in London in 1665* (London: Bodley Head, 1924.)

Bell, Walter George, *Unknown London* (London: Bodley Head, 1951).

Blackmore, H. L., *The Armouries of the Tower of London: I Ordnance* (London: HMSO, 1976).

Britton, John, and Brayley, Edward Wedlake, *Memoirs of the Tower of London* (London: 1830).

Brown, R. Allen, Colvin, H. M. and Taylor, A. J., *The History of the King's Works, Vols I & II: The Middle Ages* (London: HMSO, 1963).

Brown, R. Allen, *The Normans and the Norman Conquest* (London: Constable, 1969).

Burnet, Gilbert, *History of His Own Time* (London: Dent, 1979).

Caraman, Philip, *John Gerard: The Autobiography of an Elizabethan* (London: Longman Green, 1951).

Carlton, Charles, ed., *State, sovereigns & society in early modern England: essays in honour of A. J. Slavin* (London: Macmillan, 1998).

Charlton, John, ed., *The Tower of London: its Buildings and Institutions* (London: HMSO, 1978).

Cook, Alan, *Edmond Halley. Charting the Heavens and the Seas* (Oxford: Clarendon Press, 1998).

Craig, John, *The Mint. A History of the London Mint from A.D. 287 to 1948* (Cambridge: CUP, 1953).

Crouch, David, *Tournament* (London: Hambledon, 2005).

De Beer, E. S., ed., *The Diary of John Evelyn* (Oxford: OUP, 1959).

De Ros, William, Lord, *Memorials of the Tower of London* (London: John Murray, 1866).

Deiter, Kristen, *The Tower of London in English Renaissance drama: icon of opposition* (London: Routledge, 2008).

Doherty, Paul, *The Great Crown Jewels Robbery of 1303* (London: Constable, 2005).

Ffoulkes, Charles John, *Arms and the Tower* (London: Murray, 1939).

Fissel, Mark Charles, *The Bishops' Wars: Charles I's campaigns against Scotland 1638–1640* (Cambridge: CUP, 1994).

Groos, G. W., *The Diary of Baron Waldstein. A Traveller in Elizabethan England* (London: Thames & Hudson, 1981).

Hamilton, William Douglas, ed., *A Chronicle of England during the reigns of the Tudors* (Camden Soc., 2 vols, 1875, 1877)

Hammond, Peter, 'Epitome of England's History', *Royal Armouries Yearbook*, 4 (1999).

Harris, Tim, *London Crowds in the Reign of Charles II* (Cambridge: CUP, 1987).

Henderson, Helen W., *A Loiterer in London* (London: Hodder & Stoughton, 1924).

Henry, David, *An historical description of the Tower of London and its curiosities* (London: 1753).

Hewitt, John, *The Tower: its history, armories, and antiquities* (London: 1841).

Hewitt, Rachel, *Map of a Nation: A biography of the Ordnance Survey* (London: Granta, 2010).

Hicks, Michael, *False, Fleeting Perjur'd Clarence: George, Duke of Clarence 1449–78* (Bangor: Headstart, 1992).

Hicks, Michael, *Richard III* (Stroud: Tempus, 2003).

Holt, J. C., *Magna Carta* (Cambridge: CUP, 1992).

Hone, William, *The Yearbook of Daily Recreation and Information* (London: Thomas Tegg, 1832).

Hutchinson, Lucy, *Memoirs of the Life of Colonel Hutchinson*, ed. James Sutherland (Oxford: OUP, 1973).

Impey, Edward, *The White Tower* (London: Yale University Press, 2008).

Impey, Edward, and Parnell, Geoffrey, *The Tower of London: The Official Illustrated History* (London: Merrell, 2000).

Jones, Michael, ed., *Philippe de Commynes Memoirs. The Reign of Louis XI 1461–83* (Harmondsworth: Penguin, 1972).

Keay, Anna, 'The Elizabethan Tower of London: The Haiward and Gascoyne plan of 1597', *London Topographical Soc.*, 158 (2001).

Knight, Samuel, *The life of Dr. John Colet, Dean of St Paul's, in the reigns of K. Henry VII. and K. Henry VIII.* (Oxford: Clarendon Press, 1823).

Lander, J. R., *The Wars of the Roses* (Stroud: Sutton, 2000).

Langbein, John, *Torture and the Law of Proof: Europe and England in the Ancien Regime*, (Chicago: Chicago University Press, 2nd ed., 2006).

Loftie, W. J., *Authorised Guide to the Tower of London* (London: HMSO, 1904).

Marchand, Jean, *A Frenchman in England 1784* (Cambridge, CUP, 1933).

Marsh, Christopher W., *The Family of Love in English Society, 1550–1630* (Cambridge: CUP, 1994).

Mason, Emma, *William II: Rufus, the Red King* (Stroud: Tempus, 2005).

Misson, Henri, *Memoirs and Observations in his Travels over England* (London: 1719).

Mundill, Robin R., 'Edward I and the Final Phase of Anglo-Jewry', in Patricia Skinner, ed., *The Jews in medieval Britain: historical, literary, and archaeological perspectives* (Woodbridge: Boydell, 2003).

Mundill, Robin R., *England's Jewish Solution. Experiment and Expulsion, 1262–1290*, (Cambridge: CUP, 1998).

Murphy, Claire, and Souden, David, eds, *Prisoners of the Tower: The Tower of London as a state prison, 1100–1941* (London: Historic Royal Palaces, 2004).

Parker, Geoffrey, 'The Place of Tudor England in the Messianic Vision of Philip II of Spain', *Trans. Royal Historical Soc.*, sixth series, 12 (2002).

Parnell, Geoffrey, 'The Refortification of the Tower of London, 1679–86', *The Antiquaries Journal*, LXIII (1983).

Parnell, Geoffrey, 'Five Seventeenth-Century Plans of the Tower of London', *London*

Topographical Record, XXV (1985).

Parnell, Geoffrey, *The Tower of London* (London: Batsford, 1993).

Parnell, Geoffrey, *The Tower of London Past & Present* (Stroud: Sutton Publishing, 1998).

Parnell, Geoffrey, *The Royal Menagerie at the Tower of London* (London: Royal Armouries, 1999).

Pepys, Samuel, *The Diary of Samuel Pepys*, ed. R. C. Latham and W. Matthews, Vols IV & V (London: Bell & Hyman, 1971).

Powicke, Frederick M., ed., *Essays in Medieval History Presented to Thomas Frederick Tout*, (Manchester: 1925).

Rex, Peter, *The English Resistance: The Underground War against the Normans* (Stroud: Tempus, 2006).

Rowse, A. L., *The Tower of London in the History of the Nation* (London: Weidenfeld & Nicolson, 1972).

Rye, William Brenchley, *England as seen by foreigners in the days of Elizabeth and James the First* (London: John Russell Smith 1865, new ed. 2005).

Saunders, Ann, ed., *The London Letters of Samuel Molyneux, 1712–13*, London Topographical Soc., 172 (2011).

Seymour, W. A., *A History of the Ordnance Survey* (Folkestone: William Dawson, 1980).

Somerset, Anne, *Unnatural Murder: Poison at the Court of James I* (London: Weidenfeld & Nicolson, 1997).

Soseki, Natsume, *The Tower of London*, trans. Damian Flanagan (London: Peter Owen, 2005).

Stow, John, *The Survey of London*, ed. H. B. Wheatley (London: Dent, 1987).

Strong, Roy, *Painting the Past. The Victorian Painter and British History* (London: Pimlico, 2004).

Swanton, Michael, ed., *The Anglo-Saxon Chronicles* (London: Dent, 1996).

Swift, Jonathan, *The Journal to Stella*, ed. Frederick Ryland (London: Bell, 1924).

Thurley, Simon, 'Royal Lodgings at the Tower of London. 1216–1327', *Architectural History*, 38 (1995).

Tomlinson, Howard, *Guns and government: the ordnance office under the later Stuarts* (London: Royal Historical Soc., 1979).

Trevelyan, Raleigh, *Sir Walter Raleigh* (London: Allen Lane, 2002).

Ward, Ned, *The London Spy* (London: Folio Soc., 1955).

Warren, W. L., *King John* (London: Yale University Press, 1997).

Williams, Neville, *Thomas Howard, Fourth Duke of Norfolk* (London: Barrie & Rockliff, 1964).

Williamson, Audrey, *The Mystery of the Princes* (Stroud: Amberley, 2010).

Wilson, David, *et al.*, *Prisoners of the Tower: The Tower of London as a state prison, 1100–1941* (Hampton Court: Historic Royal Palaces, 2004).

Woolf, Virginia, *The London Scene* (London: Snowbooks, 1975).

Younghusband, Sir George, *The Tower from Within* (London: Jenkins, 1919).

LIST OF ILLUSTRATIONS

Also available from Amberley Publishing

Everyday life in the teeming metropolis during Pepys's time in the city (c.1650-1703)

'A fast-paced narrative with a real sense of history unfolding' GILLIAN TINDALL

Samuel Pepys's London was a turbulent, boisterous city, enduring the strains caused by foreign wars, the Great Plague and the Great Fire, yet growing and prospering. The London of Wren, Dryden and Purcell was also the city of Nell Gwyn, an orange seller in the theatre who became an actress and the king's mistress; of 'Colonel' Thomas Blood, who attempted to steal the crown jewels from the Tower and yet escaped punishment; and of Titus Oates, whose invention of a Popish Plot provoked a major political crisis.

£10.99 Paperback
146 illustrations
256 pages
978-1-4456-0980-5

Available from all good bookshops or to order direct
Please call **01453-847-800**
www.amberleybooks.com

Also available from Amberley Publishing

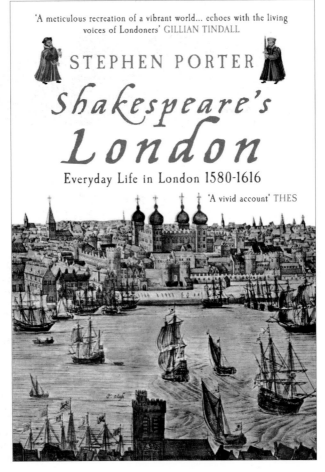

Everyday life in the teeming metropolis during William Shakespeare's time in the city (c. 1580-1616), the height of Queen Elizabeth I's reign

'A vivid account' THES

'A lucid and cogent narrative of everyday life' SHAKESPEARE BIRTHPLACE TRUST

Shakespeare's London was a bustling, teeming metropolis that was growing so rapidly that the government took repeated, and ineffectual, steps to curb its expansion. From contemporary letters, journals and diaries, a vivid picture emerges of this fascinating city, with its many opportunities and also its persistent problems.

£9.99 Paperback
127 illustrations (45 colour)
304 pages
978-1-84868-200-9

Available from all good bookshops or to order direct
Please call **01453-847-800**
www.amberleybooks.com

INDEX